HOW CITIES WORK

CONSTRUCTS

The Constructs Series examines the ways in
which the things we make change both our
world and how we understand it. Authors in
the series explore the constructive nature of
the human artifact and the imagination and
reflection that bring it into being.

SERIES EDITORS

H. Randolph Swearer
Robert Mugerauer
Vivian Sobchack

ALEX MARSHALL

HOW

CITIES

WORK

Suburbs, Sprawl, and the Roads Not Taken

UNIVERSITY OF TEXAS PRESS
AUSTIN

Sixth paperback printing, 2005

Requests for permission to reproduce material from this work should be sent
to Permissions, University of Texas Press, Box 7819, Austin, TX 78713-7819.
www.utexas.edu/utpress/about/bpermission.html

(∞) The paper used in this book meets the minimum requirements of
ANSI/NISO Z39.48-1992 (R1997) (Permanence of Paper).

LIBRARY OF CONGRESS CATALOGING-IN-PUBLICATION DATA

Marshall, Alex, 1959–
    How cities work : suburbs, sprawl, and the roads not taken / Alex Marshall.
        p.   cm.— (Constructs series)
    Includes bibliographical references and index.
    ISBN 0-292-75240-7 (pbk. : alk. paper)
    1. City planning.   2. Cities and towns—Growth.   3. Suburbs.   4. Social
psychology.   5. Social participation.   I. Title.   II. Series.

HT166.M259   2000
307.76—dc21   00-026691

TO ANDREA

CONTENTS

THE SEX

OF CITIES

CHILDREN ARE SUPPOSED to turn to their parents at some point and ask innocently, "Daddy [or Mommy], where do babies come from?" Faced with such a basic question, parents then decide how directly to answer it.

I doubt any child has turned to anyone and asked plaintively, "Daddy, where do places come from?" Or, "Daddy, where do cities come from?" But it is these questions that I hope people are asking, even if not consciously, and which I seek to answer in this book.

There's been a lot of talk over the last half-century about our cities, towns, suburbs, and neighborhoods. Through most of it has run a thick current of dissatisfaction with the galloping forces of suburbanization that have characterized the postwar era. People may love their three-bedroom home on the cul-de-sac, but they hate traffic jams, destroyed countryside, pollution, and automobile dependence. But before we start labeling places as good or bad, or attempting to design new ones, we should understand them better. This means asking basic questions. Which are: What forces produce our streets, neighborhoods, towns, cities, and regions, and the shape they take? And can we control them? To proceed without understanding is to almost guarantee ill-conceived and unwanted results.

Babies come from sex. Where do places come from? What is the sex of place? What union of people and nature produces our cities, our suburbs, and the environment out of which we make our homes? If some concede the need for more widespread sex education, might I raise the call for more universal place education?

I believe we are mixed up about our cities, our neighborhoods, and the places where we live. We don't understand how they work. We don't understand what produces them. We don't understand what starts them or stops them. We don't know how to change them, even if we wanted to. That is what I hope to do in this book. To explain to myself and to the reader why human settlement occurs, what shapes it, and how it can be shaped. *In this book, I discuss the nature of place and how the nature of places has changed. And how we can shape the nature of our places.* I do not argue to redesign our cities in a specific way. I have preferences and make them known. But my purpose is to make clear the choices available and the price tag of each. How do we change our world? What levers do we grasp if we want to change how it is constructed?

Much of the book explicitly or implicitly addresses the dualism that has developed between the so-called urban and suburban environments, between the land of the parking lot and the land of the street. These two types of places are seen as representing different ideals, and being governed by different systems. I attempt to find the Rosetta stone that will make understandable the workings of both city and suburb. Although they indeed have stark differences in their everyday life, I contend if we widen the lens, we find both urban and suburban places are governed and created by the same laws of place. If we understand those laws, we come a long way in understanding how places and cities are created and how they function.

WHAT IS PLACE?

The structure of a human settlement rests on a three-legged stool of politics, economics, and transportation. It's these forces that I attempt to understand and explain in this book. If we seek to change our world, it's these interconnected levers that must be pulled.

GETTING AROUND

Of these, transportation is the most visible and active in shaping a place. It's a simple rule: How we get around determines how we live. But it's a rule we still haven't grasped. Transportation determines the form of our places.

My neighborhood of Ghent, in Norfolk, Virginia, has the unusual structure of dense apartment buildings next to large, although skinny, homes because it was built around a streetcar line, Norfolk's first. The streetcar line inflated real-estate values so that developers could build densely and still sell. People wanted to live outside the city, yet still be connected to it, and would even live in a low-rise apartment building to do so. This was a first, and invented a new type of city.

The older, more narrow streets of Norfolk's downtown, most of which vanished under a bulldozer's blade, were created by a different transportation system. A tiny network of streets grew up in the seventeenth and eighteenth centuries around a port where everything from cotton to coffee to coal made its way in and out. These streets were so narrow because they were built primarily for the foot, which on land was the main means of transportation. The first streets were laid out in 1680 by a state surveyor at the request of Lord Culpepper, the royal governor, who had been instructed by Charles II of England to establish more towns to facilitate trade.[1] As I will discuss later, it's important to realize that a political act began my town.

The suburbs of my city were built around the car. They have no need of form, and therefore have none. Cars need parking lots and highways.

Different transportation systems produce different types of cities, and the places within them, as effortlessly as different types of soils produce different sorts of shrubbery, flowers, and trees. They determine the width of the streets, or whether there are streets. This dynamic is almost impossible to change and should be understood if we are to get a handle on our cities and places.

What's startling is how slowly the shape of the city changed before

1800. Both land and sea travel had changed very little for two thousand years, and what changes did occur were more because of the changing technology of warfare than changes in transportation. But the industrial revolution brought a slew of new transportation systems, coming about every generation, each of which remade the city with it. The pace of change has been so dramatic that most of us are still gasping. It's as if each of us, inside, had a town or neighborhood built around a main street lined with homes and services that open onto the street. That paradigm has been with us at least two thousand years. It's only in the last fifty that it's evaporated, and we have a hard time shaking it. Perhaps we shouldn't. This dramatic pace of change, unseen before, is what some call modernism. It is something we are all still trying to get used to, even after two centuries of its existence.

THE ARM OF THE POLITY

If transportation determines the shape of our cities, then who determines the shape of the transportation system? Largely the state, whether that be a king, a dictator, or a democratically elected government. A transportation system is an expression of the political will of a government, tempered by economics. In the United States, the local, state, and federal governments lay down the transportation methods that shape our cities. They build roads, train lines, ports, and airports. It is one of government's principal jobs to lay down transportation systems. The rest of the economy builds on these positive externalities.

Government has the same relationship to place as it does to private enterprise, and in both cases the relationship is fundamentally misunderstood. A common conception of government is that it stands outside the creation of places and the market economy, tidying up around their edges, moderating what are essentially natural phenomena that would continue without government. Which is false. In actuality, government creates both places and the market economy. It is the mother of these systems. It creates the architecture within which these two systems are housed.

With places, government does this by creating transportation systems. With a market economy, it does this by creating the laws within which a market economy must operate. Certainly, private enterprise is important, but its handiwork is built on top of a structural base constructed by the public, both in a legal sense and a material sense. Private business does not depend on government for much—just the indispensable. First, a system of laws and courts. Then a money supply. Then concrete infrastructure like: A water supply. A sewer system. A transportation network. A storm drainage system. Then there is the soft infrastructure like public schooling. Private businesses can no more go it alone in an urbanistic sense than they can in an economic sense go without using a government-backed dollar bill and court system. Nor can places.

CREATING WEALTH

If government determines what type of transportation system is constructed, then what determines what type of transportation system government constructs? Are there immutable rules or pressures that drive the choice of transportation, and thus the city structure, that we build? It's here we get into economics. And the nature of what cities are.

Cities exist because they create wealth. Again, by cities I mean both suburb and urban center—any human-made settlement at least one step removed from subsistence farming. The other things we love about cities—their production of culture, art, beauty—exist only because the production of wealth allows a city to exist at all.

Creating wealth means creating anything that a community can trade outside the community for other products and services. This can mean anything from the production of pottery to the production of computer chips. This doesn't have to mean heavy industry. A university town is "selling" its knowledge and teaching. I'm not saying that cities don't have other roles; they do. Humans are social animals. They get together to love, marry, talk, dance, and play Parcheesi. But people live together permanently in larger numbers because doing so allows them to make a living. This comes down to industry, not just business. Running a grocery store or a shopping center does not produce an economic base the way running a factory does. The existence of the shopping center depends on the people working at the factory; the existence of the factory does not depend on the shopping center.

Transportation is the cornerstone of cities' ability to create wealth.

It is their principal playing card. Cities are created, even in the age of the Internet, around major transportation links to other cities and the world. Before the eighteenth century, that was usually a water port. In modern and contemporary times, these links are railroads, an airport, and Interstate access. A city's major transportation links are part of its monopoly, its franchise, something it can do that no other physical place can do. They pull people and jobs to it.

But a city's internal transportation system—the layout of its streets and roads, the layout of streetcar systems and subways—determines the character of the city, how its citizens live and work. It has less to do with the direct engines of wealth creation. Build subways and people will live in dense neighborhoods and walk to corner stores; build broad suburban boulevards and they will live in subdivisions and drive to the Wal-Mart. The choice is a matter of taste, as expressed through political decisions, more than economics. The internal transportation system is built with the fruits of economic success, and so can assume a number of styles. But in saying it's largely a matter of taste, I don't mean to say that the choices are unimportant. The typical pattern of sprawling suburbs is environmentally destructive and no fun to live in; but it is sustainable in an economic sense. So is a denser, more urban pattern.

This matter of choice delights me. We all like to put the imprint of science or necessity on our desires. But cities are still art, done on a wide scale, with our paintbrushes and colors being freeways and train lines. That cities are art also means that the choices of what kind of places we want rest precisely where they should: with the public. It is a responsibility and privilege that should both delight and burden us.

CHANGING PLACES

The interplay of these three forces—transportation, economics, and politics—largely determines the shape of our cities and places. What makes our present time so confusing is that our places are less solid than ever before. The fast-moving dance of these forces in the last two centuries is producing new forms of places at an accelerating rate. First, in the nineteenth century, streets themselves changed in style. Then, after World War II, streets were banished entirely as the basic unit of place, and replaced with the parking lot and the driveway. It's a dance that is causing old characters to play new roles. It's the dance of these players that I seek to show and uncover in this book.

SUBURB AND CITY

The suburbs are one actor playing a new role. The word originally meant stuff on the fringes of a metropolitan area, external to such a place physically and secondary in importance. But the suburb now dominates. It's where most people live and work. And so it has switched places with the urban environment, and the roles they serve have also reversed. It is the suburbs that are now the center of commerce, industry, and business. In particular, this is true with emerging business and commerce, the cutting edge. Parts of the city are actually becoming suburbs to the suburbs.

This change of roles has changed how we perceive city and suburb. The suburbs were once a place of refuge for the family away from the world of commerce, greed, politics, and blind striving for more. That is no longer true. The suburban world of highways, shopping centers, and office parks is now a place of blind market forces and impersonality—exactly what the city represented in the past. The city has become the refuge; the suburbs have become the open, storm-tossed sea. As in Eric Bogosian's play *Suburbia*, the parking lot of the 7-Eleven has replaced the street corner as the place where people hang out, meet the opposite sex, and are corrupted. Like the proverbial "street" that we once wanted kids "off of," the mall and the 7-Eleven parking lot have become the places of low culture and an absence of civilized rules and learning. Exactly what the downtown or urban street corner once represented.

Meanwhile, the classic downtown or urban shopping street has become a more rarefied place, both more controlled and controlling. Downtown is now a place of specialized boutiques, art galleries, coffeehouses, cooking stores, and restaurants, perhaps most of all restaurants. Gone are the department store, the appliance seller, the barbershop, the average hash house. In their appeal, these streets aim at the more exclusive clientele that have both the money and the taste to go there. "The street," once a symbol of corruption and amorality, is now an example of refinement and civilization. The blind, unfeeling edge of capitalism has moved farther out.

xvi ■ HOW CITIES WORK

COMMUNITY

Our changing places have changed our basic relationships with other people. "Community," something you can define many ways, is different now because our places are different. When I say community, I mean the very stuff of life, our relationships with our family and friends and neighbors, and how and whether those relationships come about.

The biggest change in "community" is that it is less linked to a physical place than ever before. Several factors working together have made it so people are both less obliged and less able to be physically tied to a specific neighborhood and city through a web of family, friendly, and economic relationships. The car and the highway have produced places that are fractured physically, and in the related patterns of commerce and business. The huge explosion of wealth in the last half-century has meant more people can choose to leave a place if they choose. And a more global economy means people are less able to remain tied to a specific city or place.

Because of all this, community has become an option rather than a fact of life. It has become an accessory one can choose or buy, like a lifestyle or a Jeep Cherokee. Abetting this trend are New Urban subdivisions like Celebration in Florida, where one buys his or her way into a subdivision that offers as an amenity "community," along with the pool and the health club.

Community was once not something you chose; it was something you were a part of, that you only separated from with great effort and difficulty. That this has changed is a good thing in many ways. It's worth noting that residents of housing projects are some of the few people who remain tied to a physical place as their first community. But it's also a bad thing. We live in the physical world, not in cyberspace. We all have to come home at night and sleep in a bed, and live much of our lives within a somewhat confined circle of space. The delinking of commerce and most actions to physical place has drained and damaged us, even as it has increased our wealth as individuals. We finally need a physical place that also links us in ways that are not optional to a community. We need friends. We need our children to be educated, and also disciplined. Marriages need support. The essential threads of the fabric of society are woven not from the marketplace but those things that live outside it and are not measured by a price tag. Producing more stable physical places is part of the task of producing more stable physical societies.

FOUR CITIES

We can get a more realistic view of the choices involved in place-making by looking at the decisions of two cities and two parts of cities. Each has chosen to mix the essential ingredients of place-making—economics, politics, and transportation—in a different way, and so each of these places is fundamentally different.

I have chosen Portland, Oregon; the Silicon Valley in California; an immigrant neighborhood in New York City called Jackson Heights; and Celebration outside Orlando, Florida. All are economically healthy and prosperous. Whether they are successful aesthetically, practically, environmentally, or in other ways is a different question.

Portland is an example of a metropolitan area that has begun to grapple realistically with the actual forces that produce development. It has instituted a growth boundary, which, put another way, can be seen as a refusal by the founder of development, government, to extend basic infrastructure and services. It has torn down freeways and built train lines. It has pushed the forces of development inward, or put another way, it has chosen not to extend them outward. And it has reaped the rewards. Which is a place that is more aesthetically pleasing, less environmentally destructive, and more livable. But this has been at the price of grappling with some of our cherished illusions about ourselves. One of the illusions is the belief that the building of cities rests chiefly in the hands of the individual property owner. The second illusion is believing that smaller suburban cities are actually that, rather than appendages of a larger, dominant entity, which is the metropolitan area itself. It's a struggle that is still not won, because the myth of the independent actor as shaper of his destiny, and the difficult relationship of people and their actions to government, are tough subjects.

Silicon Valley is an example of a region that has chosen an opposite path. It has chosen to let the dominant forces of our times—the car and the highway, and a fractured political structure—play themselves out in the usual way. The leaders of the Valley have been too busy making microchips to do otherwise. A series of governmental entities have made a series of decisions, important ones, but ones which don't add up to a unified whole. Localities have extended roads and sewer lines; state transportation departments have built highways and train lines; smaller localities and bigger cities have pursued a variety of conflicting paths toward development and growth. The result is a fairly typical American suburb—with the big exception that it is home to the dominant industry of the twenty-first century, the computer. The Valley in reality is not a suburb at all. It is not the fringe of anything. It is the center of a huge industry and the producer of vast quantities of new wealth. *It is a city.* That this generation of wealth, and the spending of it, takes place in a nondescript environment of shopping centers, subdivisions, and supermarkets makes it all the more interesting. It shows how our places are really about choices. Computer chips are made in both Portland and the Silicon Valley, but these cities are utterly different in character.

Jackson Heights in New York City is what is now an anachronism—an urban place that helps create a new middle class. Urbanism in the contemporary era has become mostly the domain of the rich and the poor. Jackson Heights illustrates how an earlier form—an early-twentieth-century subway suburb—can manage, even thrive, in what is generally an era of highways and cars. It is a rarity in that it is a working-class, or lower-middle-class, neighborhood that is urban in its form. That it is a rarity shows how drastically our cities and places have changed.

Celebration in Florida is a "town," a subdivision, a community—pick your moniker—built by Disney in its holdings of land outside Orlando that are part of the Disney World world. In it, we see what happens when someone fashions a place without acknowledging the forces that actually produce a place. Celebration is a conventional suburban subdivision pretending to be a small town. It is an appendage to a freeway off-ramp. Like other freeway appendage subdivisions, it is low-density and its residents are dependent for their necessities on a suburban boulevard lined with supermarkets and chain stores. Celebration is an example of the design philosophy of New Urbanism, whose advocates are reviving the form of traditional towns and cities, both in the suburbs and the existing city. By looking at Celebration, we can start to see what parts of this design philosophy are valid.

New Urbanism is a philosophy well worth examining, for it is arguably the most influential movement in city design in the last half-century. It has attracted enormous attention and gained a large number of prominent backers. Many New Urbanist theorists and advocates start with a very agreeable concept. They say neighborhoods such as my Ghent should be used as a model for new development, both in the city and, in particular, out of town. The joys of my neighborhood can be replicated, they say, if its design is carefully copied.

Which is false.

If we want to revive or create urban places, we have to look at the design of the underlying systems that produced those places, and less at the design of the places themselves. Most of New Urbanism resembles trying to grow a rose by studying the patterns of its leaves and petals. That won't work. You have to study the seed, and the soil within which the seed is grown. If we want urban places such as those spotlighted by New Urbanists, then we build streetcars, subways, and bike paths. We stop building freeways within a metropolitan area, and, if we are really serious, we start tearing some down. Through these and other policies, we concentrate people and limit their mobility on a macro level while expanding it on a micro level. Urbanism is a result of putting people and their activities under pressure. It is a result of limiting the amount of space available for shopping, living, and every other activity. To revive or create the type of walking, pedestrian environments desired requires by definition putting more people per square mile.

But what is conceptually simple is difficult politically. Difficult because these policies involve restricting the supply of cheap housing and, ultimately, cheap goods. They are difficult because they involve changing American lifestyles, in ways such as increasing reliance on public transportation. They are difficult because they involve a level of cooperation between municipal governments and state governments that has seldom been attempted. They are difficult because they involve re-thinking what is the real relationship between government and property rights. But they are not hard to understand.

Much of the writing and thought going under the banner of New Urbanism is intelligent attempts to move planners, architects, and citizens forward in building more coherent cities and places. Because of that, to some extent, I am a New Urbanist. But what New Urbanism has mostly been on the ground is a way of building suburban subdivisions that are masquerading as something else. It is a stylistic revolution in the suburbs, like changing the hemlines of skirts, and not an actual change of their design. As a way of grappling with our places, New Urbanism has been destructive because it has offered an easy way out of the difficult policy questions that reviving actual urbanism entails. It is politically quite difficult to stop building highways. A huge coalition of home builders, road builders, and politicians is geared up to build them. Growth boundaries, and similar mechanisms like "smart growth" laws, that prohibit the extension of infrastructure represent, if implemented, huge shifts in where the political power of the state lies. With New Urbanism, instead of debating whether to prohibit the conversion of more farmland to houses, we debate whether a private developer should be allowed to build a slightly reconfigured subdivision. It is a far simpler fight than whether to impose a growth boundary around a municipal area, invest more in mass transit, or impose a bigger tax on gasoline.

If there is anything central to this book, it's that real changes in the structure of our places can be both productive and rejuvenating. But that half-measures and window dressings are neither needed nor helpful. Real changes require making real choices. I would be glad if we chose to make them. If not, however, we should recognize that and live with the consequences.

GOING PLACES

This book is more about understanding than it is about solutions. I hope we will arrive at solutions through understanding more clearly how our human-made world works. I do have preferences. I favor investing more in mass transit, which would include everything from intracity bus lines to intercity high-speed rails. I favor controlling the outward growth of the metropolitan area, while at the same time taking steps to decrease automobile use and increase other means of getting around. I favor raising the price of gasoline to reflect the actual costs of the highway system the consumption of gasoline supports, which would consequently reshape the built environment. Such policies would revive downtowns, and aging neighborhoods in general, and are the only effective way I see of protecting the environment. They could also be coupled with different agricultural policies that encourage more local farming and more local selling of what such farmers produce. But such policies come at a price, and I do not wish to mandate my tastes. Rather, I wish people to debate clearly the costs of sprawl and of controlling sprawl. Some people want less growth; some want more. Some want more highways, some less. Some want urbanism, some want suburbanism. Yet I sense people on all sides usually don't understand what the choices are, what they have to give up to get what they want. Although I have no monopoly on insight, this lack of understanding is common both in the general public and in the upper echelons of architects, planners, and policy makers.

I am not an architect, a professional planner, or a professional scholar. I am a journalist, with all the strengths and weaknesses that come with that profession. My point of view comes from roughly a decade spent observing the changing face of our cities, both suburbs and center cities, and writing about it. I have tried to understand why things occur.

For most of that decade, I was a staff writer for *The Virginian-Pilot* in Norfolk. I observed and participated in the suburban growth battles in the sprawling "city" of Virginia Beach. I observed and participated in the battles to renew the isolated and struggling center city of Norfolk. For better or for worse, my stories were often part of the battles. Various sides seized on them to support their case. And sometimes, the stories created new positions and defenders of them because the stories showed viewpoints and facts that had not been considered before. Good journalism does that. I grew up and lived in both cities, and my family goes back several generations in Norfolk, which colored my reporting.

I also write from the perspective of a journalist who has traveled a good chunk of the country and Europe. Many of the resulting stories appeared in *Metropolis Magazine* in New York and other publications. I have seen enough to know that Norfolk citizens are not the only ones who are confused. At the same time, I have also seen that knowledge and points of view vary tremendously from place to place. There seems to be a floor of knowledge and perspectives that forms a lingua franca in a metropolis. Where that floor is varies. That's why a Portland, with a relatively sophisticated base of understanding, can discuss in newspapers how to save farmland by increasing density. While a Virginia Beach, less sophisticated, will discuss saving farmland by decreasing density. Or to use another example, Portland will discuss helping downtown by limiting parking, while Norfolk will discuss saving downtown by increasing parking. In both examples, the arguments turn on exactly opposite beliefs as to how the world works, and what helps or hurts downtowns or farmland.

In my quest to determine what shapes places and cities, I find that the big choices are political ones. They allocate the resources of society differently, which is the purpose politics serves. Building fewer freeways and more trains makes people drive less and walk and use transit more. As a matter of taste, some people like this and others don't. As a matter of money, it makes shopping mall owners poorer and inner-city businesses wealthier. The same equation occurs for landowners outside town compared to those within it. These are political choices.

If we are to shape our cities more effectively, we must recognize that the fragmented character of our places and our society stems from the fact that at every fork in the road, we have chosen the individual over the collective. Our problems originate in scarcities of collective wealth, not individual wealth. If I can afford it, I am free to buy a house in the country. But my wealth cannot buy me a bike ride in the country unhindered by traffic; or easy access out of my city on a weekend; or useful public transit when I'm unable to drive. I cannot buy a crime-free city for my child to grow up in, although I can purchase a subdivision with a gate. If we want to revive the much-lauded practice of "community," then we must understand that it is obtained through shared political choices and not through private purchases in the market.

The design of cities is still a fascinating canvas on which to work. Whether we be playing with Interstates, train lines, streetcars, or bike paths, they are ultimately enormous works of art. Some of our biggest ones. What makes these works of art so difficult to produce is recognizing that they come from shared decisions, exercised through the collective system of authority we call the state. Agreeing on shared goals is difficult in any society, but particularly in ours. We hesitate to recognize that agreeing on shared goals is even one of our responsibilities as a polity. Instead, we cling to the belief that the only collective decision we need to make is agreeing we should all be free to make money.

All this is one reason why the most coherent shapers of the urban environment in the last half-century have been two movements that are largely reactionary in nature. One is the environmental movement.

Through its drive to stop the conversion of farms and forests to housing, it has shaped the urban environment more forcefully than other movements which have set their sights directly on the built environment. It's significant that Oregon's growth boundaries, which have so significantly shaped the city, were passed largely to protect farms and forests. That they would radically and favorably affect urban life was only dimly understood or appreciated.

The second is the historic preservation movement. From initial desires to save individual buildings, it has gradually evolved into a movement to conserve and promote entire urban environments. Saving an old church has gradually turned into saving the things that produce an environment where the urban church functioned successfully. Like the environmental movement, it has significantly affected urban environments because its spokespeople are some of the few that coherently say "Stop" to the raging forces of development.

A final thought occurs to me. Does it matter how we shape our places? It's the conceit of architects that places and buildings shape human behavior, rather than the other way around. Wholesome, productive communities can be built in high-rises, town houses, and houses with the three-car garage on the street. As can vicious and exploitive ones. It does matter, though. It's partly a question of beauty. Places designed with care and intent are sometimes more harmonious than those that aren't. We shouldn't be afraid to try. And though I'm fearful of cause-and-effect statements, there is at least some relationship between the nature of our places and the nature of our selves. Getting a handle on the nature of the places we produce will help us, a little, get a handle on our selves.

The burden and joy we face today is that the construction of place has to be done more consciously than ever before. We are like the method actor who, as he grows older, must do consciously what once was intuitive or reflexive. It appears to be one of the unavoidable consequences, and prerequisites, of maturity.

HOW CITIES WORK

U.S. Highway 192:
The real main street of
both Celebration and
Kissimmee. Photo by
Alex Marshall.

When you're building your own creation, nothing's better
than real than a real imitation.

From "Frankenstein" by Aimee Mann

CHAPTER 1

A TALE

OF TWO

TOWNS

Kissimmee versus Celebration and the New Urbanism

ON THE EDGE of two lakes about twenty miles south of Orlando are two small southern Florida towns. Both have old-fashioned main streets, with stores, restaurants, and a movie theater that open onto their sidewalks. Both have old-fashioned homes with front porches set on streets which lead into their downtowns. Both have parks that wrap around their lakes, where you can stroll and take in a sunrise or the night air. They both lie off a road called u.s. 192, and are just a few miles from each other.

But one of these towns is struggling. Its homes are not selling for much, and its storefronts have trouble staying full. The other town is a wealthy place, with homes that cost up to $1 million. Its downtown has rich boutiques and pricey restaurants.

The struggling town is called Kissimmee. It was founded in the mid-nineteenth century and grew as a shipping port and then a railroad and cattle town. But people stopped using the big lakes for shipping, and railroads became less important as well, and the town suffered.

The successful town is called Celebration. It is a new place, founded in 1994. It is, in reality, not a town, but a subdivision, built by the Disney corporation in conscious imitation of towns like Kissimmee. It sits next to a freeway and an exit ramp. Its homes are being bought by the Orlando upper classes, and its stores are being filled with tourists. It is an example of a much-heralded design philosophy called New Urbanism.

In learning why one town is struggling, and the other prospering, we can learn what people value, compared to what they say they value. We can also learn about what makes towns, and subdivisions, tick. We also learn about the concept and practice of community, which Celebration's owners say they are reviving. By looking at Kissimmee, we can learn about Celebration, because Kissimmee is the thing Celebration is pretending to be—a small, Florida main-street-style town. What does it say when the imitation of something is worth more than the thing itself?

Comparing Kissimmee to Celebration shows where Disney has chosen to imitate the design of a small town, and where it has not. In some aspects, like front porches, Disney has chosen to exactly copy Kissimmee. In other aspects, like the way the towns govern themselves, it has chosen not to. What we find is that Celebration is a contemporary automobile suburb pretending to be a nineteenth-century town. And that pretense, like most pretenses, has a price.

By looking at Kissimmee and Celebration, we can learn about the general thrust of the design philosophy the latter represents, New Urbanism. It is probably the most heralded design movement of the last half-century. It has been embraced as a way out of the problems of sprawl. Celebration closely resembles other New Urban developments, both in the structure of its streets and the structure of its management, although it does differ in some respects. By looking at Celebration, and the thing it is imitating, Kissimmee, we start to see just where this New Urban path, as it has generally been configured, leads.

KISSIMMEE: A HISTORY

Cities are primarily about creating wealth. At the core of virtually every human habitat is some industry or combination of industries—be it automobiles, tourism, gambling, computers, or insurance—that brings in money from outside an area and keeps a city or town going. These industries are very different from service businesses, like newspapers, grocery stores, and dentists, dependent on the wealth already brought into the area to survive.

Kissimmee has the classic history of small towns and cities. People came together because they found a way to generate wealth on an ongoing basis. And as with many cities and towns, this mechanism had to do with a basic link of transportation, in this case a port and later a railroad stop.

Kissimmee was born when an early sugarcane grower bought 2 million acres of land from the government in the 1800s and drained it, converting swamp to dry land.[1] In a few decades, a town grew up on land at the northern end of Lake Tohopekaliga, an enormous body of water that fills this already lake-studded section of Florida. Why? Because boats could travel across Lake Tohopekaliga, down the Kissimmee River to Lake Okeechobee, and then to either the Gulf of Mexico or the Atlantic Ocean. So a port grew up at Kissimmee, and with it a town. Transportation creates cities.

The city really hit its stride, though, when the railroad went through after the Civil War. Along with growing sugarcane, the region became one of the largest cattle producers and transporters in the United States. Florida is still a leading producer of cattle. The cows and steers were first driven overland, then transported by barge, and finally hauled by railroad. Millions of animals loaded onto boxcars made their way to points north. While in town, the cattlemen, the "cowboys," met with their bankers, bought supplies, shopped, talked to the mayor, and did other tasks—political, commercial, and recreational—that are at the heart of a town.

Things changed, though. The cattle industry stopped using rail. The Interstate replaced shipping things down the lake, which is now only used for bass fishing. Still, when Disney arrived in the mid-1960s, Kissimmee was a town of 7,000 people with a courthouse, a City Hall, and a high school.

In the next three decades, Disney would become the principal industry of this part of the Orlando area, as much as the port and railroad were in the nineteenth century. Disney World gave the city of Kissimmee a brand-new tourism economy, as an old industry died out. But because we now travel by road and less by lake or rail, the economic center of Kissimmee shifted from the old downtown, which was next to the rail line and the lake, and out to U.S. 192.

This broad suburban strip boulevard, which feeds into Interstate 4, is the "Main Street" of the Disney World universe. It is lined for ten solid miles with hotels shaped like alligators and giant glass-walled souvenir shops and shopping malls, all waving mile-high signs at the people driving by. The city of Kissimmee has become an appendage of Disney World, feeding on the people who want the cheaper hotel rates, or who visit a theme park called Medieval Times, rather than Disney World, for the day.

This has left the old downtown of Kissimmee and its surrounding streets as a relic, even while the city's population as a whole has quintupled. The old city center is no longer the center of anything. It's almost ten miles from the Interstate, although only a mile or two from U.S. 192. So even though the city now holds 40,000, and the county 160,000, the downtown is struggling. It does have a fabulous waterfront on a lake so large that the other side is barely visible. But this region of Florida has lakes everywhere, and so they are not that valuable.

Celebration has a school right by its downtown. Kissimmee used to. But it closed, replaced by a new one out in the suburbs. A new county library has been built, though, along with a new civic center, right off downtown.

CELEBRATION: A HISTORY

Although Disney is certainly in the business of making money, the history of Celebration is very different than that of Kissimmee, because Celebration is not about people coming together to make a living. People who live at Celebration already have a living. That's required to get in the door of the "town." Many Celebration residents work at adjacent Disney World. Others work in Orlando. Celebration is an attempt by the Disney corporation to capture a little more of the money being brought into the Orlando region through Disney World and other industries like Universal Studios. If these and other industries were to somehow dry up overnight, so would Celebration, because that's where its residents get their money from, either directly or indirectly.

Rather than being born from a port or a rail stop, Celebration was born from an exit ramp. In the early 1980s Disney World began to fear that mounting environmental initiatives would lock up use of Disney World's vast property holdings. So, in exchange for creating a wildlife conservation area, it got zoning and development rights "locked in" on the rest of the property.[2]

One of these development areas was Celebration. Disney had long thought about building a residential community, and the environmental initiatives pushed Disney to move forward with the project. At this same time, Disney had worked to improve Interstate access to Disney World. This resulted in a new Interstate link. Off one of the exit ramps, Disney carved out 10,000 acres that were split off from the Disney World holdings. The location was perfect, because a Disney employee could drive right down U.S. 192 to work, while an Orlando businessperson could hop on I-4, which leads the roughly twenty miles to downtown Orlando. But this new development of Celebration would be very different from Kissimmee, because it was not creating an industry. It was creating a housing development.

What does a comparison of these two towns' histories tell us? It tells us a lot about the thing called urbanism.

The town of Kissimmee is a relic of a now bygone transportation and economic system. Railroads and lake shipping have died, and so have their towns. Interstates and suburban highways have thrived, and so have their towns. It is this underlying economic reality that is key to understanding Kissimmee, and understanding why "urbanism" as celebrated by New Urbanists is a different animal than what it appears at first glance.

Miami architect Andres Duany, the most prominent New Urbanist, says that wherever you find great urbanism you find soaring real-estate values. Good urbanism is in such short supply that it's precious wherever you find it, he says. By urbanism, he means gridded streets, homes built close to sidewalks, and main-street-style retail. This is not only a whopper of the highest order, it confuses people about where urbanism comes from. The truth is, there are at least ten dead or dying urban neighborhoods for every alive one. The ones that are alive are valuable precisely because it is rare that circumstances conspire to create a life support system that will keep an urban neighborhood or town alive. Urban-style cities and neighborhoods originated from transportation systems and economies that came about before the advent of the car. Because, as with Kissimmee, most of those economies are now gone, maintaining the towns is difficult. A few places have managed it. Some, like New York City, are still working cities. Others, like a quaint New

England tourist town, are ornamental. But in general, urban areas are antiques, and so are valuable the same way a well-kept Model-T Ford is valuable.

Urbanism comes from a particular type of transportation system or systems. Grids of streets with a close network of stores and homes are produced by a transportation system where people rely on their feet to get around short distances, and on some type of mass transportation to go longer distances. Healthy urban neighborhoods are rare because these transportation systems have declined, and the economies designed around them have declined. Where New Urbanism errs is treating the design of a neighborhood as something done on the level of individual streets and buildings. In reality, a neighborhood is designed within the context of its larger transportation system, which, in the case of Celebration, is the network of freeways and large suburban boulevards. What Celebration is trying to do is re-create an urban neighborhood without creating the transportation network that spawned such neighborhoods. Which is not possible. So what you get is a peculiar thing, an automobile-oriented subdivision dressed up to look like a small pre-car-centered town.

One of the most misleading illustrations is the one replicated in almost every article about New Urbanism, which shows a major arterial highway with a New Urbanism subdivision on one side and a standard collection of suburban pods on the other. This is supposed to compare urbanism to suburbanism and show its benefits.

But in reality, towns, cities, and neighborhoods all grow around their central transportation artery, whether it be a train line or a road or a highway. No urban neighborhood is "off" a highway. Fundamentally, there is no difference between the neighborhoods grouped around the suburban highway and those grouped around the subway stop. Their form is different, but not the process that created them.

TWO MAIN STREETS

At first glance, the main streets of Kissimmee and Celebration resemble each other somewhat. Both have stores, restaurants, and even a movie theater that open onto a sidewalk. Both are at the center of the respective "towns." But a second glance shows revealing differences.

Content versus Style: Kissimmee's Main Street (top) and Celebration's Market Street.
Photos by Alex Marshall.

Celebration's main street is Market Street, which is at the core of its small downtown. Whatever its deficiencies, Celebration's downtown is its crowning achievement. Other New Urban communities have not been able to create even a limited commercial center. Disney pulls it off because of a unique set of circumstances and set of efforts. With a master plan designed by architects Robert Stern and Jaquelin Robertson, it has a bank, a "Town Hall," a post office, and a movie theater designed by Robert Venturi, Philip Johnson, Michael Graves, and Cesar Pelli. Its central one-block main street, designed by Stern and Robertson, has New Orleans–style balconies overlooking a palm-tree-shaded street lined with a specialty-foods-type grocery store, a bakery, two restaurants, a dress store, and a gift shop. Although Stern's work often achieves a muted elegance, here most subtlety is lost in the sea of front porches that adorn the houses in Celebration.

With the exception of Stern and Robertson's work, the downtown buildings are both assertive and comic. The Graves post office is a cartoon cylinder wearing a hat; a visitor to the Johnson "Town Hall" (more about that later) meanders through a forest of white columns; the Cesar Pelli movie theater features two spires that shoot off into the night. It is a no-holds-barred collection of contemporary architecture—set amid a Williamsburg-like collection of historical motifs that characterizes the rest of Celebration. I'm not sure it works; it's like mixing arugula and iceberg lettuce. At least it's interesting.

But the architecture is not what makes Celebration's downtown such a triumph: It is that it exists at all. Not counting a convenience store or cafe here and there, planned downtowns in other New Urban developments generally do not exist. With its incredible financial and marketing muscle, Disney was able to build the downtown first, subsidize store leases, and advertise the downtown heavily so that tourists and sightseers come in and at least partially support the stores.

Around this downtown are Celebration's residential streets. They are a mixture of classic urban styles, from the Georgetown-style row houses to Charleston-style homes with entrances onto a side-facing front porch. Most of the detached homes, however, feature big front porches with white railings, and these give the town its central atmosphere. The largest homes face a golf course which is at the end of the community, between U.S. 192 and the residential areas. These homes are like the others, with big front porches and such, only slightly bigger and grander.

In approved urban style, they are not set on the golf course but on the other side of the street. They face the course, but leave its cutting edge for strollers and bikers.

A short walk from the core of downtown is the Celebration School, with grades one through twelve. Although it is a public school, run by Osceola County, Disney has had a free hand in running and designing its curriculum, an arrangement Disney obtained by bankrolling a large part of its costs. The turning over of part of a public school system to a large corporation troubles me.

DOWNTOWN KISSIMMEE

Kissimmee's Main Street is much longer than Celebration's Market Street. It is about a quarter-mile long in its central area. It has old brick buildings, some with elaborate detailing and exterior molding. The street is lined with storefronts, most of them, to the town's credit, open for business. There's a seemingly endless number of old barbershops, all open, a wedding store, two musical instruments stores, a couple of old-style cafes, very cheaply furnished, and a quite tired-looking but open movie theater. There are some clothing stores and a boot shop.

Off the downtown fan streets, part of a grid that is filled with a variety of homes of various ages. Some are simple bungalows; others are grand mansions. The atmosphere of the town is aided by the huge oak trees that dot many streets and yards, some with hanging Spanish moss.

On one side of Main Street the perpendicular streets run quickly into Lake Tohopekaliga, with a landscaped park along its edge. It's great urbanism. City officials kept houses and other buildings off the lakefront and placed them on the other side of the roadway bordering the lake; a park and a path wind their way around the lake. This perimeter park includes small driveways every so often where someone can stop and use the picnic tables placed there. The lake is huge, with the far side barely visible.

The downtown of Kissimmee is alive, but barely. There used to be two grocery stores, I was told, but one burned down and the other closed. On the downtown streetlights are city-sponsored banners proclaiming that this is "Downtown!" lest anyone has forgotten. The place has received some municipal attention, probably for both good and ill.

A new library and a new civic center sit right off downtown. Although built unurbanistically, with parking lots out front, they are real amenities that should boost the health of the town, but appear not to have done much.

MRS. MAC'S VERSUS MAX'S

We can glimpse the distinctive characters of the respective "main streets" of Kissimmee and Celebration by looking at two eatery proprietors offering simple fare there. Kissimmee has a small restaurant on Main Street, called "Mrs. Mac's," that serves sandwiches, hamburgers, meat loaf, and pie. Celebration has a restaurant on Market Street, called "Max's Cafe," that serves sandwiches, hamburgers, meat loaf, and pie. One is a magical realist version of the other.

Mrs. Mac's on Main Street in Kissimmee has Formica-topped tables that you might find in your kitchen, a nondescript floor, and a wooden checkout counter with a noncomputerized cash register. The menu is simple. Two grilled pork chops with three vegetables for $5.95. Steak for $6.95. Homemade chili for $1.50. At lunch, I watched a nonpicturesque group of people eat there: a fat woman struggling to control her three children, a businessman here and there. The food was austere but good.

Max's Cafe in Celebration is to cafes what Celebration is to small towns: a fantasy version of a small Southern cafe. Max's has venetian blinds with thick louvers in the windows, booths inside with metallic piping, and a long soda fountain. It's really quite beautiful, although it comes at a price.

A bowl of chili at Max's costs $5.95, compared to $1.50 at Mrs. Mac's. A piece of pie costs $4.95 compared to $1.50 at Mrs. Mac's. A cheeseburger is $7.50 compared to $2.70 at Mrs. Mac's. And we don't even want to get into the entrees. But the differences between the two places go deeper than the prices and decor.

The proprietor of Mrs. Mac's in Kissimmee opens or closes when she pleases. Like the other property owners or lessors in Kissimmee, she is not under the thumb of a common management. The property under Max's, however, is owned by Disney. Every store in Celebration serves at Disney's pleasure and was handpicked by it. Celebration's management is that of a shopping mall, not a town. Disney can adjust "the mix" of the stores to optimize profits, or character, or anything it chooses.

So why do the respective characters, not to mention prices, of these two main streets differ so remarkably?

Kissimmee's Main Street was once its center, because the town itself was once a business and transportation center. It was natural for people to shop as they went to work, or got off the train, or took a boat down the lake. When the region's center shifted away from the town, its Main Street dried up.

Celebration's Market Street is no more of a center than Kissimmee's Main Street is now. But it does do a better job of fostering that illusion, for reasons I will come to.

The business district of Celebration is a curious animal. To some extent, Celebration has succeeded in overcoming what has been the Achilles heel of New Urbanism, which is establishing a commercial center within a residential subdivision. Retail is an area where fictions are exposed. Successful retail establishments have basic needs, like traffic or pedestrian counts, that cannot be dressed up or swept aside.

New Urbanists blame zoning for the segregated uses embodied in the mall, the subdivision, and the isolated schools no one can walk to. But this puts the cart before the horse. Zoning, like most regulation, usually only tidies up decisions the marketplace and the physical infrastructure dictated. Neighborhood business districts were created by the necessity to have services within walking distance of one's home. Before the nineteenth century, this was because feet were basically the only transportation for most people. To buy something, you had to walk there.

The advent of the streetcar and other forms of mass transportation changed that dynamic only somewhat. In their effects, streetcars and subways were to cities what guns are to violence: they were force multipliers. They made it possible for even more people to live in one place, and congregated businesses around streetcar lines and subway stops. Once they got home from work, people still walked to shop, visit a friend, or have a drink. They had to.

The car and the highway changed that. While mass transit systems were magnets, gathering people and businesses around central points, cars and highways were antimagnets, spreading things out as much as possible. Businesses that relied on customers with cars needed parking lots, which ate away at the street-based retail around them. Eventually, stores moved to the suburbs, where their parking lots could be as big as their owners liked. Stores got bigger and bigger because people could drive to them. So far, the country has not seen an end to this centrifugal dynamic, where businesses get larger and larger, and more and more isolated and spread out.

New Urban communities attempt to change this by resurrecting the old form of retail which existed prior to the automobile, or which was left over in its first few decades. They try to do this, however, without actually resurrecting the old transportation systems that made the old business districts possible and necessary.

To survive, retail needs an astonishingly large potential customer base, much larger than might be intuitively thought. The huge, 200,000-square-foot warehouse-style stores, like a Wal-Mart Supercenter, can require a customer base of a half million households within a twenty-minute drive.[3] But even a small restaurant or pharmacy requires high traffic volumes, whether it be by foot or car. Traffic volumes depend on transportation systems. Wal-Marts are located around key freeway interchanges because it allows them access to a regional population base. A small store can succeed in an urban neighborhood, but it requires a lot of people going by its front door, the same as such a store in a strip shopping center out on the highway. To produce those traffic volumes, an urban storefront seems to need at least 10,000 families within walking distance, which means a gross density of at least ten homes an acre. Ghent, the century-old neighborhood in Norfolk where I live, has a gross density of close to twenty homes to an acre. Some individual blocks in Ghent, with larger apartment buildings, have double and triple this density. And Ghent still has difficulty supporting a retail street. In general, the denser the distribution of stores, the denser the distribution of people. Manhattan can support retail in almost every block because it can pack 10,000 people into one block.

This point has always confused architects. Retail is not their strong point. Le Corbusier, the modernist giant of the twentieth century, imagined that shops could be put into his tall towers and persisted even after it was shown that their population was not nearly enough to support the shops.[4] Duany conceives of small shops within his low-density, neotraditional subdivisions even though they also lack the necessary population and density.

Celebration, even at buildout, has a density of fewer than two per acre. The densest part of Celebration is the Garden District, which has about five homes to an acre. These are the special, lower-priced homes, starting at $150,000, and so are off to themselves so they won't contaminate the more-common $400,000 and $1 million homes in the rest of the community. The Garden District homes, which are 1,350 to 2,200 square feet, are often only six feet apart.[5] At five homes to an acre, the Garden District has a crammed-together feel to it. I wouldn't want to live there. I bet turning into your driveway at night could be a real operation. Yet the density here is still nowhere near high enough to support a business district.

So how is Celebration able to support a downtown?

In a book about the making of the Macintosh computer, *Insanely Great*,[6] Steven Levy described the "reality distortion field" that workers said Apple founder Steve Jobs was able to create around him by the sheer force of his personality. Disney is able to create a similar reality distortion field around Celebration. Through the force of its marketing muscle, it is able to reverse the normal laws of retailing that demand that retail be placed around principal transportation arteries, be they suburban highways or subway lines. In the suburbs, this means placing retail on a heavily traveled main artery and putting big parking lots there to scoop the traffic off of it.

With Celebration's downtown, you have to drive a mile on a winding access road off U.S. 192. This should kill any attempt at retail. But Disney is able to surmount this with the sheer force of its name and presence. Tourists and sightseers are being pulled off U.S. 192 by the publicity generated by the press and advertising. Disney has heavily advertised Celebration on local television as a place to go shop. Celebration also has its own exit sign on Interstate 4. It's already listed on the one-page, low-detail maps that you get from the rental car companies.

All this is enough to bring a steady stream of traffic into Celebration to both look at the homes and walk around this novel creature, a "downtown" inside a subdivision. The tourist traffic is a twofer, for the tourists both support the stores and look at the model homes. (This has obviously caused some tension in the neighborhood. Many homes have small signs on them that say they are occupied, not a model home.)

Celebration's downtown will only succeed if it is able to be not a neighborhood business district, but a regional shopping center. That is working so far. Most of their customers, store owners tell me, are tourists and home lookers. But because of this, the stores in the downtown are nothing like those one would choose for a neighborhood shopping street. There are a fancy dress store, and upscale souvenir shops. There are restaurants, a grocery store, and a movie theater, but all extremely upscale. The Goodings market, a luxury chain in Florida, is a gourmet store. The manager says it originally tried to have a full produce and meat section. But the stuff wouldn't sell. So it scaled back the produce and eliminated the fresh meat. What you have left is a fancy store that is convenient if you forget the bottle of wine, but is not for everyday grocery shopping.

The point is that the residents of Celebration are still utterly dependent on U.S. 192, and always will be. They drive there to shop for groceries. They drive to the Wal-Mart to buy some lawn furniture. They drive to the mall to buy a computer, a lamp, or almost anything essential.

THE REAL MAIN STREET

U.S. 192 is actually the "main street" of both Kissimmee and Celebration. Kissimmee's downtown is failing because of this, while Celebration is trying to create a new downtown for itself in spite of it. Celebration is part of the sprawl of U.S. 192, as much a part of it as the alligator-shaped hotels, the glass-walled souvenir shops, and shopping malls. Celebration is part of the ecosystem of U.S. 192. Its residents depend on the highway's stores to exist. Its businesses have links to wholesalers. Their sewage and water are part of the same system that links those businesses on U.S. 192. Like the shopping centers, hotels, and other subdivisions that line U.S. 192, Celebration is one more pod off of it. This is where food comes in and wastes go out. To call Celebration a town, even projecting to the future when it will become fully built out, is a dreadful conceit. Such a designation denotes a kind of separateness. Celebration is fully dependent on U.S. 192, and could not survive without it. The irony here is that Celebration pretends to be the antithesis of U.S. 192. But if the artery from U.S. 192 were somehow severed, Celebration would die as quickly as a severed limb. U.S. 192, along with the Interstate, is

Celebration's lifeline, as vital to it as the railroad and the big lake were to Kissimmee in the nineteenth century.

To pull back the camera even farther, we see that U.S. 192 and Celebration are part of the sprawl that surrounds Disney World, and both are within its orbit. And this sprawl in turn is part of the larger sprawl that surrounds Orlando, most of it sparked by Disney's decision to locate here thirty years ago.

What Celebration very much is *not,* is a cure to the sprawl around Orlando. If Disney wanted to help combat sprawl, the worst thing to have done was to build another subdivision twenty miles outside town. Demand for housing is generated by economic development. There is only a limited market for residential housing. Center city Orlando would be more healthy if the wealth that is now going into the peripheries, where government must build new roads and other infrastructure, were forced back into the center. Celebration is destructive because it propels growth and wealth outward. All this gets back to transportation. Cities and places are products of transportation. The Interstate and the megasuburban boulevard created the possibility for Celebration, as well as its inherent advantages and limitations. Celebration is an automobile suburb. It can do little to escape from that dynamic.

If U.S. 192 is the main street of Celebration, then what is Market Street, the Stern-created hub of Celebration? It's not a main street, it's a shopping center, one more appendage to U.S. 192, as is Celebration itself. The downtown is a carefully contrived amenity to the subdivision that offers outsiders a novel place to look around, and insiders a place to get a cup of coffee and a meal, or go to a movie.

That's limited, but that's fine. Even if it ain't everything, it is something. But only Disney is likely to have the marketing and financial muscle to pull something like this off. The average New Urban subdivision developer cannot afford to spend millions on a business district up front, nor would it have the marketing power to draw in outsiders. Which is why virtually every other New Urban business district has failed. Seaside, arguably the first New Urban development, near Panama City in Florida, has a small retail district, but this relates to its status as a resort community, which again has both tourist traffic and a stranded population.

It's clear that Celebration's downtown, even with its special status, is just barely getting by. The traffic is light. Several stores have already changed over, even with Disney subsidizing the rent initially.[7]

Tension has already started to develop in Celebration between the residents and the merchants, and between the merchants and Disney.[8] The residents resent the merchants because they are realizing that the bulk of the stores are not for them, and that the merchants' need for a steady flow of tourists and sightseers conflicts with the goal of a sheltered neighborhood. The merchants, on the other hand, are angry at Disney because they are realizing that the traffic downtown will not support a store very easily.

Traffic for downtown stores could have been increased if Disney had chosen to put more offices there. Disney has built an office complex, but it chose not to put it downtown. The decision says a lot about Celebration.

Out by the main highway, apart from the downtown and residential areas, you have two large Disney office buildings designed by Aldo Rossi. The two buildings, one four-story and one nine-story, are in hypercartoon style, in soft brick red and ochre yellow. But despite their style, they are serious buildings meant for serious work. They are each surrounded by parking lots, and they are big enough—240,000 square feet in all—to have the big floor plans of the typical contemporary office. They have easy highway and Interstate access. No messing around here with faux main streets. It's here—not in the play world of the Celebration downtown—that you find the offices of Disney Imagineering, which created and supervises Celebration. It's as if the make-believe world of "main street" should not be intruded on by any hint of the adult world that created it. The overlords sit outside their creation, looking in, moving a lever when they need to.

If Disney meant Celebration to have a downtown, why not place this mammoth collection of office space within it? It would not only be appropriate in an urban sense, because downtowns are meant for work, but would also contribute a customer base to the businesses. But office buildings are a place for grown-ups, and so must have parking lots and easy access to U.S. 192 and the Interstate. Putting them in downtown would change that place into an actual working downtown where real business was conducted. Which isn't what Celebration's "downtown" is about. It is, instead, a place to play, a magical world for the children of all ages that live in Celebration, where they can have the illusion of living in a world of the past that had a main street. Real business should not be allowed to intrude.

This placement of the central offices, along with the health center, outside the downtown completes the inversion of suburban/urban functions. In this faux-urban world, the actual work of the town is placed outside it, in the suburbs, so to speak. The residential living and associated amenities are in the inner city.

GOVERNING A TOWN VERSUS MANAGING ONE

Because our political systems are even more basic than our retail or transportation systems, looking at the political systems of our two towns is even more instructive in revealing the underlying reality of each. Although "town" is a general word, it implies some sort of political structure or at least system of organization.

Kissimmee has something that is underused, ignored, and reviled by many people these days. It's called a government. The people of Kissimmee, those who care to vote, elect it. They are eligible to vote by virtue of declaring their residence there.

Where does this government exist? Well, in the City Hall on Main Street, and it's where the elected town council meets. But the government exists also in the state constitution of Florida, which lays out the power of the state legislature, including its right to create corporate city charters. Kissimmee exists in the state statute that authorized it. The town exists at the pleasure of the state legislature, which governs at the pleasure of the citizens of Florida. Kissimmee was authorized by the state in 1883. The town is a creation of the state, a political subdivision of it, with its powers and limitations on power directly stemming from the state of Florida and, through it, the U.S. Constitution as well.

The town of Kissimmee has a mayor and a town council. To vote for this government, you must have your legal residence there.

Celebration does not have a government. It has a homeowners association. The state legislature in Tallahassee did not create it. Instead, it is created by the inch-thick stack of documents you sign that is legally part of the deed to your house if you buy one in Celebration. The homeowners association and the entire package of rules that go with it are created first by the Disney corporation, and secondly by the courts, as opposed to the legislature, which have been willing to recognize the validity of stapling a package of rules to the sale of a property.

A homeowners association is usually the most visible tip of the iceberg of what have been labeled "Common Interest Developments," or CIDs. A CID is any group of properties or owners bound together through agreements and restrictions written into the property deeds. CIDs include everything from subdivisions to condominium associations. They are an enormous force now. In 1990, an estimated 11 percent of all housing in the United States was covered by CIDs,[9] almost all of which had versions of a homeowners association. There are probably about 200,000 homeowners associations today.[10] In many areas of the country, most new housing, particularly on the fringes, is in CID communities.

As Evan McKenzie details authoritatively in *Privatopia*,[11] these associations do not represent an embrace of democracy but a withdrawal from it. It's an exchange of governance for management, a submission to a kind of corporate fascism. It is an act of withdrawal from society and the messiness of democracy, in exchange for an ordered world where corporate-style management can eliminate much of the unpredictability and openness of democracy.

McKenzie says: "In a variety of ways, these private governments are illiberal and undemocratic. Most significantly, boards of directors operate outside constitutional restrictions because the law views them as business entities rather than governments. Moreover, courts accept the legal fiction that all the residents have voluntarily agreed to be bound by the covenants by virtue of having bought a unit in the development."[12]

Homeowners associations have been known to ban political signs on front lawns, as well as political gatherings in the "public" squares, McKenzie notes. They have a record of arbitrary acts like seizing pets or, in a case in Boca Raton, Florida, ordering a couple to stop using their back door because it was wearing a path down in the grass.[13] This is the form of "government" Disney has chosen to create in Celebration, where people can return to the creation of "community" and revive "public space."

McKenzie argues that the restrictive covenants on which the entire foundation of these private governments rest are actually outside the tradition of common law and ought to be illegal or sharply curtailed. In preindustrial England, courts frowned on the idea that an owner could tie restrictions to a piece of property, in effect, not fully transferring ownership. The courts particularly frowned on the idea that a property owner could determine the actions of *all future property owners* long after he had died. Considered this way, such restrictions are very strange indeed. Imagine. Theoretically, I could tie restrictions on the use of a piece of land a thousand years into the future, simply by selling it to one person who agreed to those restrictions.

The rules of homeowners associations are typically very difficult to change. Homeowners buy a package of rules when they buy a house. Amending this package, much less a wholesale rewrite, would require an enormous political effort made more difficult by the extraconstitutional nature of such bodies. Conventional governments are bound by the U.S. Constitution, which requires "one man, one vote."

But a homeowners association is not bound by "one man, one vote." It is standard for developers to get three votes in a homeowners association for every piece of property they own, and for buyers to only get one. Such a restriction would not be possible with a conventional government, but a homeowners association is not a conventional government, courts have ruled, but a voluntary contractual agreement. If you don't like this, don't buy the property, goes the argument. This rule allows the developer to control the homeowners association until three-quarters of all property is sold. In addition, to change the rules of a homeowners association typically requires a supermajority of 75 percent of *all property owners*, not just those participating in an election. Which is a virtual impossibility, given that elections for board members of a homeowners association usually have a participation rate below that of local school board elections.

Celebration covenants include the usual restriction of giving the company three votes for every piece of property. But Disney goes even further, giving the company unprecedented control over Celebration. As McKenzie spotted in a review of the deed restrictions at Celebration, Disney retains veto power over the actions of the homeowners association for as long as it owns even one piece of property in the district. So basically, Disney can control Celebration forever, or as long as it chooses, simply by allowing one piece of property to remain in its hands.

It's scary that talented people like architect Robert Stern do not, apparently, realize the difference between a homeowners association and a town, between the rules of a corporation and the laws of a municipality. Stern is quoted in *The New York Times Magazine,* December 14, 1997, that "In a freewheeling capitalist society, you need controls—you can't have community without them. It's right there in Tocqueville: in the absence of aristocratic hierarchy, you need firm rules to maintain decorum. I'm convinced these controls are actually liberating to people. It makes them feel their investment is safe. Regimentation can release you."[14]

Sure, but that's why we have governments. There's a difference between a government and a corporate management group. A homeowners association is a product of a "freewheeling capitalist society," not a defense against it. It is a private government, bought and paid for by its residents. There's a Faustian bargain going on in Celebration. For the illusion of living in a small town, you give up your right to self-government. By purchasing a life within a chimera of Democracy, including a "Town Hall" and lots of talk about community, public space, and so forth, you give up democracy itself.

Russ Rymer, in the October 1996 issue of *Harper's Magazine,* said people were buying themselves a childlike world where the real pains of governance are ceded over to the grown-ups of Disney. The yearning to come to Celebration, Rymer said, is:

> a yearning for bygone America, . . . when informed citizens reigned from every front porch over the structure of their community, and the messy responsibility of democracy held sway, and society worked. If the mythic American town had such a thing as a soul, it lay in that machinery. It wasn't a machinery meant for pretty calm, because a town had reasons for being and people had reasons for being in the town, and with those purposes came conflict. That was the strange secret of America's innocence—that its people regularly conspired to engage in government, not out of consensus but in contention over their differences. . . .
>
> . . . maybe Celebration really isn't neo-1940s or neo-traditional or, for that matter, neo-anything; maybe it is instead proto-corporate and quintessentially contemporary, a town off the

shelf, meant not to be built but to be consumed by its residents, residents who understood perfectly the equation that had eluded me: that in this new corporate city, history and tradition were needed as aesthetics to permit their absence in fact, that democracy was the disruptive god honored in elaborate ceremony precisely to keep him at bay. . . .

What Celebration celebrates, oddly, is an American community that existed precisely in that time before corporations made it their business to build communities—an era before neighborhoods became subdivisions and business districts became malls and culture in all its sources and manifestations became supplanted by the cathode-ray tube and the theme park. In that bygone America, businesses served a community built by its citizens who were enveloped in a society. Celebration wants to see if the chain can be reversed—if a true society can be fostered among people living in a community built by a business.[15]

Which is what makes the celebrated "Town Hall" in Celebration such an outrageous joke. Designed by Philip Johnson, it features a forest of columns out front, perhaps meant to remind residents of ancient Athenian democracy. But no government exists therein. What's inside is the manager of the homeowners association, the company manager hired by Disney to supervise its creation, who sends out little messages asking people not to put strong-colored curtains in their front windows.

The corruption of language that calling such management "government" entails runs all through New Urbanism and neotraditionalism. It's an interesting trend, because it reverses the usual path of bad language, which is to make simple things appear complicated. By this, I refer to calling a rich person "upper-income," or calling a library "the media center." New Urbanists, and Andres Duany in particular, do something more clever: they make complex things appear simple by stealing the labels of older, more basic institutions and concepts. The center of a homeowners association is called a "Town Hall." A subdivision is called a "village" or a "town." It's a Hollywoodization of language, with words as icons that represent something very different. In the New Urban subdivision of Kentlands in Maryland, a project by Duany, the homeowners association is called "The Kentlands Citizens Assembly." This is the embrace of the language of democracy, to serve as a front for an organization that is explicitly rejecting it.

The choice of government relates to community. Does Celebration deliver it? It does only if community is defined as excluding most of society, and controlling people in a way that goes beyond the normal powers of government. Celebration is a narrowing of the ideal of community. It rests not on self-government or cooperation, but on selective controls, achieved through an outside party that the participants recognize. Residents have chosen to be managed rather than to govern themselves.

But most people I interviewed at Celebration liked what they had bought. Celebration had delivered the package of friendly neighbors, clean community, and nearby amenities they had been promised.

"We love it," say Lauri and Paul McElroy, who live on Sycamore Street. (The street names in Celebration match what one would think an old-fashioned town would have.) They were lining their flowerbeds as we talked. "Today, the children walked to a dentist appointment downtown. They walk to school. They walk to the movies and to the post office. They rollerblade everywhere."

As the McElroys indicate, Celebration works as advertised to some extent. You do see families bicycling together downtown, even if it doesn't quite mesh that the six-year-old on a bike is in danger of being run down by the out-of-town driver who is keeping the high-end stores on main street in operation. Many people had found the tighter, friendlier community they said they wanted. They also loved Disney and had no fear about being in a subdivision under its control. And that's fine. My intent is not to blame people for their choices, but to see clearly what Celebration is, what it can deliver and at what price.

CONTINUING THE MASQUERADE: STREETS AND HOMES

Real-estate values are the ultimate reality check. They reveal at a glance what society values, versus what it says it values or thinks it values. Comparing the homes and streets of Kissimmee, versus those of Celebration, is revealing for two reasons. One, the astonishing difference in housing prices shows how much people actually value a real Florida small town, something which is allegedly in short supply. Secondly, the differences

This old mansion in Kissimmee, now housing five apartments, is assessed at a mere $125,000. "Old-home lovers" with money prefer the new old mansions in Celebration to the real ones in Kissimmee. Photo by Alex Marshall.

One of the "Estate" homes of Celebration, which sell for up to $1 million. Photo by Alex Marshall.

in the design of the homes and the streets around them show what com-
promises Celebration has made to achieve its masquerade.

For me, the contrast was most stark in comparing a grand old mansion I found in Kissimmee with one of the model homes open for inspection in Celebration. Although the Kissimmee mansion was twice
the home of the Celebration model home, both in size and style, it was
less than half the price.

We'll look at the Celebration home first. While the Disney development is reminiscent in appearance of a nineteenth-century town, the
homes are a product of late-twentieth-century power building, factory-
style home construction. That means big building companies, and model
homes with extras that you pick out like buying a Chevy Trail Blazer,
and deciding whether you want leather seats and the extra drink holder
in the back. It's a very different way of building houses than what produced Kissimmee, and produces a very different house. Touring a model
home in Celebration shows how little $400,000 can buy.

The Kentland model (named, I presume, after Duany's development in Maryland) was typical of a row of homes on Sycamore Street.
Built by Town and Country, it was $416,000, "as equipped." It was the
deluxe model, featuring all the upgrades, as the saleswoman put it. That
included the "Honeywell Home Theater Surround Sound," "fireplace
with media niche," "crown molding in living room and dining room,"
plus ceiling fans, central vac system, standing-seam metal roof, "bathroom light fixture Package D," and a tiny pool out on the back patio that
substituted for a backyard, which the house lacked. The house was one
story with twelve-foot ceilings. The extra height was used to create the
impression of a false second story from the outside. The house lacked
both a basement and an attic, which is common now in new homes. It
was not a large home, 2,300 square feet. This is not tiny, but seemed
small for $416,000.

"I love the old-time feel," said a woman from Austin, Texas. "I like
the small streets, garages on back, the village feel. The place has that
Norman Rockwell feel to it. At least on the outside. Inside, you have a
modern home."

Andres Duany could not have stated the neotraditional design philosophy more coherently. These houses have about the same relation to
the older homes they imitate as the whole of Celebration does to the
towns it imitates. They are stage sets.

Duany is unapologetic about this, although he would probably disagree with my calling them stage sets. Neotraditionalism, he says, blends old and new, taking the best from both. It is the equivalent, he says, of the Mazda Miata. The Miata might look like an old English roadster, say an MG or TR3, but the innards are utterly different. The Miata will not leak oil or suddenly stop in midhighway because of strange electrical problems. The throaty chuckle its exhaust pipe emits will be a sound carefully designed by the manufacturer.

The same goes with the New Urban subdivision. Its proponents say it is unapologetically not the old thing, but a new thing, that looks like the old thing and functions like it in the good ways and not the bad. This is a pretty good sales job. But the New Urban creation is less a blend of old and new than a masquerade. New Urbanism is really more comparable to the wood-grained strips of plastic that used to be put on station wagons in the 1960s. The New Urban design philosophy is akin to dressing up a car to look like a horse-drawn carriage, and then saying you have brought back the intimacy and community of carriage life.

The house I fell in love with in Kissimmee was as different from the Kentland model home as a Steinway grand is from a toy piano. It suggested a richness and depth that went beyond its fine brick exterior into its interior structure. Built in the early 1920s,[16] it had bulging bay windows, soaring white columns, and a second-story balcony that cut under its Paladian trim. It's solid brick, said the owner, whom I later contacted, with heart of pine floors and wood throughout. It was a huge house, with about 5,000 square feet of space.

It originally had five bedrooms. But it now has five apartments. In the 1950s, as its original owners aged along with the town, the house was chopped up. The original owners' daughter, now aging herself, still owns it and manages the apartments. Still, the house is in rock-solid condition, and an enterprising couple could buy it and convert it back into a house. It might not cost much. The house is assessed for a mere $123,913. It might sell for even less. At $123,913, it would be double or triple much of Kissimmee real estate. Most houses go for between $40,000 and $80,000.[17] That's an astonishingly low price, especially considering the $400,000 the average home in Celebration appears to be selling for.

The $125,000 my mansion might cost in Kissimmee would not even get you in the door in Celebration. The cheapest model home open for inspection was $195,000, and it was a cramped, small place on a tiny lot. The Kentland model home—at $416,000—was half the size of the Kissimmee mansion and arguably far inferior in construction. To get a home even roughly comparable to the mansion in Kissimmee, you'd have to move up to the "estate" homes, which go for from $500,000 up to $1 million. For the price of a home in Celebration, you could buy a home in Kissimmee, tear it down, and build a brand new one, and still have money left over. And you would have a real main street within walking distance, with a greater variety of stores, plus a larger, more stylish waterfront.

But the Celebration clients are not buying homes in Kissimmee. "We are trying to encourage people to buy some of these older homes and restore them," Mark Durbin, Kissimmee's city manager, said. "A couple of people have bought them, but it's not happening as quickly as we would like." What does this tell us, that people are buying homes at two, three, and four times the price in Celebration instead of bigger and arguably better homes in exactly the same kind of environment they are seeking out in Celebration?

Real-estate values are a reality check. The lesson they teach us here is that *people don't want to live in a real Florida small town!* They want to live in a fake small town where they can pretend to live in a real one. There are too many intrusions of reality into Kissimmee. There is no homeowners association to control your neighbor's habits. There's no preselection of housing types, so just the upper class can live in your preordered community. No, better to buy a home in Celebration at five times the price, and lament how small-town values have faded in the United States.

What's so ironic is that Kissimmee has everything Celebration does, except more so. Kissimmee has a central, but larger, main street, with more stores that you can walk to. It has a beautiful and larger lake to walk around, with a well-designed and urbanistically appropriate park. It has fine old homes that you can buy and fix up, or tear down if you choose. The town also has a brand new library, with an accompanying civic center, right off downtown. It has an Amtrak rail stop. But Kissimmee is a tired old town, just barely getting by, while Celebration is thriving.

It's not supposed to be this way, of course. The domed ceiling inside the Celebration sales center lists all the blue-ribbon small towns that have inspired it. Along with Savannah, Nantucket, and Easthampton is named Kissimmee. Think about it. Kissimmee is considered such a fine example of urbanism that it has a place of honor inside Celebration. Its name on the domed ceiling might be considered in part a sop thrown to the home team. But it wouldn't be listed there if it didn't have some admirable qualities. And its homes are selling for a fraction of the price of homes in Celebration. What gives?

If, as Celebration advertisers and New Urbanist prophets say, people are really hankering for a return to small town America and "great urbanism," then Kissimmee should be a boom town, with soaring real-estate prices and swanky restaurants. Celebration, in this world, would be the imitation for people who could not afford the real thing. But the reverse is true.

If we look at wider Orlando, we'll see what a foreign element Celebration is in its prices. Driving around the rest of Orlando often means driving down dirt roads lined with simple one-story houses. Like much of the South, Florida is not a rich state at heart.

There's a lot of talk about how Celebration and New Urbanism include a diversity of housing. It's part of the theory that New Urbanism does not segregate classes like the suburbs. It's true that Celebration does have some mix of housing, but it is a mixing of the upper class. In early 1998, Celebration had about 600 homes built, including apartments. Of these, about 50 were "Estate" homes that cost between $500,000 and $1 million; about 125 were "Village" homes that cost between $275,000 and $425,000; about 225 were "Cottage" and "Garden" homes, which cost between $190,000 and $300,000; about 75 were town houses costing from $160,000 to $200,000; and about 125 were apartments, which rented for about $1 a square foot, or between $700 and $2,000 a month.[18] The homes in each of these categories were generally built separate from each other on different streets, although the streets were sometimes adjacent, and the lower-priced "Garden" homes were in an entirely separate district.

By any estimation, this is a very upper-class place. To get in the door costs $200,000 if you want to buy a house. If you rent, you are paying big-city prices in a Southern city whose economy is based on low-wage service jobs. I understand why a Kissimmee city assessor told me Celebration "isn't for the people of Osceola County."

To succeed financially, Celebration needs to capture 25 percent of the top 10 percent of the housing market that is its potential clientele, said Disney executive David Pace in a briefing to a group from the American Institute of Architects in 1998.[19] Notice also how radically this language clashes with the standard preaching of New Urban diversity. By Disney's own words, its market is the top 10 percent of the housing market. That's not very diverse. And the Disney mix of housing at Celebration is about what I have seen at the other New Urban developments. In Duany's Kentlands, outside Washington, the mix is almost identical. There you also have a wide swath of $400,000 homes along with $1 million ones and a sprinkling of lower-priced ones in the $200,000 range. The "low-income" people I met there were two young attorneys, who complained that people snubbed them because they lived in a $175,000 condominium instead of a $500,000 single-family house.[20] The New Urban idea of diversity is almost exactly the opposite of what exists in the real world. If the real world is 80 percent poor and middle class, and 20 percent upper class, New Urban developments are generally 80 percent upper class, and 20 percent middle class. Forget poor. The New Urban idea of diversity is to sprinkle a handful of middle-class residents within a solidly upper-income subdivision.

STUFFING A TOWN INTO A SUBDIVISION: A TIGHT FIT

When Ron Dickson parks his car underneath the carport behind his London-style town house on Campus Street, he has to carefully stop his car at the right position between the Jeffersonian columns that support it. The carport is so narrow that if he does not, he cannot open his car door. His neighbor has an even worse problem. Because her carport is on the opposite side of the accompanying garage, she has to back her car in to be able to open her doors, provided she still parks exactly between the supporting columns.

Celebration has essentially rammed a late-twentieth-century, automobile-dependent subdivision into the shell of a nineteenth-century, pre-automobile town. Something has to give, and it does.

Cramped, awkward spaces are what New Urban developments create through their attempt to have the car and get rid of it, too. The communities that New Urbanists love, like Savannah or Charleston, were all founded before the automobile. Homes were built close to the street

Town house owner Ron Dickson shows how he cannot open his car door inside his carport unless the car is carefully lined up between the columns. Photo by Alex Marshall.

because there was no reason not to. No driveways or garages were included because not only were there no cars, but walking was the principal means of transportation. Only the wealthy had carriage houses with separate driveways. In contemporary times, these historic places have been made to work with the automobile with great difficulty, but successfully, because there was no alternative and because the historic qualities of these places were so unique and valuable.

What Celebration and other New Urban communities do is try to imitate the design of a Charleston and a Savannah, only modifying it to squeeze in a two-car garage for every family, along with parking lots for stores—while still retaining at least some of the tight structure of an eighteenth- or nineteenth-century town. It is a tight fit. Postal trucks have problems negotiating the narrow, ten-foot-wide alleys, sometimes meeting garbage trucks going the other way. It's an article of New Urban faith that the wide streets of standard subdivisions are unneeded. But in a world designed around the automobile, this may not be true.

The fatal flaw of New Urban design may be that it has killed off the classic suburban backyard, where the barbecue is held, the neighbors invited in, and the drink after work consumed. New Urbanists have done this by making a priority out of establishing a ceremonial street facade. They push houses close to the street and ban front driveways and garages. But because the car must still be accommodated, all the support services for it, like driveways and garages, have been pushed into the alley and the back of the house. Where the nice open backyard used to be. So what you get are homes that have neither front, nor back, yards. Older urban homes usually have small, unrestricted backyards because they had no need of driveways and garages. They were built close to the street because that was where the traffic was.

Alleys are a nice device in communities that are not completely automobile-dependent. In Savannah, or many urban cities like Norfolk, alleys provided a way to get some services off the street, while the bulk of humanity still went in and out the front doors. But in a completely car-dependent environment, alleys simply become tiny, narrow streets that are handling all the traffic of a neighborhood. The ceremonial front door and the street it is on become a vestige, there only for appearance.

What you get in Celebration is a type of design where form perversely does not follow function. Residents get a ceremonial street with front porches and an unbroken line of facades, which appears urban. But the real work of the street goes on in the alleys. It's here where cars enter, exit, and park; it's here where mail is delivered and garbage picked up.

It's this structural fact that may kill New Urbanism. Americans like backyards. The classic suburban home with the double-wide garage doors facing the street is a symbol of suburban banality and the triumph of the car. But in an automobile-dominated setting, this is an appropriate and honest way to build. The car is the principal means of transportation. Therefore, put access to it directly in front of the house on the street. If you don't like houses with garage doors on their front, then you have to change the overall transportation system. It doesn't work in reverse. Putting alleys and garages behind houses will not magically create a streetcar system. It will just mean that residents have sacrificed both their front and back yards for the sake of appearances. It's a triumph of style over substance. Hiding the driveway is a kind of urban puritanism, hiding the real workings of our society.

The classic suburban home, with the two-car garage facing the street, is an example of honest design. We depend on the car. Therefore, we put its home right out front, where it can be easily used. If we don't like this, then we need to start by changing the transportation system, not working at hiding the garage.

In New Urban subdivisions, hiding the car has perversely meant reducing activity on the street, the vaunted public life that such projects are meant to bolster. Because the car is still the main means of transport, all the action of the neighborhood goes on in the alleys. Such projects usually have wonderfully picturesque streets that are deserted.

I visited Southern Village, a New Urban development in Chapel Hill, and strolled around its confusing New Urban grid and talked to folks. One of the most striking comments came from the manager of the struggling cafe, which had recently changed ownership.

"Where I grew up, I saw kids playing in the street, and a lot of activity. You know what's strange here, you never see much activity in the street here, because all the activity is in the back. That's where you see people getting their mail, the garbage trucks, and all the other stuff."

Brent Herrington, the Disney-paid community manager of Celebration who operates out of the Town Hall in Celebration's downtown, said fitting cars, garages, and services into the narrow alleys and lots behind the town houses has been difficult. Because of this, the company recently retroactively widened the ten-foot alleys to eleven and a half feet. This widening will make it easier for service vehicles, as well as make it easier for residents to turn into their driveway or garage. Right now, they often have to make a three-point turn. But the more expensive, single-family homes, which are built on bigger lots, have not suffered these difficulties, he said.

"The town homes have been a challenge, that's no question," Herrington said. "But it would be unfair to characterize these alleys as anything but a success overall. It does keep the garbage trucks, the service vehicles, and the going-to-work traffic off the main streets, which means kids and parents can walk in the streets without worry."[21]

Leaving aside the street design of Celebration, a close inspection of Dickson's home again raises questions about the quality of houses produced on an assembly line. It is unfair to blame Disney for these problems, but it does call into question the contemporary method of building homes.

Dickson, whom I met completely by accident while knocking on doors, has suffered huge problems with his town house on Campus Street. He has waged a steady campaign to have either Disney, or Town and Country, the building company that produced it, fix them. Dickson showed me where his dining room ceiling caved in because workers forgot to solder the pipes together in the upstairs bathrooms. His kitchen flooded because the downspout dumped directly beside the exterior porch, thus flooding both it and the kitchen when it rained. He had rigged up an effective, but unsightly, piece of black tubing to carry the water farther out into the yard.

One error that stands out in my mind is in his back carport, where Dickson has problems parking his car. The clear-plastic corrugated roof was held up with, in best New Urban tradition, white Greek-style columns. But, as Dickson pointed out, and, being unusually tall myself, I could see, the makers had not closed off the tops of the columns. They were open to the elements, with a supporting piece of lumber only covering part of the open hole. Consequently, rain was pouring in, filling up each column, rotting the wood, and already leaching out a brown stain through the white paint. It seemed emblematic of the entire stage-set nature of New Urbanism: a hollow white column, rain leaching it brown, holding up a carport.

Dickson had complained of endless delays in trying to have these problems fixed. He had organized a group of dissatisfied residents, many with homes by Town and Country. But when interviewed in the spring of 1998, he was happier because Disney had stepped in and pushed the company that manufactured many of the houses with problems to fix them.[22] Dickson credits this to a certified letter to Michael Eisner, the Disney chairman, but Herrington said this was not the case.

"For whatever reason, Town and Country has had some problems on the town homes," Herrington said. "They took a long time to complete them, and there was a lot of time waiting to complete punch list items. There was a point when Celebration met with Town and Country" and worked out a plan to have the problems taken care of.[23]

NEW URBANISM: CURE OR DISEASE?

The questions I have raised about Celebration raise a natural follow-up: How much of what I perceive as the flaws and limitations of Celebration are part of the design philosophy it represents, New Urbanism? The answer is important, because New Urbanism is the most heralded new philosophy of city planning in quite a while. Its proponents believe they are leading the way out of the wilderness of sprawl, and into a more peaceful and ordered land where things work right.

The answer is that most of Celebration's drawbacks are also drawbacks in many of the theories and practices of many New Urbanists. Celebration is unique in many ways, particularly the existence and operation of its downtown. But in the way its streets and homes are laid out, in the demographics of its home buyers, in the way it manages itself, in its relationship with the highway it sits near, it is like dozens of other New Urban subdivisions around the country.

As it stands now, New Urbanism is more destructive than not in its effect on city planning and design. It often represents the worst of America in its hucksterism, in its promise of avoiding difficult choices, in its proffered option of buying one's way out of problems, in its delivery of image over substance.

Many New Urbanists resist recognizing that the communities they admire and copy were produced by transportation systems that no longer exist. One cannot copy the design of such communities—Charleston, Annapolis, etc.—without copying the transportation system that produced them, or building some modern facsimile of it. A neighborhood or place lives within the transportation system that spawns it, and can no more escape this dynamic than a creek can escape the watershed it is part of.

New Urbanism has a chance to become a more positive force in urban design the more it recognizes a hard truth: that there is a hierarchy of neighborhood, city, and regional design that cannot be escaped from. To build a good neighborhood, one must first build a good region. One must address the choices that shape a region, particularly its transportation structure, which usually means addressing the structure of its government. The dynamics of a metropolitan area are reflected in the dynamics of each of the neighborhoods within it.

Historian Robert Fishman, in a paper analyzing the antagonism between Jane Jacobs and Lewis Mumford in the early 1960s, said leaders of American cities should understand how "a vital and intense central city can strengthen and draw strength from a planned and coherent suburban periphery."[24] This is one of the best summations of the proper relationship between city and suburb. It is also a relationship that New Urbanists honor in word, but not usually in deed.

I speak of New Urbanism as singular in number. But the fact is, New Urbanism is plural, with many different adherents, thinkers, and streams of thought within it.

One of those different New Urbanist thinkers is Peter Calthorpe, the California-based architect and planner. Calthorpe's conception of good design is extremely close to my own. He recognizes the importance of transportation, regional dynamics, and government in determining the shape of the places where we live. In his 1993 book *The Next American Metropolis,* Calthorpe begins by saying: "This book is about the American Metropolis; by which I mean the sum total of the city, its suburbs, and their natural environment. The three are inseparable and the failure to treat them as a whole is endemic to many of our problems. . . . They are each interdependent and connected at the root by our concept of community."[25] He coined the phrase and title "transit-oriented design," or TODs, which, in its word structure, recognizes the primacy of transportation.

The minimum gross density to make any form of mass transit work is ten units to an acre, Calthorpe says. *The minimum.* No suburban New Urban development in the country that I know of comes close to this density, much less exceeds it. The strength of Calthorpe's work is laying out a coherent philosophy of regional, city, and neighborhood design. He speaks of regional planning, urban growth boundaries, when new towns might be built as opposed to urban infill, and how all these things work together.

Architect Douglas Kelbaugh, author of *Common Places* and formerly of Seattle, says he and Calthorpe typify the "latent schism" between "West-Coast" and "East-Coast" New Urbanists. The West-Coast New Urban movement, Kelbaugh says, grows more out of the environmental movement. It emphasizes transit and takes a macro viewpoint, recognizing the importance of things like gas prices in affecting the form of cities. The East-Coast New Urbanism movement, typified by Andres Duany and Elizabeth Plater-Zyberk, grows more out of European formalism, Kelbaugh says, and emphasizes design and aesthetics more.

The trouble is that Calthorpe and Kelbaugh are listened to in inverse proportion to the strength of their ideas. People hear readily the talk of front porches and narrower streets, but become increasingly deaf to the words of mass transit, regional planning, and more realistic gasoline pricing. Yet without those things, the mixed-use neighborhoods and other goodies of New Urbanism do not follow. And Calthorpe contributes to this confusion, for he never quite comes out and says in *The Next American Metropolis* that transit must come first.

Despite a variety of different voices within New Urbanism as a whole, in its public face and its effect on the culture of city planning, New Urbanism is almost monolithic. To most city councils and zoning boards, New Urbanism represents the option of solving serious urban problems of sprawl and center-city decline by the application of front porches, alleyways, and other devices in new developments far out of town.

Indeed, the most prominent of the New Urbanists, Duany, has steadily opposed urban growth boundaries, which Calthorpe praises, and which I believe are the single most effective tool in revitalizing existing urban areas. Duany opposes growth boundaries on the logic that they are not natural or "organic," a phrase which in concept subverts the recognition that cities are not organic, but political, creations.

No examination of New Urbanism would be complete without examining Duany and his wife and partner, Elizabeth Plater-Zyberk, who lead the architectural firm of Duany Plater-Zyberk & Company in Miami. They are bright and articulate spokespersons for their viewpoints and together have catapulted neotraditional design into the forefront of public attention. The founding of the neotraditional community Seaside in the late 1980s was like inserting a live wire into the business-as-usual profession of architecture and design. Duany in particular is a master polemicist, and, what is even rarer, is aware that he is a polemicist. In his well-attended lectures and slide shows, he speaks in broad generalities, marshaling concepts and facts to the aid of whatever viewpoint he is advocating. I favor this as a way of making a point, but it can also sweep subtleties under the rug. One of his favorite tricks is converting whatever flaws that are pointed out in his New Urban subdivisions into assets that others should emulate. So his subdivisions have homeowners associations? So should older urban areas, and it is to their discredit that they don't. So his main streets operate as shopping centers, with unified management and corporate structure? So should real main streets, he says. So his subdivisions selectively borrow from the urban places they copy? This is just because New Urbanism stands for "the best of everything," an idea which is difficult to oppose, as Harvard Professor Alex Krieger pointed out in a debate with Duany in Orlando in February of 1998. I admire Duany's and Plater-Zyberk's skill as politicians, even while the elasticity of their thinking, particularly Duany's, bothers me. I don't see him as close to admitting that to really re-create the urbanism he loves, many of the new subdivisions he designs should not be built.

The couple's Seaside in northwest Florida, however, does stand as a testament to their skill as designers and the more limited possibilities of their ideas. With its front porches, picket fences, and statuesque houses, Seaside early on came to be the symbol of New Urbanism and the alternative to conventional suburbia. It was the first neotraditional "town" built, and it launched the New Urban revolution. My sense of Seaside is that it works better than most New Urban subdivisions. But this is so precisely because it is principally a resort, and not a place where people make their year-round homes and live their daily lives. While on vacation, people have less need of the trip to the dentist, of buying a new washing machine, of making their way among a dozen vital deeds in a day. Precisely because of this, Seaside can avoid the pitfalls inherent in its pre-automobile structure that still is dependent on the automobile. It can function well the same way a college campus can, because its tenants have very different needs and sets of circumstances than the wider public around them.

New Urbanism has seeped into just about every state, and is making inroads into Australia, Canada, and other countries. There are several hundred New Urban projects now in the United States and Canada either in design or under construction. The vast majority are on the fringes of a metropolitan area, adding to, not subtracting from, the problems of sprawl.[26] They make no change in the system of sprawl that produces them.

What's difficult to accept about New Urbanism is that it is so far more of an illness than a cure. It is yet another design movement that focuses its attention outward, and gives the rationale for new suburban building that this time, we will get it right. In this, it is the spiritual descendant of both the New Town movement of the 1960s and the Planned Unit Development movement of the 1970s. Reaching further back, its root ancestor is the Garden City movement of Ebenezer Howard, which promised an end to urban ills by building new places outside urban cities.

New Urbanism is typically American because it suggests no limits. Under its rubric, Americans are told they can eat their cake and have it, too. They can both continue outward development, and have all the joys of urbanism. It can be compared to a fad diet in its proposition that we can build our way out of the excesses of sprawl. It's the equivalent of eating your way to thinness. But the only way to build a more coherent environment and metropolitan area is to do the urban equivalent of exercising more and eating less. That means such things as growth control, a big gas tax, investment in mass transit, prohibitions on parking. None of which are sexy advertising slogans.

What New Urbanism has done effectively is to market the ideal of urbanism. It has placed before the public and before the world of architects and planners the image of a tree-shaded street with houses close to it and a cafe on the corner. As an image of urbanism, it certainly is a good deal better than windowless buildings and a sidewalk covered with crack vials. This image has enormous appeal at a time when there is no "there" there for many people. The average citizen's life lacks any nexus for home, family, business, child rearing, church, feeding and clothing oneself, or playing. All these activities exist in fragmented, isolated form that the individual must "consume" and move on from. There is a hunger for a nest that will provide a place, a home, for life. Such is the promise of New Urbanism, one that I hunger after as well.

Urbanism is a result of pressure. It is produced by confining people, places, and economic activity within a limited area. No New Urban development I have seen recognizes this. In fact, all are attempts to work their way around this painful truth. Urbanism comes with a package of pains and pleasures that cannot be separated. I get to walk to my neighborhood store, but have to sometimes drive a block from my house before I find a parking place. I cannot have both an easy place to park, which comes with the low-density suburban development, and the activity and commercial environment that come with an urban one.

Norfolk and Portsmouth, the two inner cities of my metropolitan area, have probably between them a dozen urban neighborhoods that are falling into disrepair. Most of these neighborhoods have all the attributes New Urbanists love. If we want urbanity, they are where we should go.

Like a slowly turning battleship, the Congress of New Urbanism, the umbrella group that serves as a forum for the design philosophy, shows signs that it is beginning to focus more on public policy and infrastructure development than on promoting the construction of new-fangled subdivisions. Leading members are calling for studies on the hidden subsidies of sprawl, for example. Members are backing "smart growth," which is more coherent in its philosophy of limited extensions of the metropolitan area.

If this trend continues, it would shift New Urbanism to a more productive force within the debate over the direction of the American landscape. But it might also promote a schism within New Urbanism, because much of the money and power of the movement come from the excitement around having a new product to sell: the New Urban subdivision. If we reduce sprawl subsidies, for example, we would also reduce the construction of neotraditional suburbs like Celebration.

It's possible that New Urbanists are turning this corner. The 1998 Congress of New Urbanism in Denver focused on infill development. Yet, with the exception of Calthorpe, New Urbanists have generally not acknowledged that choosing urbanism means setting priorities and choosing one thing over another. But it is possible that with time, New Urbanists will begin to see the path they must take to re-create the classic walkable street they have held up as an ideal.

LEADING US ASTRAY

Celebration delivers much of what it advertises. It has walkable streets, a school kids can walk to, and a downtown that you can reach on foot.

True, its downtown is really a pricey boutique strip shopping center. But you can walk there from your house and have a bite to eat, even if it is an expensive one. If Celebration could be replicated, the town is arguably an improvement over standard suburbia.

But most of Celebration's improvements over the standard subdivision lie in the existence of its downtown, which probably cannot be reproduced elsewhere, and may not be able to survive even in Celebration. When the glow fades from Celebration, the daily tourists might disappear. And so might the downtown.

The bottom line on Celebration is that one is paying dearly for something that could be had far more cheaply, and fully, somewhere else. It's not just Kissimmee that has old urban homes at low prices. Orlando has dozens of gridded-street, urban or semiurban neighborhoods. Many have shopping streets within walking distance. Many are closer to where at least some of Celebration's residents work, in downtown Orlando. Why buy a thin, tepid version of what one supposedly desires at a far greater cost than the real thing? The answer says a lot about people's desire for control and to be controlled, and their fears of race and class. This same bottom line on Celebration applies to New Urbanism as a whole. For every New Urban development being built on the edge of town, there are multiple real urban neighborhoods decaying or in need of attention within the same metropolitan area. Why go outside of town to buy something that could be had more fully, and more cheaply, within it?

Actually addressing the subjects Celebration and New Urbanists raise—community, public life, and the incredible isolation of most Americans—means addressing far more difficult subjects than most New Urbanists acknowledge. It means addressing the design of an entire metropolitan area, the overemphasis on highway spending, the price of gasoline, and the desire of many Americans to buy their way out of social problems. It means looking at our political structures, including things like school funding, and whether they are fair and honest. Until these are addressed, Celebration and most New Urban developments will remain winking ornaments on the more gritty reality of American urban life, make-believe worlds that, like Disney's theme parks, lure a public and society away from addressing the challenges such developments advertise with their image.

A suburban boulevard outside Lyon, France, shows the galloping suburbanization that has occurred even in Europe. Photo by Alex Marshall.

CHAPTER 2

THE END

OF PLACE

THIS EXERCISE WORKS best in Europe. Begin in the oldest part of a city, say Florence, Barcelona, or Lyon, and walk outward. You'll start in the center, in the medieval section, with narrow, tiny streets built for the foot. You'll move into the Renaissance, where the streets and plazas gain more stature and nobility. Then you'll arrive at the nineteenth and early twentieth centuries, where you come to wide, tree-lined boulevards built for carriages and streetcars. Then you arrive at the bulk of the twentieth century, where the streets . . . fall apart, lose themselves, become patternless.

The same thing works in New York or almost any American city older than a century. It just lacks the European drama. You'll start on a main street, with shops built for people to walk up to their doors, and then you'll eventually come to the parking lots, subdivisions, and malls designed for the people who drive. It's a world of looping freeways and roads accompanied by a random placement of homes, shopping malls, and businesses. All visible sense of order and structure is lost.

What's different about the postwar places compared to all that went before? How do a strip mall in Kansas City and a warehouse-style supermarket in Lyon—a hypermarché—differ from a traditional "main street" in either place? What has changed?

They lack what I think of as a sense of order or place. In almost any space created before World War I, a sense of enclosure and stability is part of its fabric. Newer places have no fabric at all. It's the difference between a well-knit sweater and a pile of yarn. The modern structure of highways and assorted destinations tied to it lacks any sense of being there. And it's not just an American phenomenon. French sprawl looks a little different than American, and there isn't as much of it, but it's still sprawl.

Our cities have become unbound, and with them, our sense of place and home. And this horrifies us. I know of no one who receives the sight of car dealers and Wal-Marts on a busy boulevard with a warm glow. We look around, whether we are in Cleveland or California, and say, "What have we wrought?"

I am here to give us absolution. Our contemporary cities both are, and are not, our fault. We have created them, but their placelessness was not a consequence that we could have avoided unless we understood the dynamics of their components far more thoroughly.

Before World War I, cities produced a feeling of place as effortlessly as a tree produces bark. It was an inherent attribute of their existence, not something that had to be consciously designed into them. All places were designed as accessories to the human foot and various forms of mass transit, from sailing ships to train lines to carriages and streetcars. The street was the bottom line of place, even though its form changed some over time.

The car changed all that. The parking lot and the tire, not the street and the foot, became the baseline of a city. And with that, everything changed. The best, most elegantly designed shopping center lacks a sense of place. The most mechanistic, reflexively built nineteenth-century company town will have it. The context was different.

James Howard Kunstler, in his seminal book *The Geography of Nowhere*, says in an oft-repeated statement, "Eighty percent of everything ever built in America has been built in the last fifty years, and most of it is depressing, brutal, ugly, unhealthy, and spiritually degrading."[1] This is basically true, but also basically beside the point. Our automobile suburbs could never have created the sense of place that Kunstler loves. Even if Frank Lloyd Wright, Thomas Jefferson, and Vitruvius had designed them, they would still have the "Nowhereness" that Kunstler decries. The designers of a Woolworth's or pharmacy in 1910 had no more aesthetic sense than a designer of a Wal-Mart or a Revco today. But they did have a different context.

The challenge is to understand this dynamic, and then decide how much we want to grapple with it. Changing it is possible, but it involves taking on our entire transportation system.

THE NATURE OF PLACE

Before the car, or more particularly before the highway, the essential challenge of cities was to keep everything from being in the same place. The city was centripetal. Like a black hole, the nature of a city or town was to suck everything to one point. People needed to be near the railroad, the port, the factory to get to their jobs, and factories needed to be near the people and transportation links. This was why reformers championed public parks. Called the lungs of the cities, they were spots of greenery in the tightly packed clumps of buildings and streets. And it took real community effort to put them there. Valuable and scarce land, which could have been converted into homes and businesses, had to be set aside by the public. The tendency of the pre-automobile city to suck people to specific points only intensified with the transportation advances of the nineteenth century, which drew people, machinery, businesses, and money toward the subway stop, the streetcar stop, the railroad terminal.

Just the opposite conditions prevail today. The city is centrifugal. The city is more akin to a giant salad spinner, spraying growth out over the countryside indiscriminately. Growth still clusters around transportation sources, except that it is now the freeway off-ramp rather than the subway stop or train station. But the growth circle of a streetcar is measured in blocks because people have to walk there. The growth circle of a freeway off-ramp is measured in miles, because people drive there, and need places to put their cars at each end. Consequently, there is no particular advantage to being right near one's workplace. In fact, there is considerable advantage to being as far away from work or other necessities as possible. The person who locates himself on the fringes gets the advantage of bigger lots and more peace and quiet, while still being able to "raid" the jobs and commerce of the metropolis as a whole. Thus the city expands ever outward, with each person and developer reaching the short-term gain of being the farthest out.

The drive to establish parks is anachronistic now, because we no longer live packed in a block with no green space nearby. Now, most of us live surrounded by green space, from our backyards to the berms and shrubbery that surround the shopping mall and local gas station. We are enveloped in greenery, because the low-density environment has plenty of spaces for trees, shrubs, and spare land that is left as forest or fields. Now, a park is just about providing recreation, not relief from crowding and congestion.

The essential dynamic of cities and places has changed. The fundamental challenge of cities today is to keep everything from being everywhere at once. The modern push to establish growth boundaries can be compared to the drive in the past to establish parks. Each movement is attempting to check a fundamental tendency of the form in favor of the public good. The public good now concerns containment, whereas before it was the reverse. Kenneth Jackson, a historian of the suburbs, said, "The effect of the auto on the city is analogous to what astronomers call the big bang theory of the universe."[2] In the past, cities sucked inward. With the car, they exploded outward.

This big bang has increased exponentially the rate cities consume land. Urban historian Robert Fishman noted, "The basic unit of the new city is not the street measured in blocks but the 'growth corridor' stretching 50 to 100 miles. Where the leading metropolis of the early 20th century—New York, London, or Berlin—covered perhaps 100 square miles, the new city routinely encompasses *two to three thousand* [square] *miles*."[3]

A news article about contemporary Atlanta, a particularly acute case, gives a glimpse of the dynamic. "Over the past six years, Atlanta has gobbled up more land than any metro area, anywhere. Each year, the region's suburban boundaries grow by 38 square miles. . . . As a result, commuters . . . pile up more car miles each day, per capita, than residents of any U.S. metropolis, including Los Angeles. They also breathe the worst air of any city in the Southeast." The fastest-growing county, Gwinnett, has tripled in population in sixteen years to 460,000. "Seen from the air, Gwinnett looks like a vast sea of cul-de-sacs—an estimated 9,000 of which are spread across the county." The growth of Atlanta, the writer correctly observes, was fueled by three Interstates built in the postwar era that converge on the region.[4]

Victor Gruen, father of the first enclosed shopping mall, in Minneapolis, precisely describes the centrifugal nature of suburban development in a long piece, which he apparently writes with some regret, about the children he has sired. In a chart entitled "The Vicious Circle," he shows an arrow from "Sprawl" leading to "Increased Use of Automobiles" leading to "Decreased Use of Public Transportation" leading to "Separation of Urban Functions" leading to "Increased Road Surfaces" leading back to "Sprawl."[5]

The End of Place saddens us, I believe. We have had thousands of years living with "walls" around us in the form of streets and buildings. It's only in the last fifty that most of us have been able to leave them. Now, like a prisoner yearning for his old jail cell, we miss the places that once involuntarily confined us. Although we chafed at our old constraints, we find now that we might need them. The car and the highway have allowed us to leave our old confines, but they also have meant we could not go back.

Is the End of Place an unavoidable consequence of the car? To answer this, we need to understand why one method of transportation is chosen or can be chosen.

WHERE PLACES COME FROM

Cities and places are created by the methods we choose for moving people and goods and services from place to place. In other words, their transportation systems. How we get around determines how we live. It doesn't work the other way around. Cities are born from their transportation systems. These systems drive the economy of a city, and determine how people live. If James Carville, the fast-talking Cajun who led President Bill Clinton's 1992 election campaign, had been a city planner, he would have reworded his campaign message of "It's the economy, stupid" to read, "It's transportation, stupid."

In many of the efforts to redirect city planning, there has been a misplaced emphasis on zoning, as if zoning caused our cities to be laid out a particular way. This mistake is understandable, because this appears to be true at first glance. Usually, zoning and codes require the standard suburban form of separated uses, mucho parking, and so many curb cuts. But in reality, zoning no more causes this than a posted speed limit causes cars to drive fast. Like most government regulation, zoning just tidies up what would be the basic form of the city anyway. The essential dynamic of the suburbs, which is separation of uses, and the essential dynamic of inner cities, which is mixed uses, are determined by their transportation systems. No amount of rewriting zoning codes will change this.

New York City can be said to be its subway system. Its network of dense buildings would be impossible without it. In a similar way, the network of highways in a suburban metropolitan area makes possible both cheap, big houses on half-acre plots of land and the big-box stores with huge parking lots. If a region could control nothing else, controlling the transportation system would still be an adequate tool to shape development. Land-use laws, like zoning, are secondary to the effects of a transportation system.

"Housing patterns, land utilization, and employment and commerce centers are all shaped by the transportation system. . . . The rise and fall of cities throughout history and especially in the United States can also be accounted for largely through changing technology in transportation," say Delbert A. Taebel and James V. Cornehls in *The Political Economy of Urban Transportation*. Cities built around railroads have risen and fallen, they note, while "the boom towns of America today are frequently located at the intersections of the major interstate highways."[6]

Every city built has grown from the spine of its transportation system, like flesh around bones, whether it be a river, a trail, a railroad, or a highway. If we want to shape a city, we have to shape its transportation system.

Why do I speak so loudly about this? Because so many efforts dealing with cities do not recognize this. If we want a particular type of place, then we have to look at what kind of transportation system produces that kind of place. If we want to control or shape the type of development in a metropolitan area, we have to grapple with the highways, rails, and other systems that move people around within it.

GETTING AROUND VERSUS GETTING AWAY

So who decides the transportation systems of a city, state, or nation, and on what is the decision based? It is primarily a political act. From the Erie Canal to the Interstate Highway System to the Manhattan subway, the way we get around has primarily been determined by politicians and the public will, even if with the cooperation and participation and profiting of private developers.

These political efforts, and their effects, can be broken down into intercity transportation, which is necessary for economic growth, and intracity transportation, which determines living styles but which is a secondary system that is dependent on the economic growth of the former.

Cities are born from intercity transportation—that is, major transportation links to other cities, regions, and countries. New York was created by its natural harbor to the Atlantic, and by the Erie Canal, which opened up the entire Midwest to shippers bringing goods to and from Europe. Detroit was born from its position at the headwaters of the Great Lakes. My own city of Norfolk and the surrounding region are a product of a great port. This isn't to say that great transportation links automatically create great cities, but they are a prerequisite.

The contemporary city is at the center of Interstate crossings. Interstates are our modern rivers of commerce, and proximity to them is probably more important now than being on a train line or a river. Major transportation links create the possibility for industry, which in turn brings people and money to a city. Industry depends on the transportation links to the outside world.

The vital transportation components of the contemporary city, both here and in Europe, are a major airport, an Interstate highway link, a train line, and a port. A city must have at least two of these to thrive, and preferably all four. It is these external links that are necessary to ship products and bring them in. Improving these links is the quickest way for a city to generate economic growth.

Cities are export entities, said Jane Jacobs in *Cities and the Wealth of Nations.*[7] They exist because they provide people a way to make money, or in more abstract terms, to gain wealth. When two or more people are gathered together, you usually do not find religion but a way of producing wealth.

It's important to understand this, because only when there is industry present can we then begin talking about housing and shopping malls and dentists' offices and accountants and newspapers. These are all secondary activities, dependent on the export industries of a city, whether producing grapes or producing computer chips. Residents of the same place buying and selling things to each other will not produce a city.

People discuss growth as if it were fueled by available land, or by the presence of a road. Opening up more land for development in a region will not fuel growth, it will only shape the pattern of growth.

"New residential development is usually cited as the reason for growth, but no one moves here because there is a new subdivision. They move here because of job opportunities," said Jim Wahlbrink, executive officer of the Home Builders Association of Raleigh–Wake County, in commenting on that region's explosive growth.[8]

A true statement. Of course, a city or even a small town is in a constant churn as people start businesses and close them, move into town and leave it. But the basic dynamic is still there. To observe this, just look at any ghost mining town in Wyoming. Or remember how people talked about "the last people leaving Seattle please turn off the lights" when a slump in Boeing triggered a vast exodus from the city.

People come to a region because there are jobs and money, not because there is available land. Montana and South and North Dakota are still among the least-populated areas in the country because no one has figured out how to make a living there yet, even though these states have some of the prettiest countryside in the nation. The Dakotas actually have fewer people in them today than in 1900, when expectations of a big farm economy fueled the last of a homesteading boom.

STREETS VERSUS TROLLEYS VERSUS HIGHWAYS

The internal transportation of a city is a different question. It determines how people live, and is more a matter of taste. These internal transportation decisions—whether to build a beltway-style freeway, whether to widen a road, whether to build a commuter train line—determine the pattern of homes, offices, and shops. The people who make computer chips in the Silicon Valley could live in row houses and take a streetcar to work, or live in automobile suburbs and use the freeway, as is the case now. The important thing is that the chips have a way out of the Valley by either Interstate or rail. Which they do. Internal and external transportation systems overlap, but the distinction is still useful.

By using the word "taste," I don't mean that a city's internal transportation system is unimportant; only that there is choice. The pattern of sprawl that most American metropolises have chosen is environmentally destructive, harmful to the poor and elderly, inflexible, and less livable than a more compact form. But sprawl is compatible with Interstates, airports, ports, and train lines, and so is supportable economically.

Talk by reformers of how we have "subsidized" suburban development obscures the true nature of growth. In reality, government "subsidizes" all forms of growth because it makes the principal transportation decisions and pays for them. The construction of subway lines in New York City, with government help, "subsidized" the manufacture of Queens and Brooklyn and the Upper West Side. The construction of streetcar lines in Norfolk "subsidized" the creation of my neighborhood of Ghent, an old streetcar suburb.

It is true that the federal government fueled the growth of big highways. But then, it did the same with construction of railroads, which produced a series of railroad towns. Government builds place through its choices of transportation. Most of the changes that have so radically altered our ways of living have had to do with internal means of transportation within a metropolitan area. That being the case, they have been more a matter of choice than necessity. The classic street was murdered by the car and the highway. The seminal modern architect Le Corbusier predicted and advocated this when he scrawled on a drawing, "We must kill the street!" And without a street, there is no sense of place. Bringing back the street is not possible unless we bring back the types of transportation that once made it essential.

THE HISTORY OF PLACE

Mark Kingwell, writing in *Harper's*, noted that both "Alexander the Great and Napoleon moved through their respective worlds . . . at precisely the same speed. Top velocity for them, or anyone, was the gallop of a horse."[9] Before the industrial revolution in the latter part of the eighteenth century, cities and their dynamics hadn't changed much in several thousand years, because the technology of transportation had not changed much.

There were stylistic differences among the Italian Renaissance city of Florence and the Arab city of Fez and the streets of London. Defense strategies shaped the exterior of cities and squeezed people within the mandatory walls. But the basic form of a city or town—tiny, narrow streets built mostly to accommodate people on foot—stayed the same for five thousand years.

The industrial and technological revolutions changed all that.[10] Their innovations initially would catapult the form of the classic city to its zenith, and then swiftly bring about its downfall with the invention of the car and the subsequent decision by governments to build roads for it. In between, one saw the steamship, the railroad, the horse-drawn tram, the streetcar, the elevated train line, the elevator, and the subway, all inventions that would torque the form of the traditional city into new shapes, while keeping the street built around pedestrians as the bottom line.

Each of these past revolutions—the canal, the railroad, the subway—remade the city, although within the context of a traditional grid or other urban street pattern.

People despaired when trains entered the heart of the great cities in the mid-nineteenth century, Mumford wrote, destroying and transforming places where generations of people had lived and died and loved. "The rushing locomotives brought noise, smoke, grit, into the hearts of the towns: more than one superb urban site, like Prince's Gardens in Edinburgh, was desecrated by the invasion of the railroad."[11] The earlier introduction of canals, said Mumford, beautified cities. "With their locks and bridges and tollhouses, with their trim banks and their gliding barges, [canals] had brought a new element of beauty into the rural landscape, the railroads of the paleotechnic phase made huge gashes."[12]

It's an ironic statement to read, because urbanists now praise railroads as preservers of urban form, which they are in the contemporary context. Colonial cities and towns of America were wrenched into new shapes by the forces of "coal, iron, and steam,"[13] which swept away the time of simple agricultural markets, craftsmen, and handiwork. Along with objecting to early skyscrapers blotting out the church steeples in New York, Henry James found Paris in 1904, freshly urban renewed by Baron Haussmann, to be marred by "The deadly monotony that M. Haussmann called into being . . . its huge, blank, pompous, featureless sameness."[14]

But the lesson is not just that things change, get used to it. While cities and place changed in the past, they did not change as fundamentally as they have with the introduction of the car and the freeway. While the train, the streetcar, the canal, and the subway transformed the city, they did not end the primacy of the street. The car, on the other hand, would eventually kill it. Railroads tore at the fabric of cities, but would ultimately reknit and enhance this fabric, making it even more essential, more packed with life. Highways were different. They would serve as giant antimatter objects, repelling everything around them. To be compatible with them was an impossibility for cities; it would mean altering every one of the basic urban characteristics—reliance on feet, density, and structuring around the conventional street and sidewalk. Most cities destroyed themselves trying unsuccessfully to make this leap. Can we blame those cities for not foreseeing this? Their planners were just doing what every other generation of planners had done: thrusting the latest transportation innovation into the heart of the city. In past generations, the city would regroup around the new system. This time, it could not.

NORFOLK

My own city of Norfolk is a particularly egregious example of this. In 1951, it had the dubious honor of being the first city in the country to apply for and use urban renewal money.[15] Authorized by the misnamed U.S. Housing Act of 1949, the federal program gave money to cities to tear down older areas and redevelop them. The feds paid 80 percent, the cities merely 20 percent, and even that 20 percent was construed very loosely. Norfolk pursued the policy with a vengeance. Over the next decade, this city that dated back to the seventeenth century would tear down roughly a thousand acres in and around downtown. The first phase, begun in 1951, tore out mostly decrepit shacks. But as the taste for destruction was whetted, the destruction grew indiscriminate. In 1958, the city tore out two hundred acres in the oldest part of the city, destroying more than five hundred commercial buildings and displacing twenty thousand people.[16]

By the early 1960s, gone were the century-old burlesque theaters, the old train station, and the fabulous city markets, one built Art Deco–style in the 1930s and the other with medieval turrets in the 1880s. Gone were the often elegant buildings near the water where brokers and other businessmen bargained over the tons of coffee and coal that made their way in and out of the port. Most of all, gone was the tiny network of streets, many of them still cobblestoned, that invoked the memory of the city's oldest days, dating back several centuries. As one historian put it, "Nothing remained to suggest that the city had not descended full-blown from the sky from the 1940s, a place with no discernible past."[17]

While tearing stuff down, the city was facilitating the insertion into downtown of giant freeways, many of which were laid atop the oldest neighborhoods. As part of the redevelopment, the old city hall and courts, which formed a central square at the city's heart, were closed, and a giant, windswept plaza with modernist skyscrapers of concrete and glass was built as the new municipal center. It sat at freeway's edge, with the mayor's and councilmembers' parking spaces appropriately placed under a freeway off-ramp. The downtown was left with only a few old churches that the city couldn't quite bring itself to wipe out. They sat like lonely monks, ornate spires in a sea of concrete, refugees from a massacre.

And what can we say about Norfolk's action? First, that it was a tragedy, if a common one. Norfolk went farther and further with its urban renewal than perhaps any city in the country. But most cities did something similar to Norfolk. More importantly, however, we should understand that it was a tragedy not only because it occurred, but also because *it didn't work!*

In its actions, Norfolk was merely doing what other cities had done over the past two centuries of industrialization and technology—which was inserting the latest transportation methods into the city and facilitating the reconstruction of a city around that method of transportation. In the 1950s, this was the Interstate-style highway. Norfolk was acting no differently than London or Paris in the nineteenth century, when they destroyed some of the prettiest parts of their cities by laying down train tracks into their cities' hearts. With the introduction of every other transportation advance—canals, trains, subways, and streetcars—buildings would be lost, the city would change, but the city would ultimately re-knit itself around the new method of transportation. The king is dead, long live the king. But that didn't happen this time.

Norfolk tore down its oldest, most historic quarters, and then stood back . . . and nothing happened. The consultant Charles Agle, who led the process, had painted grand visions of a Corbusier-style city, with tall towers springing up from plazas while the gentle curve of an elevated freeway passed nearby. But it was a false vision. Oh, the city built a lot of stuff. A municipal center, a sports arena, a concert hall. A new traditional urban office sector would emerge. But the heart of the city, a windswept parking lot of twenty acres where the city foresaw its grandest visions emerging, would stay vacant for almost forty years. Finally, in the spring of 1999, a three-story, enclosed suburban shopping mall, flanked by giant parking garages bigger than the mall itself, opened. It was built by the Taubman Company and seeded with $100 million of city money.

What Norfolk and other cities did not foresee was that the new transportation system—the limited-access, Interstate-style highway—was too radical for the city to ever re-form around it. Their intended savior would destroy its intended beneficiaries. What development around highways needed was plenty of open land for giant parking lots, vast separation of uses, and giant cloverleafs. With space demands this extreme, older city centers, built on the scale of the human foot, could never compete. They killed themselves trying.

The beloved status of older, urban-style neighborhoods and city centers today derives precisely from our realization that they are a past art form that will not be built anew. In the words of Joel Garreau, they are "antiques," and like that seventeenth-century rocker, we can bestow love, care, and attention on them.

CITIES MAX OUT

The nightingale's song is most brilliant and sweet near its death, goes the saying.

Such was true with the early-twentieth- and late-nineteenth-century city. The streetcar, the subway, and the railroad pushed the classic city form to its summit. The streets themselves were at their most fetching, as cities played with Beaux Arts–style circles and avenues. It was a hyperdense but dramatic place of grand apartments lining streets that led to magnificent department stores and train stations. It was the city of Haussmann's Right Bank, Grand Central Station, and the first skyscraper. The city was the center of the world.

The new transportation technologies created the classic streets that surround the older cores of cities in both the New and Old Worlds. Every major city in the latter half of the nineteenth century saw what were essentially new cities created outside or, in the case of the Right Bank of Paris, on top of their older cores. They include the Eixample in Barcelona, the lovely grid of soft-cornered streets that has Antoni Gaudí's creations in it. The bulk of New York was created during this same time period and into the early twentieth century. In fact, what's fascinating is how relatively new are such urban icons as Las Ramblas in Barcelona or Fifth Avenue in New York or the Champs Élysées in Paris. They were all products of the latter half of the nineteenth century and the explosive new forces of the train, the steamship, the streetcar, and the elevator that were "force multipliers" for the classic form of the street.

The narrow medieval and Colonial-era street, often built just a few arm's-lengths wide, broadened into the boulevard and the avenue and carried loads unimagined in centuries past as trains, streetcars, subways, and elevators put more and more people on it. Rather than relieving congestion on streets, as in centuries past, the new methods of transportation increased it. In paradoxical fashion, "every major advance in transportation merely made the streets more crowded."[18] Water and rail terminals provided central locations for industrial and commercial activities. People lived near these activities because they had to walk to work. Factories and houses were jammed together, and both workers and managers lived near the factories. Cities like New York achieved a hyperdensity in the late nineteenth and early twentieth centuries never seen before or since. In 1905, New York's lower Manhattan district housed 742,135 persons on 2,415 acres, or 195,000 people per square mile.[19]

In a fashion identical to today's highway construction, the building of a streetcar or subway line generated its own demand. The new housing, businesses, and apartments created by building a new line were enough to crowd the line and to further crowd the center city, where the lines ended. Social reformers hoped that the streetcar would open up the suburbs to the poor, but "the poorest remained the least mobile, locked into their ghetto area."[20] As with white flight in the 1950s and 1960s, the middle class left the poor behind. A half-century later, the rich and the middle class would leave their new neighborhoods to be taken over by the poor.

A glimpse into urbanism around 1900 shows how clearly new forms of transportation—in this case the streetcar or its brethren—create new forms of living. The effect of streetcars, trains, and subways to increase density prompted the rich and upper classes to live in apartment buildings, rather than individual houses. As Elizabeth Hawes notes in her excellent book *New York, New York: How the Apartment House Transformed the Life of the City*, before 1870, only the poor and the working class lived in multifamily buildings. They were called tenements, or for slightly better dwellings, "flats." By 1930, that had all changed, and 95 percent of even the upper classes in New York City lived in apartments—which was a new word imported from France to make respectable a lower-class custom.[21] Similar changes were happening in established cities all over the country as the invention of streetcar lines both extended and densified cities.

Although the apartment revolution started in New York, it gradually spread to the provinces. Smaller cities in the South, East, and West were also building their first streetcar lines, and developers attempting to profit off this new form of transportation looked to the major cities and copied what their colleagues had done there.

At the turn of the century, elegant apartment buildings with lavish molding began to sprout around the new streetcar lines in Norfolk. An unsigned article from *The Virginian-Pilot* in Norfolk, dated October 15, 1911, speaks of the origin of these new places. The unnamed author speaks with clear knowledge of urban cause and effect, as if he were a trained urban historian rather than a low-paid, ink-stained wretch.

"The age of the apartment house life has come here to stay. It is a recent institution even in the larger centers, this apartment house living. It is new for the reason that there is a distinction between an apartment and a flat, just as there is between a flat and a tenement. And the first is an outgrowth of the second, which evolved from the third." The writer says that in these new, more luxurious apartments "any stigma that might be attached to a tenement dweller, any social descendency that be held against the flatite has no reflection upon the apartment house family."

The car and the highway killed the urban apartment building and its broad, graceful avenues. The city was cut down at the top of its form.

The age of the car separates into the era of the road and the era of the freeway. Although they extended and enlarged the city, the first paved roads did not immediately kill the street. If you look at Seattle and parts of other cities formed in the early twentieth century after the car had been introduced, you'll still see a coherent grid of streets and shopping districts formed around businesses fronting on a sidewalk and street with minimal accommodation for parking. This was partly because this was a transition stage between forms. But it was also because the car can be accommodated in a limited way within an urban fabric. San Francisco was rebuilt after the earthquake and fire in 1906, and so largely in the age of the car. It's surprising, but makes sense, how relatively low in density the city center is, and how many of those beautiful Victorians have garages carved underneath them that were part of their original construction. The relatively low density of San Francisco is one reason why it's more difficult to make a public transportation system there work, in comparison to New York, Boston, and Chicago.

It was not until the introduction of the raised, limited-access freeway after World War II that the era of place, of urbanity and cities, was truly swept away. An Interstate highway is incompatible with any form of street-based activity. This postwar invention swept away streets and the need for them. We enter a world of pods placed off freeway ramps, the pods ranging from subdivisions to shopping malls and office parks.

COULD IT HAVE BEEN DIFFERENT?

Were there alternate paths the form of the city could have taken, rather than that it took which so destroyed the primacy of the street? I think so. Certainly the car had to have been adopted, but the elimination of all other forms of transportation, and the accompanying physical changes to the form of cities, were not predestined.

As so often is the case, Mumford was an unheeded Cassandra on the subject. He was particularly prescient in his brilliant essay "The Highway and the City," originally published in 1958 in *Architectural Record*. It was written after Congress had passed and President Dwight Eisenhower had signed the Federal Highway Act, which would kick off the Interstate Highway System. Over the coming decades, the federal government would spend hundreds of billions of dollars for what some say is the largest public works project in history. Mumford deplored the approval of such a monochromatic transportation system, and he laid out how it would lead, paradoxically, to more traffic congestion and dysfunctional places that offered residents no alternative to the car. This essay is unnerving to read because it is so insightful, yet apparently so ineffective.

"What's transportation for? This is a question that highway engineers apparently never ask themselves: probably because they take for granted the belief that transportation exists for the purpose of providing suitable outlets for the motorcar industry."

Mumford answers his own question.

"The purpose of transportation is to bring people and goods to places where they are needed, and to concentrate the greatest variety of goods and people within a limited area, in order to widen the possibility of choice without making it necessary to travel. A good transportation system minimizes unnecessary transportation; and in any event, it offers change of speed and mode to fit a diversity of human purposes."[22]

His opening question should be stapled to the head of every policy maker in every city hall and state capitol. With it, he opens a door which can lead one to a sense of how transportation shapes the overall dynamic of a place. Mumford saw that each transportation system is like a medium in art or music, producing its own peculiarities in tone, style, and color. He says a page later, "The fatal mistake we have been making is to sacrifice every other form of transportation to the private motor-car—and to offer, as the only long-distance alternative, the airplane. But the fact is that each type of transportation has its special use and a good transportation policy must seek to improve each type and make the most of it. This cannot be achieved by aiming at high speed or continuous flow alone."[23] Mumford saw that highways should not be "thrust into the delicate tissue of our cities";[24] that within metropolitan areas, as opposed to between them, a freeway has little use.

It's interesting to contemplate what America's landscape would be like if Congress had divided the money for the Interstate Highway System between it and improving and upgrading the country's rail system. If this had been done, then the passenger-train lines like Penn Central might not have gone broke, and our cities would not have sprawled so widely and far.

Looking to the future, there are some chances that cities may end their outward orbits, and recoalesce around new centralizing forms of transportation. The most likely is the high-speed train line. Tom Downs, former head of Amtrak, makes the accurate observation that rapid rail "will be the first urban recentralizer of our time."[25]

In France, the world's most extensive rail network, whose high-speed trains travel at close to 200 miles per hour, is actually altering life in that country in new and unexpected ways. When I was in France in 1996, a university student on a conventional train in Tours blithely commented to me that she seldom saw her professors outside class, because they all lived in Paris. The professors, preferring the more cosmopolitan city, *commuted* roughly 150 miles each way to their classes at the university in Tours. They took one of the high-speed trains that depart on the hour from Paris, and arrived in Tours fifty-eight minutes later.[26]

These trains would be perfect on the East and West Coasts, where the bulk of the population lives and the cities are close together. But they may never happen here. The extended form of our cities makes building them much more difficult. Secondly, the airlines and highway builders are sure to mightily oppose their construction. A high-speed train between Washington and New York would cut airline traffic in half, if not more.

High-speed trains are the first major new form of transportation in almost a century. Both cars and planes have been around since the 1920s. Air travel has improved since then, it's true, but cars, except in exceptional circumstances, travel the same speed they did in the 1920s, or perhaps even more slowly. It actually takes me longer to drive the 20 miles from Norfolk to the oceanfront in Virginia Beach than it did my father in 1928. He traveled a two-lane road with little traffic. I have an Interstate but face traffic jams and a gauntlet of stoplights and intersecting boulevards.

THE DEATH OF PLACE

Contemplating the Death of Place and the fractured, incoherent places our cities have become, we have the choice, as with so many things, whether to groove on it or gag on it, to quote comic-strip artist R. Crumb. I myself am undecided. There are times when I look around at the boundless boxes of suburbia, the sweeping freeways, the glittering signs, and say, "Ain't it a gas?" You'll notice I don't say, "Ain't it wonderful?" I can't quite bring myself that far. It's more like admiring a good car crash.

Is it possible to admire our distended cities and places without irony? I come to the same doorway that Robert Venturi, Joel Garreau, Deyan Sudjic, and others have arrived at. These commentators have walked through the doorway and learned to love that which they once feared and loathed. Sudjic notes with approval that "we have begun to see the first steps towards an urban architecture that accepts the contemporary city for what it is, a fractured, incoherent place."[27]

I myself am not able to. Not yet. I am still unable to look at a K-Mart with the same fondness that a Woolworth's on a downtown street would inspire, even though both have the same mission—to deliver basic goods cheaply. I do see that the suburbs are a new form of city and not a product of malevolent forces. But the disappearance of place is not something I love.

The ancient Greeks may have poisoned themselves by the smelters that produced the lead that they put into the bronze that they relied upon. In a similar way, we may be poisoning ourselves in our pursuit of the most and the cheapest, and by resisting any attempt to examine whether those efforts have the side effect of destroying something we may vitally need. A place, a square, a home.

It's tempting to ponder whether the Death of Place is linked with some general withering away of coherency and structure in nearly every field of artistic endeavor. Poems no longer rhyme. Sonnets are a dead art form. Representational painting is one small side road in contemporary painting, rather than a central avenue. Architecture, as we have been told so many times, has dropped any sort of rules or structure. Contemporary classical music jettisons melody, harmony, rhythm, and sometimes even the standard fifteen-note chromatic scale.

In a similar way, the narrative line of cities has broken down. Streets, which have been the pages on which the storylines of cities have been written, have been traded in. They are no longer the continuous theme on which human settlement is built, moving on up from tiny walkways, to wider streets, to boulevards and avenues. No longer.

The death of the street has in turn killed related unifying devices, like the central town hall and the neighborhood bar. At the same time, transportation and technology have globalized industry and capital, which means people and industry move more, and communities are even less confined to a physical place. Our communities are becoming more conceptual than actual, as characters and actors move in and out of job descriptions like "mayor," "newspaper editor," and "industrial leader," only to be replaced by someone else a few years later.

People no longer know their neighbors. One could write a book on all the reasons why this is true. My own hunch is that a variety of societal trends have added up, building to the "tipping point," as statisticians say, where suddenly it's just too difficult to walk the few feet to the homes around you and get to know their inhabitants. People move frequently; family patterns have fragmented; religions are diffuse and many, with no one faith dominant anymore in a community, the way some towns were once ruled by Episcopalians or Methodists. If you make that walk, carrying a home-baked pie to the newcomers, chances are they'll like different music than you, different art, different religions. And even if you were to hit it off, they would probably be gone, moved to another job, just as the friendship flourished.

Unfortunately, the storyline for people has not broken down. It's still pretty simple. We live, we die. We do some stuff in between. Handling this simple narrative line, in the midst of a society where all is possible, is difficult and often tragic. Riding the tiger of modernity, as Marshall Berman says in *All That Is Solid Melts into Air*, is a tough job.

This difficult ride continues in the forms of city and community. We live . . . anywhere, anywhen, with anybody. Much of the alienation and anger harnessed by New Urbanism comes out of this. The incoherence of our places matches the incoherence of our lives. This disgust with our physical form comes with having no narrative line on which to hang our hat.

But if we want to build order into our world, then having a family leave policy and universal health care may be as important as a good street system. To really build a more ordered world we have to tackle those forces that contribute to disorder, which is as much about our economic and political life as it is our urban or suburban life. Can you decrease the fluidity of capital and the rate of business change, in order to increase other choices, like the possibility of staying in one place, and getting to know one set of people?

Even though the traditional "place" has died, it remains embedded in our collective memory. It's fascinating how many standard television shows and movies still organize characters and plots around a Main Street, with a corner store or bar, even though those things don't exist in most people's lives. A standard television show, like *Beverly Hills 90210*, still has its pretty teenagers Jason and Kelly hang out at an urban-style soda shop, which wouldn't exist in the automobile-oriented Beverly Hills. The camera never shows the exterior, but one imagines Jason or Kelly walking in from a traditional sidewalk through a traditional front door. The show gets away with it by stylizing the retro soda-and-hamburger joint as one that is being consciously nostalgic. Feminist writer Naomi Wolf talks about this when she notes that disaster movies seldom show tract housing or a suburban shopping center getting blown up, flooded, or burned. "The 'edge city' is practically invisible right now in movies and TV. Why is that? Because, on the visceral level at which we recognize archetypes, we all know that the bleakness of American life is connected to the hideous artificial environment No one can work up a good goddamn about whether the lava is going to get the Wal-Mart."[28] She has a point, although I part company with her about the "bleakness of American life" being connected to its "hideous artificial environment."

A Wal-Mart is no more artificial than the brick department store downtown. It just comes from a different system.

Bart Simpson is one of the most honest characters on television. He and his cartoon family, the Simpsons, relentlessly peel away the white lies and fig leaves of American life. Yet this cartoon world is a curious mixture of suburbia and a traditional Main Street–style town. The Simpsons live in the prototypical two-story-with-attached-garage suburban home, and shop at the Quiki-Mart run by the Indian clerk. Bart skateboards to school, almost surely an impossibility in the suburban community that the Simpsons live in. And on this skateboard journey, he passes traditional storefronts built on traditional-style sidewalks and streets. His school occupies a central square in a park. The town of Springfield is seen as possessing a classic city hall and square, rather than a faceless office complex on a parking lot, which is the style in so many suburban cities. It's as if a town were impossible to construct conceptually without a Main Street, even though Bart's counterpart in real life almost surely does not know one.

The classic form of the city, and its clear order of town square, neighborhood bar, etc., still serve as a unifying narrative even if in reality its thread has been erased. We have lagged in producing art that accurately reflects the Death of Place. Film director Michael Tolkin, writing in *The New Yorker*, notes that there is a dearth of novels or literary works that take place in Los Angeles.

> For a city to produce a great novel, more than a few people have to agree about the city, and Los Angeles does not offer a clear harmonizing of its themes. This is why our literature fits onto a short shelf, and why the movies can grow here, unencumbered by a shared social history. . . . A great novel might yet be written if a song could take the I-10 [expressway] for granted the way the world takes Central Park or the Champs Élysées or the Nevsky Prospect for granted, those real places that exist for everyone because someone saw them and loved them.[29]

Joel Garreau is right in saying that the new formless places, like Tyson's Corner, are cities. He calls them Edge Cities. But I think he is wrong in predicting that with time, the patina of age will soften their sharp corners and turn them into places that we can love. Tyson's Corner, the classic Edge City, is approaching a half-century in age. By that time, a place like the East Side of New York or midtown Manhattan had acquired the seeming permanence of centuries. Tyson's Corner still feels like an afterthought, a nowhere land. The places we are creating in this latter half of the twentieth century are fundamentally different than those before. Their incoherence, which is a product of the transportation system that produced them, makes them difficult to love.

Cities with a sense of place go back to the dawn of recorded history. The stories of cities without a sense of place began about 1945. We are in a new era, one that poses new challenges and the opportunity for new narratives.

A glass-faced office building hovers over Deborah
Olson's cherry and apricot
orchard, a remnant of
what used to define the
Santa Clara Valley. Photo
by Alex Marshall.

CHAPTER 3

THE

DECONSTRUCTED

CITY

The Silicon Valley

WHAT MAKES THE SILICON VALLEY so remarkable is that it's the perfect example of a city without form, without any center of any kind, be it physical, political, or economic. It's a real Nowhere Land that just happens to be the center of an industry—computers—that is at the heart of the twenty-first century. Which isn't to say that it's a bad place. It's a wonderful place in many ways, full of wows, gees, and by gollies, of incredibly intelligent people, great food, great weather, and material comforts. It just has all these things within the context of no place in particular. There is, generally speaking, no "there" there. It's a perfect example of the End of Place, the contemporary, deconstructed city that the forces of the car and the highway produce. It's a land of highways, shopping malls, subdivisions, and business parks, and not much else. It's less than the sum of its parts, much less. Anywhere you stand in Silicon Valley has the feel of being off edge, on the periphery, a stop before arriving to where you are planning to go. But you never arrive.

The Valley shows the changing role of old urban places, be they old small towns or old big cities. The few sidewalks and street-level store-fronts here are for the wealthy. The poor, who lack cars, are the ones who lack urban environments structured around walking. The major cities here, San Jose and San Francisco, are becoming appendages to the wealth, power, and industry of the Silicon Valley, dogs being wagged by their once agricultural and suburban tails. Politically, the Valley is formless. It sprawls across a dozen different political jurisdictions, each shaping the Valley's structure, but none in control or dominant.

The Silicon Valley is suburban in form—sprawling, patternless—but it is a city in function. It is a center of wealth, business, industry, finance, education, and research. It's not "sub" anything. It is not a bed-room community. It is a city by every definition except politically and urbanistically. If the borders of the Silicon Valley were sealed tomor-row, it would have everything it needed except enough waitresses, jani-tors, and gardeners, and hotel managers, food service clerks, and assistant book store clerks, who come from over the hills in places where a mod-est house will only cost you $250,000 instead of $500,000.

CHERRIES AND CHIPS

Where to start to show you the character of this fragmented place? At Deborah Olson's cherry farm? Or among the brown-skinned, Spanish-speaking residents in East Palo Alto? Or in the wine section of Draeger's Supermarket in Menlo Park, among the seven-hundred-dollar bottles of Chateau Margaux, set a few aisles down from the frozen peas? Each comes at the Valley from a different, but valid, angle, giving one bite of a piece of the pie.

Let's start with Olson. The woman runs a fruit stand and accom-panying orchard on El Camino Real, the long boulevard that runs through the Silicon Valley and gives it an approximation of form. Her great-grandparents, born in Sweden, started the orchard at the turn of the century. Rows of cherry and apricot trees stretch behind the farm of sixteen acres, which is what remains of a once larger orchard. There are machinery, farm equipment, a row of beehives, and an open packing plant where the cherries and apricots are dried and packed. There's a row of old shacks where the farmhands evidently still live. On the wall behind the checkout counter of the fruit stand is a large aerial photograph of the farm in 1956. It shows a barn and a sea of fields near an old country road. It is a farm in the middle of open countryside.

Smooth highways with sculpted curbs and curves, office buildings, fast-food restaurants, and shopping centers now encircle the farm. A Porsche dealership is one of the farm's immediate neighbors. Olson's fruit stand is on one of the last working farms in a region that once had almost nothing else. In a generation, the Silicon Valley has gone from producing apricots and cherries, to producing . . . sand. Silicon, that is, which is made of purified sand. You can see these dark, missile-like ingots inside the Intel headquarters.

It's hard to imagine that Silicon Valley was once almost as famous for fruit as it was for computers. But before World War II, most of the apricots grown in the United States came from the Santa Clara Valley, the precomputer name for the area. With up to "40 feet of alluvial soil," and warm days and cool nights, the climate and soil were perfect.[1] The valley produced plums, Bing cherries, walnuts, and dozens of other fruits. Dole, Del Monte, and other fruit companies had their packing plants on waterways here, canning peaches and throwing the waste into the rivers. This agricultural past colors the region. The towns around here— Mountain View, Sunnyvale, and others, with San Jose as the capital— existed because of it.

Now, houses and offices sit on that double-score of topsoil. An agricultural paradise was paved over.

Stanford and Palo Alto were the different drummer that gradually changed the rhythm of the entire valley. They helped incubate and bring in Hewlett-Packard and Xerox, as well as the defense jobs, the NASA center, and the best minds that would stick around to invent computer stuff. This new crop of ideas pushed out the old crops of peaches and apricots. Steve Jobs, founder of Apple computers, grew up here and when he was twelve years old, as a well-publicized story has it, called up Mr. Hewlett of Hewlett-Packard and got some advice on his first experimentations in electronics.[2] Although computer centers would arise in Boston, Seattle, and Texas, the heart of it began and prospered here.[3] The computer companies would march southward from Palo Alto, until they arrived at the edge of San Jose and filled up the Valley with people, jobs, and money.

Olson's farm is much beloved in the Valley as a link to the past. But it will soon be gone. Olson is now working out the details of a development plan that would turn fruit groves into offices or housing. Cherries and apricots are history anyway, she says. The climate's been too warm in recent years to produce good cherries, and Turkish apricots have undercut the market in that fruit.

Still, you have to ask, could it have been different? Paving over this land is the equivalent of paving over the finest vineyards in Bordeaux for a freeway interchange. While the economics might make sense locally, on a broader scale, the United States lost some of its best fruit-producing land for the sake of houses and offices that could have gone anywhere. With a less car-dependent development style, the Silicon Valley still could have arisen here but in a way that kept most of the agriculture. Once the Olson farm is gone, so, too, will vanish almost all evidence of the Valley's agricultural past.

Almost all. A half-mile away from Olson's fruit stand is the Orchard Heritage Park. It's a small grove of apricot trees, run and maintained by the city of Sunnyvale. It is a conscious preservation of the city's history. The trees sit in neat rows, and are still tended and cropped. The grove sits next to a new civic center, a performing arts center, and an indoor sports arena, all signs of the Valley's wealth, and a row of suburban houses. An apricot grove as a public park is a good demonstration of the transience of both life and the objects we create in this world. What a great piece of public art! How wise to keep a piece of the past around as a reminder of where you have been.

EL CAMINO: THE BROADWAY OF THE SILICON VALLEY

One of the few unifying features in the Santa Clara Valley is El Camino Real. The highway was laid out by the Spanish missionaries and stretches from the lower part of the state into San Francisco itself, turning into Mission Street—which makes sense, because El Camino was the road that connected the Spanish missions. (A great way to enter San Francisco is to drive up El Camino Real and see the city of Victorians and hills suddenly emerge from around a bend.) This street/road/highway is Silicon Valley's Broadway, the old country road around which a city grew, just as the grid of Manhattan grew around Broadway, which cuts a diagonal from the bottom to the top of the island.

Driving along El Camino Real in the Silicon Valley is an urban historian's dream, revealing layers of the Valley's built environment, like a fresh cut in an archaeological dig. Old warehouses and slowpoke stores with single-width parking lots sit next to Blockbuster Video and the other accouterments of late-twentieth-century sprawl. Near Palo Alto, an old, still-used movie theater fronts directly on the road, as if this were a walkable street. Down the street are upscale malls fronted by mammoth parking lots, structures that are fully in this century in their embrace of the automobile. And of course there's Olson's cherry orchard, a working farm that still fronts on this highway of shopping malls and everything else. I love El Camino Real. It's unhomogenized, unneat, and uncontrolled. Although essentially suburban in character, it is as diverse as the classic urban street praised for its mix of rents and clientele by Jane Jacobs in her classic, *The Death and Life of Great American Cities*.

The "cities" of Silicon Valley shoot off El Camino Real like branches off a tree. You have Redwood City, Menlo Park, and Palo Alto, next Mountain View and Los Altos, then Sunnyvale and Cupertino, and finally Santa Clara and San Jose. These places, once separate towns, now form one big blanket of sprawl.

Lying atop this shattered pottery of sprawl are the contemporary bones and arteries of the Silicon Valley, the network of freeways that brings the cars in and out. Parallel to El Camino are U.S. 101 and I-280, both Interstate-style highways. Cutting across at right angles, more or less, to El Camino are other elevated, limited-access highways, like the Stevens Creek Freeway. These roads are a mixture of state and federal, but all are Interstate in style—mammoth, multilane, restricted-access arteries—and make the whole place go. Together, this loose assortment of freeways forms a mammoth and awkward grid, stretching out over hundreds of square miles, and composing the architecture of our contemporary city. Who is the architect of the Silicon Valley, its L'Enfant? The state and federal transportation departments.

The economic engines of the Valley—Netscape, Apple, Intel, Novell, Sun, Adobe—spill off the exit ramps of these freeways like orchards on an irrigation system. Apple in Cupertino, Intel in Santa Clara, Netscape and Silicon Graphics in Mountain View. They are not grouped together in one municipality or even on one street, like the jewelers row in New York City, or the garment district. The buildings of the computer companies are clean and corporate—the architecture varying in its boldness—set on well-trimmed lawns. The old agricultural towns followed the path of El Camino Real and the train lines. The new industries, instead, spring up along the path of the Interstate-style highways, which are the present central arteries of commerce.

INTEL INSIDE

If there's a center in this sea of sprawl, it is the Intel headquarters in Santa Clara. The sale of the Intel chips that are the guts inside 90 percent of all personal computers pulls a billion dollars into the Valley every two weeks. Other industries in the Valley feed off this wealth, with side companies and related ventures. With its gargantuan, monopoly-level profits in 1997 of 28 percent on revenues of $25 *billion*, Intel has plenty of cash to pass around.[4]

If Intel is the heart of the Silicon Valley, though, it's a metallic and soulless heart. The Intel building, all reflective blue glass and steel, is one of dozens of nondescript office buildings standing in parking lots off twisty suburban roads. It's a generic suburban landscape, giving back nothing to the passerby. A giant Marriott hotel looms at one corner, stark and soulless. I can tell, without entering, that it would be a terrible place to stay, with windows that don't open and horrible food for an ungodly sum per night.

This generic landscape is the real Silicon Valley—nondescript office buildings spread out on soft-curving suburban roads, punctuated by bland suburban eateries and bland corporate hotels. Even though the greatest wealth of the Valley is concentrated here, the landscape is tentative. It glows with forced boosterism in names like the Great American Parkway. There used to be a downtown here. Santa Clara bulldozed it off the map, clearing the way for a new future. It's fitting that the new fragmented city was built on top of an old coherent one.

The only human-scale thing I find in this landscape is a mobile eatery, which has pulled up to a queue of office workers in a parking lot on the edge of a group of office buildings. The ice-cream-truck-style eatery, staffed by Asians, sells Mexican, Chinese, and American lunch food. The office workers line up to buy tacos, fried rice, and ham sandwiches. The directness of the human contact—people preparing and serving food to hungry people outside on their feet—stands in sharp contrast to the hermetically sealed glass boxes around them, and the bland shrubbery and cold gray of the asphalt parking lots.

But if Intel is the financial center of the Valley, the intellectual and organizational centers lie elsewhere.

Palo Alto is the intellectual center of the Valley. There you find not only Stanford University, but also Xerox's Palo Alto Research Center (PARC), where much of Apple's Macintosh technology has roots. Also in Palo Alto and nearby Menlo Park are collections of lawyers and venture capitalists, including the prominent Kliener, Perkins, Caufield, and Byers (KP to insiders). It is an interrelated ecosystem that makes this city work as an economic enterprise. The start-up company grabs some money at venture capitalist KP, gets some nearby lawyers to draw up a corporate charter, drops by a software company in Cupertino or Santa Clara to hire away part of its staff, and is off and running. These components are spread out over miles of roads and different municipalities. In Manhattan, all the players would be within a few blocks of each other. Here, they are sprawled across a dozen cities and counties. But the synergy of a city is still there.

SPENDING IT

I had seen good wine before, but this was incredible. A bottle of 1986 Chateau Margaux for $699. That's a *bottle*, not a case. A bottle of 1990 Chateau Latour for $899. A 1975 Chateau Latour for a mere $250. I was staring at these jewels not in the cellar of a famous collector, not even in a fancy wine store, but in the *aisle of the local supermarket*, Draeger's, in Menlo Park. Besides the wine, the store had high-end cheeses flown in from France and Italy, racks of special sausages and hams hanging in the well-staffed prepared food section, and flesh from the carcasses of pampered animals in the butcher department. The store nestles all the goodies under warm spotlights hung from the warehouse-style ceiling. No harsh fluorescent lights here.

Many people have made many piles of dollars from the computer industries that dot the Valley. More wealth has been created in the Silicon Valley than in any other place and time in history, say some observers.

But the wealth here is not apparent at first. You have to poke beneath the bland carpet of suburbia to find it, in the aisles of the supermarkets or on the price tags of the nondescript homes.

Housing is where the Valley's immense wealth is contorting pricing and cost most extremely. A forty-year-old, 1,000-square-foot bungalow in Palo Alto costs $600,000. While I was visiting the Valley, a news article included a quote by one resident of an even pricier section of town, who said she was glad a new developer was including affordable housing in his new development. Affordable housing, it turned out, meant houses costing $500,000.

The astronomical prices are an example of the unusual dynamics of housing, which separate it from other goods and services. Unlike purchasing almost anything else in our contemporary world, you cannot buy a house in Kansas City if the ones in Palo Alto are too expensive, or import them from the Dominican Republic. You can buy one town over, but you reach a limit of possible daily travel pretty quickly. That's not true with other products. A piece of beef, a computer chip, or a dinner plate, even a fresh vegetable, can be had from Argentina, Japan, China, or Chile as producers and consumers search out the best value for the lowest cost. Not so with housing. This is why housing costs vary so dramatically around the country.

The housing costs in the Silicon Valley are its Achilles heel. While it's a self-proving maxim that in aggregate, Valley residents can "afford" to pay $600,000 for a 1,000-square-foot bungalow, a substantial portion cannot. First of all, the people waiting tables and managing restaurants need places to live. Secondly, even a young software engineer can't afford such prices. Workers at NASA's immense AIMES facility, one of its premier installations, are starting to resist coming there because they can't afford housing on the fixed government salaries. The federal government has talked of moving some facilities away from the Valley because of housing costs.

The solution? I'm not sure.

URBANISM AND UNDERWEAR

Anne (not her real name) had worked at the small used bookstore in Menlo Park since 1967. During this time, she watched the downtown change around her. It used to be a place where the city's politicians came to meet, a place where the average person came to buy a television, some furniture, or some shampoo. Downtown was the area's commercial, political, and economic center. Then, hard times hit. The furniture and appliance stores closed or moved out to the malls. McDonald's out on the highway replaced the everyday restaurants on Main Street.

Then, about a decade ago, things picked up again. New restaurants began to move in. Lots of them. The local supermarket, Draeger's, opened an enormous upscale supermarket. Fancy boutiques blossomed. Menlo Park had come back. Only, things were different. Downtown had once been a place where you went to have your daily needs met. It was as comfortable as an old shoe. Now, it was fancy. Although she liked the downtown's success, she wished . . . that there was a place to buy something more ordinary. A smattering of older stores remained—a hardware store, a pet store, a dry cleaner—but their days seemed numbered. And all these restaurants! You could have too much of a good thing. So one day, Anne went and counted all the restaurants in this roughly two-block-long downtown.

There were thirty-seven.

"I just wish there was someplace to buy a bra or some underwear," she said. "I'd trade a half-dozen of these coffee shops for one place to buy something practical."

The trajectory of Menlo Park, from up to down to up again, is similar to that of the other downtowns of the Silicon Valley. They include Mountain View, Sunnyvale, and small shopping streets like California Avenue in Palo Alto. They have gone from ordinary building blocks of an economy, to outmoded appendages, to luxury ornaments. These old-fashioned downtown streets, many of them once centers of farming communities, are very alive now. They are also unnecessary. Their luck is that they exist in a suburban territory that can afford to keep them alive. They play a role for their areas, similar to what San Francisco does for the region, as beautiful antiques.

What role do these old downtowns play in this new city? They are the depository of place in the region. They are where you go to experience it. It is their franchise. As such, they punctuate the suburban monotony of the region. Every few miles, you come across another old downtown where you know you can get out, walk around—and of course find something to eat.

Eating out seems to be the main function of these new centers. They are one long dining table. In Palo Alto, the downtown is lacquered over with high-priced Italian restaurants, and more open all the time. On a Thursday night, lines stretch out of every other restaurant. In a world where people are young and work long hours, eating out is one of the main forms of recreation. For some reason, Italian restaurants threaten to suffocate you. Every other doorway offers aruguled this and balsamiced that. San Francisco is known for its French restaurants. In Silicon Valley, they love Italian.

What has happened is not simply the upscaling of an area. Something more structural has happened. The downtown of Menlo Park is now an appendage. Its businesses are able to survive precisely because they are unnecessary. You don't go to Menlo Park to buy a pack of Fruit of the Loom, a computer, a television, or some shoelaces. You go to the mall down the road, or the warehouse-style power centers. Nor do you go to Menlo Park to see your attorney or take out a loan; those functions have moved to corporate office parks behind well-bermed lawns. The older downtowns instead have become like an art museum, a luxury that gives you a taste of a different time, and a welcome respite from your usual hectic surroundings. And as with an art museum, only the wealthiest and most upscale areas can afford one. They are luxury items, dispensable but nice to have around. They give young people a place to court with more atmosphere than the mall. But they carry no significant economic freight. If they were blown off the map, people's palates would suffer but not much else. These old downtowns no longer function as cities, under my definition, because they no longer create wealth. Sure, their restaurants and pricey supermarkets have value, but they exist by taking the dollars that have been created elsewhere, and cycling them through. They are a secondary tier of an economy, not the primary one. If the chip plants and computer labs closed tomorrow, the pricey boutiques would go dark in a week.

It is true that some people can meet their daily needs in Menlo Park, but this is an example of the bifurcation of our society. The wealthy can afford to shop at Draeger's. They can pay for the privilege of a supermarket within walking distance, and for an older, more personalized form of service. They can order steak for $30 a portion at Dal Boffo instead of a hamburger at a mom-and-pop cafe. It's urbanism for the rich. The masses are left to the car and the Wal-Mart and the Food Lion. Anne may eventually get a place to buy underwear. But it would likely be a boutique lingerie store, with Aubade bras for $100 a pop. Not Hanes.

It's significant that one place that does not have a downtown is East Palo Alto, home to the poor, who are the people most in need of an environment that functions without cars.

DOWNTOWNS—A LUXURY NOT ALL CAN AFFORD

The standard image of a poor area of a region is a crumbling inner city, an example of traditional urbanism gone to hell. Not so in Silicon Valley. Here, the old inner cities—well, really old inner towns—prosper. The poor have their own poor suburb to live in. East Palo Alto. It doesn't have a downtown. Walking environments are for the rich, who don't need them. These people, many who lack cars, subsist on scattered strip shopping centers.

The "downtown" of East Palo Alto is a suburban intersection at University Avenue and Bay Road, with multiple left-turn lanes and prominent traffic lights. On one corner is a McDonald's and behind it, oddly, is the town's City Hall. It is partially concealed by the McDonald's and seems an appendage to it almost. Someone tells me later that the city worked out a land deal with McDonald's, where the fast-food chain gave the land for the City Hall. Kitty-corner to the McDonald's is a small strip shopping center with eight parking spaces. If East Palo Alto has any "downtown," I was told, this was it. The concrete block has a living-room-size grocery store, a Laundromat, a video store well stocked with Spanish-language titles, and a taqueria. All the essentials.

The guy in the taqueria says things have improved considerably in recent years. In Spanish, he tells me that when he opened the place twenty years ago, he wouldn't leave his apartment in the small brick buildings behind the store for fear of being shot. Now, crime is reduced considerably. There's still a drug trade, but not as bad. Clearly, the inflow of massive wealth in the Valley has helped East Palo Alto, if not proportionally.

What's striking is that in appearance, East Palo Alto looks almost exactly like the superrich Palo Alto that is literally on the other side of the tracks, as well as the other side of the freeway. Both have low bungalows on square parcels of land on old gridded streets. The homes in East Palo Alto have scruffier paint, and less-manicured lawns and shrubbery, and For Sale signs in Spanish, but are otherwise very similar.

This low-rise, suburban "bad neighborhood" is an example of the Californiazation of slums. It was once axiomatic to think of slums as being dense places where the poor lived stacked on top of one another in badly ventilated apartments. The single-family home, as a slum, was a non sequitur. If a family had its own house, it could not be poor or its neighborhood a bad one, right? But in California, particularly Los Angeles, you have street after street of single-family homes that are dangerous and poor. It's something that would have once been unthinkable, like a poor man in a tuxedo. With these areas, we see how being poor is less about being deprived of decent housing than about the overall social conditions that often come with it, particularly crime, a worse educational system, and an exclusion from other parts of society.

One can err by typecasting a particular type of building or place with a particular type of community, lifestyle, or income level. Historian Eric H. Monkkonen says: "Buildings and their inhabitants are often wildly out of sync. Some ghettos of Los Angeles look like pleasant suburbs, while the desirable Park LaBrea apartments in the same city look like 1930s public housing. In their basic shape and to the unwary, luxury apartment towers in New York look just like awful high-rise housing projects. Renovated nineteenth-century warehouses make elegant inner-city housing throughout the older cities of the United States."[5]

The residents of East Palo Alto are the gardeners and maids of Menlo Park and other richer areas. Each morning in Menlo Park or Los Altos or Sunnyvale, the Silicon executives wash out and the gardeners and maids wash in. Particularly gardeners. The growing season in the Silicon Valley is all year long, which gives plenty of opportunity for the landscape-obsessed. Of course, it's not just gardeners but roofers, plumbers, tree surgeons, electricians, and all the other support staff that keep the twelve-hour-a-day, both-person-working, career-first couple game-ready.

In East Palo Alto, we see the unfairness of the fractured political structure of the Silicon Valley. The local governments should merge into one, or the state should force them to. East Palo Alto is an integral part of the Valley. Its residents clean the floors, cut the shrubbery, and make the tacos and veggie burgers for the high-watt thinkers. Yet, because it is legally a separate city and dependent on its own tax base, it has lousy schools, an underfunded police department, and a chronically stressed municipal budget. The Cesar Chavez public school in East Palo Alto, for example, is a grim-looking brick building. It has a sparse asphalt playground out front, and little landscaping. It's especially stark compared to the well-manicured public buildings in the rest of the Valley.

As always, real-estate prices are a great reality check. The small bungalows in East Palo Alto are identical to the ones in neighboring Palo Alto. Yet a forty-year-old, 1,000-square-foot, two-bedroom-two-bath house could be mine for a mere $178,000 on the east side. That's a lot of money, but not compared to $600,000, which is what the house would sell for in Palo Alto. What do you get for the extra $425,000? A better public sector. Better schools, better services, as well as different neighbors.

THE BIG CITY

San Francisco and San Jose, two major older cities in the region, bookend the Silicon Valley. San Francisco lies to the north, a white hill of Victorians on hilly streets, teeming with street life of all sorts. To the south is San Jose, which is, despite its best efforts and a heapful of money, basically a tired industrial city searching for a purpose.

San Francisco illustrates the role our successful center cities are evolving to. It's a mixture of city and suburb, center and periphery. "The City," as people in the Valley refer to San Francisco, is the place you go for culture, beauty, and harmony. In contrast to the hustle and bustle and chaos of the Valley, the City is a place of order, quiet, and repose. It is generally not the place you go to start a new company or close a business deal. It is an example of the morphing roles of city and suburb. San Francisco, like most cities, is no longer a center of industry. The ship-yards, the ports, the labor, have moved out of town or out of the country. The high-tech companies have chosen the suburban soils of the Santa Clara Valley for their efforts, evidently finding them or thinking them more fertile. Even softer trades, like banking, where San Francisco used to dominate, have declined in importance. San Francisco is not really comparable to New York, because it's not the economic hub of the state or West Coast. Some industries, like book publishing and journalism, do remain centered in the City, but they are fewer and fewer. And a few parts of the computer industry are there, principally some of the artsier, multimedia companies. But it lacks the turbulence of the Silicon Valley.

The center city of the region economically is now the Silicon Val-ley. San Francisco is becoming "a bedroom community" of the Silicon Valley, in the words of one local. In an odd reversal of roles, housing costs in the Valley are pushing up those in the City as Valley residents look for "cheaper" digs in the most expensive city in the country.

San Jose, the other old urban city, plays a different role, or better said, is searching for a role. It is a postindustrial city struggling to find a reason for existence in the absence of the industry and transportation systems that created it. No one in the Silicon Valley referring to "the City" ever means San Jose. Although San Jose calls itself "the capital of the Silicon Valley," the locals haven't gotten the message. It is actually on the edge of the Santa Clara Valley, and outside most of the high-tech centers.

In the 1920s, it was a bustling center for the agricultural economy. But since World War II, its economy has slowly dwindled. By the 1970s, its downtown, that bellwether of a region, had become the typical scarred, lonely landscape of parking lots and isolated buildings created by a com-bination of disinvestment and urban renewal. What neighborhoods had hung on were bad ones. Over the next two decades, the city spent by one estimate a billion dollars on its downtown. The money came in part from the high-tech companies that refueled the tax base. San Jose has never been the center of the Silicon Valley, but it has captured enough of the wealth not to be completely isolated. Many of the companies went onto city-owned land, from which the taxes were required to go into downtown development.

San Jose now has the best downtown money can buy. It has a performing arts center, a technology museum, and a bunch of other gleaming buildings that sit in their isolated lawns and plazas downtown. A light rail threads between them.

But the downtown as a whole shows how little money can buy. An active, bustling downtown cannot be purchased. For crowds to walk sidewalks from store to store in the traditional way, a downtown must draw people to it from multiple sources, not just from a few single-note city projects or even a football stadium. And this can only happen if downtown is an actual center of something, particularly retail. Being a retail center means a center city has not lost its role as a center. That can only happen in the context of how a center city fits within the larger region and its land-use and other dynamics. Via the Oregon and Portland model, a center city can be repressurized, the energy of a region turned inward until the downtown streets begin to fill up again.

That hasn't happened here. For it to occur, the dynamic of growth in the Bay Area would have to be changed, with growth sharply restricted around center cities until the pressure of the housing and retail markets turned inward to the older center cities.

But since that hasn't happened and is not likely to happen, San Jose is using a different strategy. It is an example of what David Barringer, in an article entitled "The New Urban Gamble" in *The American Prospect,* called the carnival city strategy. Cities build a performing arts center, an aquarium, and a sports stadium and hope that the crowds will materialize to fill in the rest of the city. I am extremely dubious about this strategy. Things like art museums and aquariums are great as the capstones to successful places, as amenities and accessories. But trying to make them an economic foundation is to confuse the role of the foundation of a building with that of a decorative window on it. A museum can be a great reward to a successful region, as can central libraries and other public works. But, even if the crowds appear, they will not replace or even draw the people or businesses that make a center city truly a place. It does not build pressure. Which isn't to say that I'm against what San Jose has done. Absent effective regional design management, I guess this massive subsidy is as good as anything.

San Jose's downtown has some "real" life. There are a few neighborhoods coming back. Simple Victorians that avoided the urban renewal bulldozer. There is an eighteen-story Adobe office tower going up downtown, built by one of the first computer companies to go vertical and stray from the campus-style headquarters beloved by most high-tech CEOs. There are new condominiums being built in approved New Urbanist fashion with street frontage and such. The city also has a good plan for an attempt to create more urban districts by restricting outward growth, and increasing density. This ties into the light rail line that runs through downtown and out to Santa Clara. The cars always were almost empty when I saw them, although the system reportedly has 25,000 riders a day. All these are good things to do; but their limited scope and context should be seen for what they are.

A PATH NOT TAKEN

Could it have been different? Could the Silicon Valley still have been a center for the computer industry, yet developed in a different urban pattern instead of the hypersprawl it has achieved. Instead of low-density suburbs, could it have become, say, a series of neat urban towns with defined streets and centers, surrounded by still-working farms and forests?

Sure, says James Derryberry, the San Jose planning director who picked up my line of questioning immediately. Together, in his office in an awkward building in San Jose, we spun this fantasy out. Instead of cloning Interstates, the state could have built rail links between the existing towns of Mountain View, San Jose, Sunnyvale, etc. Travel between towns would be on these trains, maybe high-speed trains, which would make it far faster than on either surface or elevated roads. Within town, or really new cities, streetcars could carry residents around dense urban rows of streets, rather than the current pattern of low-density ranch houses set on green lawns. The computer companies would be located on railroad sidings instead of off-ramps. As the Silicon Valley types are fond of saying, its principal product is knowledge and ideas. These can be produced off an Interstate or a railroad track. Silicon chips can be shipped either way as well.

Some might think that without an automobile pattern of development, the Silicon Valley could never have developed as loosely, and therefore as informally, as it did. And that informality, that spontaneity, was necessary for its success, they might say. But one can build as spontaneously around a rail line as a freeway. Rails don't necessarily imply vast government supervision.

An appealing vision? I think so. It would be a fairer, more harmonious living pattern. The poor would not be so car-dependent, stuck in isolated sprawl chunks. Nature would be immediately available to residents inside the city. Great agricultural land could still produce great fruit. Perhaps those apricots and cherries of Olson's really were the best in the world, and, if so, it is a great shame to plow them up to become another house for another software designer. But Derryberry says the alternate past never had a chance. The highway is too much part of the California spirit to be put in second-tier status. "That is California. The serpentine highway that takes you where you want to go. In the postwar boom, there wasn't that much interest in fully planning."

Although Derryberry says the Silicon Valley was not planned, I think that is not quite accurate. Perhaps it was not consciously designed, but big governmental entities laid out big highways and expanded once-country roads into six-lane suburban boulevards. Mass transit was built. Zoning decisions were made. It's perhaps true that these decisions were not made with a clear plan, and were made by a dozen or so different entities, from the town of Mountain View up to the state transportation department to the San Francisco BART system. But made they were. They were a product of industry and government working together, with government as usual doing the heavy lifting.

What's interesting about the Bay Area, which Silicon Valley is a part of, is that, despite its sprawling characteristics, it does not lack for trains, buses, and streetcars. It has a semicoherent system of mass transit. There is Cal-Train, run by the state, which goes up the coast through San Mateo, Gilroy, and Palo Alto, and on up to San Francisco. There is BART, the regional mass transit system, which is run by a regional entity headquartered in San Francisco. There is a light rail line in San Jose that runs into Santa Clara County. There is a regional bus service run by something called the Valley Transportation Authority. There is the Metropolitan Transportation Commission.

All these systems lie over and on top of each other, as do the entities that run them. They change the life of the Valley, but they don't add up to a coherent mass transit system, or not enough to substantially change the physical structure of the Valley.

The region's investment in mass transit makes it more livable, but the system is not coherent enough to produce a different place. The various mass transit systems are mostly afterthoughts, laid down here and there, with better and worse results. They provide an alternative to the car to the poor, the elderly, and others who for some reason don't want to or can't drive. They keep the traffic out of gridlock and alter the land use some, although not much. What's lacking is a state and regional framework to fit development into a clear hierarchy of land use, which in turn would fit with a hierarchy of transportation decisions.

SILICON VALLEY: OUR PARIS?

What's central to understand about Silicon Valley, I think, is that new industry has always created new cities. The same goes for great explosions of wealth, which are usually based on new industries. The railroad and accompanying new industries created the Right Bank of Paris. The new dominance of national companies and centralized management created midtown Manhattan, which sprang from the earth in just a decade or two, almost overnight. From 1900 to 1930, Manhattan went from a city of generally genteel, earth-bound structures to one of soaring skyscrapers, including the Empire State Building.

The Silicon Valley is our new city. But unlike Paris or New York, it may never be a place in the traditional sense. The technology it was based on—the car and the highway—does not create place. The center, in an iconic sense, has stayed in the older city. I suspect no poems or songs will eulogize the Intel headquarters near the Great American Parkway. I didn't see any Georgia O'Keeffe out sketching the campus-style headquarters of computer companies the way the real O'Keeffe did New York skyscrapers in the 1920s. A different story has begun in the Valley, and an old one has ended.

Few people realize how young the places we now idealize really are. The East Side of New York didn't exist until the turn of the century, and the midtown Manhattan of skyscrapers was essentially created

in the 1920s and the previous decade. Yet these blocks almost instantly became places, memorialized in theater, film, song, and deed.
Midtown Manhattan was almost instantly a setting for novels, movies,
and plays. But artists ignore the landscape of the Silicon Valley. It's a
non-entity.

In the January 1998 issue of *Wired* magazine, writer Po Bronson
wrote an insightful article about the Valley, though after summing up
the Valley's landscape in a few phrases at the beginning, he then abandoned the subject. As Bronson described it: "Entangled superexpressways
pass over industrial megaparks and shady 3BR/2BA ranch-style homes and
provide occasional vistas of scorched tan acreage protected as natural
habitat for scrappy, trash-can-scrounging coyotes."[6]

Compare that to New York City. Writers nail you down to a sidewalk, a street, a building on Fifth Avenue and East Sixty-seventh Street,
or Washington Square Park. With Silicon Valley and its brethren, you
have entered the land of placelessness.

The River Walk in San Antonio—quaint and historic, but unreal—illustrates the ornamental nature of center cities in many regions. Photo by Stefanie A. Wittenbach.

The sloughed-off environment becomes a work of art in the new invisible environment.

Marshall McLuhan in a conversation with William Irwin Thompson;
quoted in Thompson, *Coming into Being*[1]

The bloodthirsty national merchants and the Chamber of Commerce have pretty well gutted the place I remember and taken and hucked the town's original character into the overall commercial park. The center of town, which when I was a kid hadn't changed much in the century, and was pleasingly timeworn and functional, has now either been torn down or renovated for artificial preservation as an example of itself.

description of Lexington, Kentucky, from Richard Hell's autobiographical novel, *Go Now*[2]

CHAPTER 4

TRADING

PLACES

The City and the Suburb

THE KING WILLIAM neighborhood in San Antonio is an elegant place of huge turreted Victorians sitting on expansive lots. German immigrants built the homes in the mid- and late nineteenth century, after they had grown rich industrializing the city. In San Antonio then, you were as likely to hear German on the streets as English or Spanish. An old photograph from the 1880s shows a sign on a bridge warning people to walk their horses. The notice is given in three languages—English, German, and Spanish.

Like many beautiful old neighborhoods, King William now mixes entrenched urban homesteaders with tourism. In one count there were more than seventy bed and breakfasts in the neighborhood, and tour buses cruising the streets have been regulated. It's ironic, because in the 1960s, the neighborhood was nearing abandonment, with the huge old homes falling into disrepair. But a wealthy believer bought and renovated a handful of homes, and suddenly a reverse exodus was on.

The tourism load is heavy in part because the neighborhood sits just a stone's throw from downtown and the city's famous River Walk, the winding subterranean path along water's edge now lined with restaurants, stores, and souvenir stands. Aboveground are the city's largely turn-of-the-century streets and buildings, which also include the ancient Alamo Mission and the modern shopping mall built a few years back. The mall gives armies of conventioneers another place to spend money.

I stayed in King William in 1997, in one of the ubiquitous bed and breakfasts. I was there on a magazine assignment, and I began my morning around the dining table with two couples who were there on vacation. They were from New Orleans, but the husbands knew San Antonio well because they traveled there frequently on business.

Knew the suburbs, that is. Like most businesspeople in the area, they conducted the bulk of their business out in the peripheries of the metropolitan area, in an environment of sprawling highways, office parks, and shopping centers that was casually called, no kidding, "Loopland." The name came from the beltway that encircled the metropolitan area and spawned the subsequent sprawl. It was a maddening, unholy place. Glass buildings were shoved right up to the high-speed freeway, and the system of exit ramps seemed like something out of a *Mad Max* movie. But this was now the true Main Street of San Antonio, the place where the wealth of the metropolitan area was produced, and where the bulk of new businesses and industries were formed.

In fact, so strong was Loopland's pull that the two businessmen, despite having traveled to the city for years, had never been downtown before or to any of the adjacent picturesque neighborhoods. The entire downtown, which includes the Alamo, the River Walk, and the business district, was a mystery to them. It was only now, on vacation, accompanied by their wives and children, that they were taking the chance to see "the city."

The couples' relationship with downtown is a good example of how contemporary center cities and suburbs have traded places. Older center cities—*when successful*—tend to be small, precious places with a limited function and market. The downtown of San Antonio was a make-believe world suitable for wives and children, who could pretend or believe they were seeing the real San Antonio.

The real San Antonio, of course, was out in Loopland. That's where the wealth of the region was being produced, that is where new businesses were being formed.

The parts of San Antonio's downtown that had been unable to convert themselves into tourist centers were dying. That included lovely but abandoned nineteenth-century office buildings and grand old theaters. Why? Because the business and essential living of the city were no longer being conducted in the center, and so the streets and buildings were no longer able to make a go of it by being utilitarian tools. They could only make it, to paraphrase Richard Hell, as artificially preserved examples of themselves.

The suburbs and city have reversed historic roles. The city now represents order, stability, community, and the human scale. The suburbs have become the example of constant change, gigantism, uncontrolled technological forces, and the rule of the marketplace. Whereas once the city symbolized a merciless, soulless world, and the suburbs calmness, family, and nature, the two worlds have almost completely traded places in what they represent.

Marshall McLuhan's statement "The sloughed-off environment becomes a work of art in the new invisible environment" is an accurate description of why this has occurred. The urban grid of streets grouped around a port or a train station or a streetcar line has ceased to be the central marketplace of society. It has been replaced by a tangle of streets built around freeway exits. And so the older form has gone from something utilitarian, a tool, to something whose aesthetics and value can be seen more clearly and admired because we are now outside it. The urban street is, to quote Joel Garreau, author of *Edge City*, an antique. And like an antique, it is seen as valuable merely for being, not for what it does. In San Antonio, the downtown plays an important role in the economy by nurturing tourism and the convention trade. But this is a passive, more gentle function than serving as the central arena of industry or the marketplace.

An antique, whether it's an object or a process, can be studied, perfected, and honed, similar to blues music, basket weaving, or the construction of handmade paper. But the form is not alive in the same way as suburbia. We can love cities because we are no longer *in* them.

From society's collective new home in the suburbs, we look back on them in wonder. I wonder when this will happen to the suburbs? When will we admire a cloverleaf, an off-ramp, and a gas station with an attached convenience store simply for their form and style?

I am not scoffing at the task of reviving the city. Ultimately it is not just the urban city but the metropolitan area that is, or can be, "a work of art," perhaps because we are now mentally outside of it in our global marketplace and Internet-enveloped world. If we are to grapple effectively with the artistic challenge before us, then we must understand city and suburb together and how they interact as a whole.

What I seek to do in this chapter is to understand the dynamic between our more traditional urban forms and the newer suburbs, and how this in turn relates to the dynamic of the metropolitan area as a whole. To understand city and suburb—and I use these words more in an iconic sense than a literal one, for I believe the true cities today in a practical sense are entire metropolitan areas—we need to understand how city and suburb have been viewed in history and what goals they have represented. When twelfth-century Italian princes built great urban piazzas, and when nineteenth-century park designers built great suburban subdivisions, what were they striving for? What heaven were they reaching for, and how far did it exceed their grasp?

URBANISM AS ORNAMENT

I make my home in what was once a designer's vision, Ghent, a hundred-year-old streetcar suburb in Norfolk. It was considered Norfolk's first suburb because it allowed the moderately prosperous to live outside the city for the first time. They commuted by streetcar the half-mile into downtown, and returned home to apartments and houses packed tightly around the streetcar line. When they needed to shop they walked to Colley Avenue, the neighborhood shopping street, or took the streetcar downtown to the department stores. They didn't have cars.

In the wake of a wave of much more extensive suburbanization that has taken place in the last fifty years, and in the wake of changed systems of transportation, this once suburban niche is now considered urban because, compared to the contemporary automobile-produced subdivision, it has a far tighter and more finely grained mix of living, working, shopping, and recreating. It is still a walking environment, and so is immediately distinguishable from anything built in the last half-century. It still has streets. The casual observer now lumps Ghent into the orbit of the downtown it once considered itself separate from.

The neighborhood both prospers and struggles because it is an anomaly. People like me love its urbanism, which is now a rarity, even as this status makes its systems difficult to support. It illustrates the paradoxes that many contemporary urban neighborhoods and downtowns struggle with.

Colley Avenue has always been the neighborhood's spine, both physically and commercially. The grid of streets is grouped around this shopping street. It has a movie theater, restaurants, some gift shops, a cooking store, a gourmet food store, some antique shops, and some more utilitarian businesses like a shoe repair shop and a small, struggling pharmacy.

Notice the trend here? With the exception of the pharmacy, all the businesses tend to be small ones that have managed to carve out a safe haven from the winds of megacapitalism blowing out on the beltway a few miles away. We have, rather than a corner grocer, a gourmet food shop. Rather than a five-and-dime, a high-priced children's clothing store. The strip offers a thin selection of luxury goods and entertainment services. The exceptions are the few neighborhood-centered service businesses that remain, like the dry cleaners and the shoe repair place and a struggling, single-proprietor pharmacy that is on its last legs.

Restaurants are a big winner. Making distinctive food is a domain where the big corporation has not yet taken over. So urban shopping streets have often become the equivalent of one long dining table. Corporations have turned food for the lower and middle classes into the assembly lines of Bennigan's, McDonald's, and Olive Gardens. The food is cheap, plentiful, and generic. Eating original food prepared outside the factory systems of the national chains is now a benefit reserved for those who can afford it.

Grocery shopping is also becoming a two-tiered system, separated by class and wealth. The rich and the educated shop at new supermarkets that blend the gourmet market with the hippie natural foods stores.

They buy vine-ripened, pesticide-free tomatoes to adorn a chicken breast from a hen that has wandered leisurely around a yard, at least in theory. The masses buy plastic tomatoes and factory-produced eggs from the Food Lion. Once, a ripe tomato that tasted like the thing that gave it its name was an item everyone enjoyed at some point, even if it was more expensive or available only at certain times of the year. Now, it is a luxury, available only to those who have the time, money, and discrimination to seek it out. I myself cannot obtain a good tomato, even during the height of summer, unless I grow one. The luxury supermarkets have yet to reach my down-market city, we have no farmer's markets near us, and the local supermarkets will not stock real tomatoes.

Making good tomatoes more available to everyone is akin to fixing our cities. We need—dare I say it—more centralized government oversight. If the government required, for example, chickens to be housed in certain more humane conditions, then all chickens would be "free-range" and their price would drop to a fraction of what such chickens cost now, although they would cost more than non-free-range chickens did before the government oversight. State and federal agricultural policies could also be reshaped to encourage supermarkets to take wares from local farms. It's not a question of a free market, because agriculture is already one of the most heavily regulated industries. But it's a question of regulation for whom. As it stands now, a decent tomato is becoming akin to a New Urban subdivision—a special, precious thing, available only to a limited market, that imitates something once available to everyone.

But back to Ghent. Colley Avenue is somewhat unusual in that an old Art Deco movie theater, The Naro, has managed to make a go of it and anchors the street commercially. I say unusual because older individual theaters have died everywhere, even in far more enlightened towns than Norfolk. And the lovely Naro is threatened even now by a huge multiplex scheduled to come to a suburban-style shopping mall being plunked downtown with city funding. Around The Naro are restaurants, gift shops, antique stores, and other businesses.

Notice the absence of anything practical on Colley Avenue. Try finding a pair of underwear, or a TV set, or almost any of the quotidian objects found at the local K-Mart that seem to be necessary for contemporary living. To get these objects, one must travel "out," to my area's equivalent of Loopland in San Antonio. To convert Colley Avenue back into an actual utilitarian shopping district, rather than the specialized mecca it has become, the transportation systems and the growth policies of the entire metropolitan area would have to be reworked. Some of the big highways would be torn down; the development of new subdivisions farther out would be restricted; money would be put into bus service and light rail. Then, as other older neighborhoods revived under the pressure of a more limited housing market and the structure of commerce changed, you'd actually see more practical stores reappear in the center city. As it stands now, even luxury items are hard to find. In the entire center city of Norfolk, for example, including downtown and surrounding older neighborhoods like Ghent, there is not a decent record store. Luckily, a good suburban music store arranges to deliver CDs to a downtown bookstore, or otherwise I would have to drive to the suburbs.

Meanwhile, big box stores and giant malls multiply around the cloverleafs in the suburbs. This is where a more chaotic and dynamic version of capitalism goes on. The suburbs have become the central marketplace of society, where laissez faire capitalism rips through the gleaming office towers on their spacious lawns, and down into the shallow boxes of the malls with their ever-changing ranks of stores. The suburbs, the Edge Cities, are where the action is.

This reversal in roles has reversed how city and suburbs are viewed. The city and its orderly pattern of gridded or semigridded streets appear humane and enlightened in comparison with the monolithic cloverleafs tieing themselves in knots in the suburbs. Whereas once the city's grid symbolized impersonality and an antlike existence in the service of Mammon, it is the suburb now that represents impersonal market forces, of an uncivilized land barely constrained by human guidance. As an operating system, the city is a Macintosh to the suburb's Windows, a clearer, more understandable system, as opposed to a more chaotic, but more robust, system, at least commercially. The gentrified urban neighborhoods, and usually the downtown itself, have a calmer, more orderly, cuter, and more comprehensible pace. They are an ornamental world, built for the amusements of their patrons, with their collection of fancy cooking shops, art galleries, and bookstores. It is a long way from the unsentimental cauldron of capitalism in the suburbs, where businesses remake themselves daily it seems.

This view of the city as an island of order amid more turbulent forces probably began with Jane Jacobs and the description of her Greenwich Village neighborhood in *The Death and Life of Great American Cities*. Jacobs emphasized the city as a dynamic, changing place. But the image one is left with is of the children playing under the watchful eye of the shopkeeper who takes the mail and guards the key for the apartment dweller upstairs. This chunk of the world's capital city resembles a small village. It is the city as sanctuary. It is an accurate picture in many respects. Older urban neighborhoods do have an intimacy that the modern suburban areas lack. But they have the role of sanctuary now in part because living in them is more of a choice and less of a requirement.

But only a minority of urban centers have made the leap from being the engine of a metropolis to its ornamentation. For every gentrified downtown and small town, there are a dozen dead urban districts, semiabandoned downtowns, and lonesome small towns where Main Street is a collection of shuttered-up shop fronts reflecting the lights of the fast-food joints and the shopping malls on the outskirts of town.

EUROSPRAWL

This trend of the suburbs becoming the workhorse of society while the center city becomes either the playground or the forgotten dump, is not peculiar to the United States. It is universal among the first tier of prosperous industrialized countries. The trend is present even in China as it begins to have the resources to suburbanize. Japan has been in love with the shopping mall for decades. Many planners, architects, and writers mistakenly describe Western Europe as a place where the bulk of living and working still goes on in traditional urban neighborhoods and business districts. Not so. Europe has experienced its own urban exodus and suburbanization. It's important to understand this, because as we do, we understand that sprawl and inner-city decay are not just products of white flight, or American bad taste, but products of changing transportation systems and the resultant places they produce.

Copenhagen is a good place to see these changes because it is, on first glance, so lovely, well-ordered, and prosperous. Cities in the Netherlands and Scandinavia, from Amsterdam up to Stockholm, are probably the finest examples of well-ordered and attentive urbanism in Europe and possibly the world. Well-ordered mass transit systems deliver people to and fro, and growth policies have held suburbanization far more in check. In Copenhagen, more than half the people travel daily on bicycle, and the sight of these fleets of urbane cyclists—a man in a business suit, a grandmother with some groceries—is winning indeed. Trams and buses carry much of the rest of the people around the city that appears prosperous, safe, and beautiful.

But a closer look, and a trip out to the suburbs of Copenhagen, reveal that most of the middle class, particularly those with children, have moved into the suburban ring, which is now far more populous than Copenhagen itself. In this suburban ring, you find shopping malls, office parks, and gas stations with Quicki-Marts, albeit with bike lanes and transit stops nearby. The city has been largely left to the young, the old, the students, the artists, and the tourists. More importantly, when you look at Copenhagen proper, you find declining neighborhoods and the bulk of the region's poor, working class, and immigrants—and a city struggling to make ends meet.

"We have the oldest and the poorest housing," said Jens de Nielsun, assistant urban planning director. "We have the students, the poor and the unemployed. The suburbs have the rich. We have the problems."[3]

The city has twice the percentage of unemployed as the rest of the metropolitan area, de Nielsun said. Since 1960, the number of jobs in the city has dropped from 460,000 to 310,000. The population has also dropped dramatically, in part because of a planned program to dedensify the center city. In 1950, de Nielsun said, 770,000 of the region's 1.4 million people lived in Copenhagen proper. By 1994, the city's population had dropped to 470,000 while the region's population had risen to 1.7 million. This drop in population, though less drastic, is comparable to that in the declining center cities in the United States, like St. Louis or Detroit.

Tellingly, Copenhagen's mix of old to young was exactly opposite that of the surrounding suburbs. As in the United States, many families want to raise children in the suburbs. In Copenhagen proper, 12 percent of the population were children under sixteen, and 20 percent of the population were over sixty-six. Outside Copenhagen, 20 percent of the population were under sixteen, and 12 percent over sixty-six years of age.

All these changes aren't readily apparent when one is walking Strøget, Copenhagen's main shopping street. This all-pedestrian street, which snakes from the nineteenth-century brick City Hall to the opera house, is crammed with tourists and overheated luxury shops. The side streets are full of trendy night clubs and Danish design stores. But outside this immediate ring of hipness one comes to long rows of warehouselike brick apartment buildings. Despite a century of age, these long buildings with small windows and stark facades have acquired only a smattering of charm with time. They still look like what they first were— worker housing. The best are still working-class neighborhoods, not trendy, but getting by.

This is becoming the standard pattern in many European cities. A city will often have an elegant shopping street that tourists visit. Nearby are noted museums, a cathedral. But around these bright lights are marginal neighborhoods that remain invisible to the average visitor.

These problems aren't readily apparent to us because most Americans don't go to Europe to visit shopping malls or decaying neighborhoods. But it's also because American cities are so much sicker by comparison, and the degree of suburbanization so much greater, that European cities seem idyllic by comparison. The situation tends to be like a dying man looking at someone in the next bed with the flu. By comparison, the neighbor looks in perfect health. Europe exercises far greater restraint in suburban development and far more conscious design in planning. Its continued investment in mass transit and trains has kept the urban form more vital. And its more egalitarian income structure means that what decaying neighborhoods there are, are not as visible as they are in the United States. What's striking is that even with those key differences, the basic dynamic—inner-city decay and specialization, suburban exodus and growth—is the same.

"Most of us do not need to be reminded again that our cities are in disarray," editor Suzanne Keatinge said in the introduction of the first issue of *European Urban Management* in 1994. "We do not need more pages about urban blight, poor housing, poor education, inadequate health services, security and transport systems and a thousand-and-one other issues."[4] The starkness of this quote contrasts pointedly with the starry-eyed views that many Americans have of European cities.

Europe's cities resemble more those of the United States in the 1950s. The suburban revolution has struck, but the center still holds. Families go downtown, although irregularly. And the more homogeneous population keeps the middle-class flight from becoming a panic, although immigrants play the role of the American blacks and Hispanics to a degree. Basically, everything designed after World War II in the United States and in Western Europe looks and feels the same. Sure, there are differences between the shopping mall outside Lyon, France, and the one outside Detroit. But both, and their surrounding homes and businesses, are fragmented and deconstructed. That is the nature of the contemporary place.

Deyan Sudjic, in his book *The 100 Mile City*, writes how, despite an authoritarian planning strategy, the new business district on the edge of Paris "has mysteriously contrived to echo North American individualism run riot. Mirror-glass office buildings erupt from pavementless roads in Marne-la-Vallée just as they do in Tyson's Corner" outside Washington.[5]

It's true that European sprawl is not American sprawl. The European suburb has fundamental differences with its American counterpart. Mainly it remains tied to the center by some form of mass transit. At least a bus line, and often train, subway, and bike lanes as well. This means that the overall stain of suburbia on the landscape is less than in the United States. In Lyon, you can travel from the Beaux-Arts-style City Hall to open farm fields in fifteen minutes on a good day.

Europeans pay a price for this. In exchange for tighter, more cohesive cities, they in general live in smaller, meaner spaces than Americans. They pay more for their washing machines and appliances, because there is less room for a Wal-Mart or warehouse-style store to elbow its way in beside the nearest freeway. Americans, with their uncontrolled development, have bought themselves the biggest living rooms and cheapest appliances in the world. Of course, they have also bought themselves monochromatic cities so dependent on the car that you might as well put yourself on an ice floe to die should you lose your ability to drive.

But the similarity of Europe to us also means that we can learn from them. Sprawl should not be thought of as a uniquely American problem. All of Europe has a heavier state hand shaping development, but even given that, the countries differ dramatically both in the tools by which they shape growth and how much they do so. Generally, the preciseness of control is most acute in Northern Europe and the Scandinavian countries, and diminishes as one travels south, being most relaxed in the southern countries of Italy and Spain. But even the best state control cannot get rid of the suburban/urban dynamic, though it can lessen the whiplash.

THE CITY IN HISTORY: STREETS NURTURE SIN

The shift in the roles city and suburb are playing is so fundamental that it helps to understand how each has been viewed through history. Both city and suburb have been dreams for men and women, but they have represented different dreams. And the city has been for many their nightmare.

In 1800, Thomas Jefferson, this country's philosopher-king, symbol of enlightenment and preeminent architect, put down a few sentiments about cities in a letter to Benjamin Rush. The letter concerned a yellow fever epidemic that had recently swept through some urban areas.

> The yellow fever will discourage the growth of great cities in our nation & I view great cities as pestilential to the morals, the health and the liberties of man. True, they nourish some of the elegant arts, but the useful ones can thrive elsewhere, and less perfection in the others, with more health, virtue & freedom, would be my choice.[6]

It's chilling to hear Jefferson praising a lethal epidemic because it will scare people away from urbanizing. This letter might be an odd footnote in history were Jefferson's view not so common among his contemporaries. It's also common in Anglo-Saxon thought, and to a lesser degree in Europe. Through much of history, urban centers have been regarded by many as necessary evils. They packed men together unnaturally and bred disease, crime, and unnatural social behavior. They were not works of art but things to be escaped from and eliminated if possible. The great places of cities that were considered art, from the Piazza San Giovanni in Florence to the grand avenues like the Nevsky Prospect, created in St. Petersburg in Russia in the nineteenth century, were valued because their air, light, and openness stood in such contrast to the dense, dark places around them.

In contemporary times, as the roles of city and suburb have reversed, so have our views of them. The difference is choice. As Mark Twain remarked, work is whatever one is obliged to do. And even without dirt and disease, living in cities was burdensome when one had no other choice. In their 1962 book, *The Intellectual versus the City*, Morton and Lucia White sum up the traditional hostility of the elite toward the urban center and form. From the practical to the aesthetic to the spiritual, they say, the city was seen as a debased and debasing place.

> Enthusiasm for the American city has not been typical or predominant in our intellectual history. . . .
>
> Of course there were some like Walt Whitman and William James who could at times speak affectionately about New York, but . . . [t]he volume of their voices did not compare with the anti-urban roar produced in the national literary pantheon by Jefferson, Emerson, Thoreau, Hawthorne, Melville, Poe, Henry Adams, Henry James, and William Dean Howells.[7]

The intellectuals criticized the city for both not being natural enough, and not being civilized enough, the Whites point out, a criticism virtually identical to that of the suburbs now.[8]

It wasn't just poets and philosophers that hated cities. The founders of urban sociology, like Robert Park and Jacob Riis, invented elaborate theories as to how the city dehumanized and depersonalized humans. In 1938, Louis Wirth published an influential essay entitled "Urbanism as a Way of Life" in the *American Journal of Sociology*. The essay built upon a theory by George Simmel that metropolitan life made people overly aggressive and overly intellectual by stimulating their nervous system too much.[9] In 1962, John Calhoun wrote his behavioral-sink essay, later canonized by Tom Wolfe in his high-velocity prose, which said the high density of the contemporary city was driving people crazy, like rats in an overcrowded cage, and thus producing the steadily rising crime rates and social disruptions of the postwar decade. Calhoun ignored or didn't notice that city density had actually been falling steadily since the turn of the century, a slight blow to his theory. Crime rates were actually much lower in 1900 in New York, when density was at its highest.[10]

Of course, the end-all of city haters was Frank Lloyd Wright, who, in his pompous prose, saw the city as a prison and its inhabitant as a slave. "To look at the cross-section of any plan of a big city, is to look at something like the section of a fibrous tumor."[11] "Like some tumor grown malignant, the city, like some cancerous growth, has become a menace to the future of humanity."[12]

The suburbs, as identified with Wright's Broadacre City, were for him and many others the converse of the city. Here families would live happily on an acre of land apiece, each traveling peacefully in its private automobile. Wright failed to do the math that would show all these cars would produce traffic jams and mammoth, dehumanizing parking lots.

"Where is your 'poor' man now? No longer poor because his soul again grows to be his own. . . . Birds sing, the grass grows for him, rain falls on his growing garden while the wheels of standardization and invention turn for him not against him where he lives. Because his devoting to the machine in these circumstances means increased life and opportunity for him, so it must mean increased life and opportunity for all concerned with him."[13]

Lewis Mumford was probably the best analyst and historian of the city in the last century, yet his view of the city at times was almost pathological. By the 1950s, he began to value the classic urban form more as its existence became threatened. But in his Depression-era book, *The Culture of Cities*, he wasted few words of praise on urbanism. In his chapter "Rise and Fall of Megalopolis," Mumford goes on and on about the deadly quality of cities, as if they were a special project of Lucifer himself.

"Within its endless streets, the metropolis provides shelter from prying eyes: here the drunkenness that would be a public spectacle becomes a private foible: here the liaison that might disrupt a provincial family can be consummated with a minimum of exposure. A man and a woman incur less danger from gossip by going to bed together in a metropolitan hotel than they would if they merely dined together in the restaurant of a small provincial town."[14]

Mumford views everything darkly. His book presents a photo of the beautiful Art Nouveau, wrought-iron subway entrances in Paris, which have become a symbol of elegant urbanity; Mumford titles it without irony: "Descent into Hades."[15]

In what might be viewed as prescient by some of the food devotees of Manhattan, he speaks of the "oral erethism" of metropolitan inhabitants, who gorge themselves with food and drink, saying that through "stuffing, gormandizing, sipping, [they achieve] a momentary euphoria that obscures the eventual physiological derangement."

Indeed. He sums all up by saying that because city dwellers tended to be preoccupied with mechanical or intellectual abstractions, they took "an almost equally abstract interest in the stomach and the sexual organs, divorced from their organic relations. To counteract boredom and isolation: mass spectacles . . . In short, the metropolis is rank with forms of negative vitality."[16]

Mumford has a lot to say in this vein. He says labor disputes of his era were put down with excessive force by the bourgeoisie to satisfy the populace's demands for violence and blood, similar to giving circuses to the Roman masses. "The tameness of the metropolitan routine must have its compensatory mobilizations of ferocity."[17]

Mumford's views remind me that, in the analysis of cities, there is a lot of pseudoscience, some of which I'm probably committing myself. Fixed rules of cause and effect are difficult to come by. From Mumford to Jane Jacobs to Andres Duany, a whole lot of ham-handed maxims are spoken that often have a half-life of less than a decade or two. These rules in time take on the sepia and absurd tones of solemn pronouncements by orthodox Marxist economists.

Jacobs, for example, spent quite a few pages in *The Death and Life of Great American Cities* describing how cities are natural generators of diversity. She goes on about the special qualities that make an urban area more diverse, including old buildings serving a vital role as nesting places for new businesses because of their cheaper rent.

Today, there is nothing so diverse as an aging suburban boulevard, like Silicon Valley's El Camino Real or one almost anywhere. On these aging roads, you will find million-dollar shopping malls planted next to comic book stores in aging suburban strip centers. If it's cheap rent you want, there's no better place than the suburbs now. As the suburbs age, abandoned shopping malls are being turned into municipal complexes. Low-capital theater companies have opened in storefronts in older shopping malls.

In the city, there are still plenty of vacant and underused buildings with low rent. But their form now appeals only to the limited market of art galleries, boutiques, and restaurants that have managed to make a home of city business. Jacobs is correct in saying that old buildings provide cheap rent. But once the suburbs aged, they had plenty of old buildings, too. Cities do need a diversity of old and new to be healthy. But Jacobs's maxim applies to any type of city, not just an urban one. Old buildings, no matter how cheap their rent, cannot overcome the wider dynamics of an urban or suburban marketplace.

THE SUBURB IN HISTORY

In 1957, John Keats wrote the satirical portrayal of life in the suburbs *The Crack in the Picture Window*. It tells the history of the then burgeoning suburbs by profiling the unsubtly named "John and Mary Drone," who take up residence in a series of awful developments around Washington, D.C. In its scathing, vitriolic language, it was a rifle shot across the bow of the battleship of suburbia that was proceeding at full pace. Keats wrote in part:

> For literally nothing down . . . you too . . . can find a box of your
> own in one of the fresh-air slums we're building around the
> edge of America's cities . . . inhabited by people whose age,
> income, number of children, problems, habits, conversation,
> dress, possessions and perhaps even blood type are also precisely

like yours. . . . [They are] developments conceived in error, nur-
tured by greed, corroding everything they touch. They destroy
established cities and trade patterns, pose dangerous problems
for the areas they invade, and actually drive mad myriads of
housewives shut up in them.[18]

In 1993, almost forty years later, James Howard Kunstler wrote
The Geography of Nowhere. It was, well, a rifle shot across the bow of
the battleship of suburbia that was proceeding at full tilt. Kunstler's prose
is more discriminating and amusing than Keats's, to my taste, but the
tone of contempt and disapproval is the same. Kunstler speaks of "the
jive-plastic commuter tract home wastelands, the Potemkin village shopping plazas with their vast parking lagoons, the Lego-block hotel complexes, the 'gourmet mansardic' junk-food joints, the Orwellian office
'parks' featuring buildings sheathed in the same reflective glass as the
sunglasses worn by chain-gang guards . . ."[19]

When we examine the writings on suburbia, what's striking is how
similar the criticism of it has been in style and substance over the last
century. Since the 'burbs first began to be a home to the middle class,
they have been criticized as soulless, vapid places that depreciate the
finer things in life and turn their residents into mindless robots of shopping and lawn maintenance. Comparing Keats to Kunstler is so interesting because the bulk of what Kunstler is criticizing hadn't even been
built yet when Keats was writing. As Kunstler says, "Eighty percent of
everything ever built in America has been built in the last fifty years,"
and that includes most of suburbia. I wonder what Kunstler thinks of
the subdivisions that Keats criticized, now shaded by trees and their roads
worn by use?

There are several ways to look at these criticisms. One is that intellectual leaders have always recognized the flaws of suburban growth,
and have tried to avert it. But the bulk of America's political and economic leaders, being unable and unwilling to do what's necessary to
change course, have clucked their tongues, made a few cosmetic changes,
but done nothing to seriously slow the rush of converting farmland into
freeways and houses.

Another way to look at the Keats-Kunstler axis of criticism is that the intellectual classes have had a snobbish aversion to granting the middle and working classes what the rich have enjoyed—space, a decent-size home, privacy, and an abundance of consumer goods that the suburbs deliver more cheaply.

Still a third line of analysis is to conclude that Keats and Kunstler are criticizing the suburbs for something they can never have, which is a sense of place. Fragmentation is the nature of cities built around the car and there is no way to change that.

All three viewpoints are correct. We can understand them better by looking at the history and nature of the suburbs.

WHAT IS SUBURBIA?

Robert Fishman, quoting Lewis Mumford, described the suburbs in his classic study, *Bourgeois Utopias*, as "a collective effort to live a private life."[20] Fishman describes suburbs as embodying the ideal of the primacy of private property and the individual family, separating themselves from the city or urban world, even though it is "the ultimate source of that wealth."[21] I think this is accurate.

This ideal was a pretty good one until the middle class caught on. As Fishman says, the first suburbs date back to the late eighteenth century. That's when the successful banker or merchant uprooted his family from the din of central London to a mini–manor house with turrets on a cul-de-sac on the edge of town. He would take his carriage into town, leaving his wife and children secure in the harmony of God-filled nature and far removed from the godless realm of man.

The suburbs for their first century and a half were imitations of the sheltered domains of the landed gentry before the industrial revolution. Said Mumford:

> From the beginning, the privileges and delights of suburbanism
> were reserved largely for the upper class; so that the suburb
> might almost be described as the collective urban form of the
> country house—the house in a park—as the suburban way of
> life is so largely a derivative of the relaxed, playful, goods-
> consuming aristocratic life that developed out of the rough, bel-
> licose, strenuous existence of the feudal stronghold. . . . To be

your own unique self; to build your unique house, amid a unique landscape; to live in this Domain of Arnheim a self-centered life, in which private fantasy and caprice would have license to express themselves openly, in short, to withdraw like a monk and live like a prince—this was the purpose of the original creators of the suburb.[22]

The suburbs earned no vast contempt of either the intellectuals or the general public until the middle class began to get the means and inclination to enjoy them, a process which started roughly at the turn of the century, but did not hit its stride until after World War II. City-haters like Mumford condemned the suburbs as soulless, decultured, banal places, while still condemning cities as breeders of immorality and decay. It left people without much of a choice.

"The [suburban] man is a man without a city—in short a barbarian," said Mumford in an essay, "The Wilderness of Suburbia," written at the early date of 1921. "Small wonder that bathtubs and heating systems and similar apparatus play such a large part in his conception of the good life. These are the compensations that carry him through his perpetual neurosis."[23]

Listening to the complaints, it's hard not to conclude that what the critics resented was the middle classes enjoying things previously reserved for the elites. Like indoor plumbing. They resented the incredible downward flow of wealth in the postwar era.

Housing is a good example of this. Many urban observers have noted with concern that the standard size of the American house is growing larger, even while families shrink. And it does seem absurd at first to have a family of four in a 5,000-square-foot house. Until you realize this has always been standard for the well off, and nothing compared to the mansions occupied by the truly wealthy. So the suburbanites have a bedroom for each kid, and a study for the husband and the wife.

Of course, customs and habits of the rich and the better off may seem debased and cheapened when practiced by the upper middle class. And perhaps are. But with the flow of wealth downward over the last half-century, it is not only the rich who live in big houses, eat too much, and are excessively individualistic.[24]

The suburbs have deficiencies their residents either ignore or discount because they like bigger houses and cheaper consumer goods. But it takes skill to distinguish between the deficiencies of the suburbs caused by their form or structure, and those caused by social and other factors.

Herbert Gans, in his classic study of Levittown in New Jersey, said critics of the suburbs confused attributes of class with the attributes of a physical setting. As the working and middle classes have come to live in the suburbs instead of the city, their characteristics—a certain vapidity and anti-intellectualism—infused the suburbs as well. "Their confusing of settlement with way of life is no different from that of Anglo-Saxon critics one hundred years ago, who blamed the city for the existence of the crime, vice, and degradation that are found among lower-class populations wherever they live."[25]

He gives here a coherent defense of suburbia. The people who live in the suburbs, he says, basically have no need of the city.

> Their major recreation is the care of home and children; their social life is focused on friends and neighbors, rather than on relatives; and they swell the membership rolls of churches and voluntary social organizations. Their culture has always been anti-urban even when they lived in the city, and they made little use of city culture even when it was easily accessible.[26]

But some deficiencies of Levittown appear to exist outside of class and culture. Gans notes it took him a year to meet his neighbor across the street. He quotes a working-class Philadelphian who lamented that he had known everyone within a four-block area there, while after moving to his new home at Levittown, he didn't know the people on his own street. Gans noted the replacement of Jewish bakeries and delis with 7-Elevens.

One observation stands out for its clarity and lasting validity today. Teenagers did not like Levittown, Gans says, because they could not live a full life there. "The adult conception of Levittown's vitality is not shared by its adolescents. Many consider it a dull place to which they have been brought involuntarily by their parents. Often there is no place to go and nothing to do after school. Although most adolescents have no trouble in their student role, many are bored after school and some are angry, expressing that anger through thinly veiled hostility to adults and vandalism against adult property. . . . The commonest gripe is the shortage of readily available transportation."[27]

TOO MANY MACHINES IN THE GARDEN

Despite my sympathy with suburban befrienders, like Gans, Garreau, and Sudjic, the suburban cities where most of the country now lives have inherent limitations that cannot be washed away by squinting and seeing them in a new light. The basic problem is that the suburbs only deliver the goods when a few people are buying them. When everyone tries to buy a house in the garden, you get a house in the middle of sprawl instead, and sprawl which does not add up to a coherent system of living, working, playing, schooling, and shopping.

"The basic concept of the suburb as a privileged zone between city and country no longer fits the realities of a posturban era in which high-tech research centers sit in the midst of farmland and grass grows on abandoned factory sites in the core," says Robert Fishman in *Bourgeois Utopias*. "As both core and periphery are swallowed up in seemingly endless multi-centered regions, where can one find suburbia?"[28]

When everyone attempts to live like a prince, as Mumford said, things get complicated. Suburbia for everyone meant its benefits— isolation, refuge, and being outside of the center—went to no one. Mumford shows his great vision by recognizing this dynamic at the beginning of mass automobile-oriented suburbanization, rather than today, a half-century after its commencement.

"Thus the ultimate effect of the suburban escape in our time is, ironically, a low-grade uniform environment from which escape is impossible," Mumford said in *The City in History*, published in 1961. "Thus, in overcoming the difficulties of the overcrowded and over-extended city, the suburb proved to be both a temporary and a costly solution. As soon as the suburban pattern became universal, the virtues it at first boasted began to disappear."[29]

This accounts for the phenomenon, familiar to every suburban reporter or civic leader, where everyone attempts to be the "last one in" to a particular section of town. No matter that my house or subdivision just went up two or five years ago, the one across the road on empty farmland should be prohibited as environmentally destructive and leading to more taxes.

This simple truth is key to understanding the ills of contemporary life, as well as the public-policy rationale for growth control as in effect in Oregon and Portland. The whole of suburbia is different from the sum of its parts. Our growth policies could be transformed if we could understand this so thoroughly that it would reflexively shape our public policies.

But we don't. It runs counter to the ethos and paradigm of American capitalism. We are trained and tutored virtually from birth in the Adam Smith truism that everyone pursuing his optimal benefit leads to a maximum benefit for everyone. The invisible hand lifts all boats, to mix metaphors. Of course, the converse is often true. That everyone seeking his own self-interest pushes down, and sometimes sinks, all boats. Degradation of the natural environment is one example; traffic jams are another. Traffic engineers will tell you that there is a point at which, when more cars are added to a highway, both the speed *and* the volume of traffic past a set point diminish. Still another example of this phenomenon is the increase in violent crime caused by the proliferation of guns. One person with a gun is arguably safer; but many people, each with a gun, are all collectively less safe. But we don't understand this simple truth as deeply as its converse, because its collectivist orientation is so contrary to our American myth and ethos of individualism.

Mumford, in his brilliant essay "The Highway and the City," published in 1958, berated the designers of the Interstate Highway System for not understanding the nuances of the transportation system they had just set in motion. What's shocking about this essay is how clearly he lays out cause and effect, and how futile his words were. He wrote:

> For the current American way of life is founded not just on motor transportation but on the religion of the motorcar, and the sacrifices that people are prepared to make for this religion stand outside the realm of rational criticism. Perhaps the only thing that could bring Americans to their senses would be a

clear demonstration of the fact that their highway program will, eventually, wipe out the very area of freedom that the private motorcar promises to retain for them. . . . That sense of freedom and power remains a fact today only in low-density areas, in the open country; the popularity of this method of escape has ruined the promise it once held forth. In using the car to flee from the metropolis the motorist finds that he has merely transferred congestion to the highway and thereby doubled it. When he reaches his destination, in a distant suburb, he finds that the countryside he sought has disappeared: beyond him, thanks to the motorway, lies only another suburb, just as dull as his own.[30]

What we see in the last fifty years of complaining about sprawl is a consistent inability to confront Mumford's analysis. The suburbs might be awful, but don't make us stop building them, or the highways that lead to their creation. Like a fat man told to push himself away from the ice cream counter and onto the exercise bicycle, we have not been willing to do it. Instead, we bitch and moan and order up another scoop of Chocolate-Crunch-Rocky-Road-Double-Fudge-Chip-Swirl, please. We try different styles of suburbia, we try New Towns and New Urbanism. We try ordering up more berms, more shrubbery, or more front porches. Save for a few brave cities and states like Portland and Oregon, we try everything, except saying no more.

Rather than stopping the outward sprawl, there is a curious phenomenon of redefining what the suburbs are, as people seek to avoid being labeled as living in them — or designing them. As with, at times, the labels of "Feminist," "Liberal," or "New Age," increasingly no one wants to be called a promoter of suburbia. Even its designers disavow their creations. James Rouse, designer of the planned, ultrasuburban community of Columbia, Maryland, declared passionately in the 1960s that the suburbs were the worst form of development. He was not building suburbs, he said, but "a city."

In *Business Week* in 1966, Rouse sounds like architect Andres Duany, leader of the neotraditional school of suburban development. Rouse says that "Sprawl is inefficient, ugly. Worst of all it is inhuman. . . . There has been too much emphasis on the role of the architect as an artist, not enough on his role as a social servant. . . . The suburb is the most controlled environment you can have. A kid can't do anything without a parent. How many kids in the massive sprawl around the big city can walk or bike to school, to a concert or music lesson, to a stream to fish, or to the movies?"[31] Duany would repeat his words a generation later, while again building automobile-oriented suburbs that masqueraded as something else.

Driving today around Rouse's planned community of Columbia, with its swooping curves, separated shopping centers, and a big enclosed mall as the "downtown," one can see Columbia is the embodiment of the suburban ideal and form. Will the same be said of New Urban subdivisions like Seaside and Celebration in twenty-five years?

The New Urbanists shun the label "suburban" and call their creations dug out of farm fields "urban." That these places, located miles from the center city, low in density, completely isolated, limited in their income appeal, composed almost entirely of homeowners and without businesses, could be called "urban" is the height of absurdity.

Robert Fishman says Ebenezer Howard, Frank Lloyd Wright, and Le Corbusier all hated the suburbs. In their attempts to create new city forms, none considered what he did suburban.[32] But all designed the contemporary suburb to one degree or another.

Ebenezer Howard, with his Garden City, helped propel the cities outward, toward the New Towns like Columbia, which to any contemporary eye are quintessentially suburban. Frank Lloyd Wright, with his Broadacre City, with one house per acre sprinkled on a vast grid, predicted and helped promote the low-density, automobile-dependent sprawl that consumes so much of our landscape. Le Corbusier, with his big highways swooping by tall towers in a park a la Radiant City, anticipated almost perfectly the Edge City environment of Tyson's Corner in Washington or the outskirts of almost every city, where tall office buildings on lawns sit by either superhighways or swollen, dynamic suburban thoroughfares.

We are left with the places we have created. These places, where the bulk of Americans live, function well neither as cities nor as country nor as an in-between environment. They will not function otherwise until we acknowledge we are building cities, and that the sum of the parts must be considered when making additions to the whole. We must turn our attention to the only entity that can consider the sum of the parts, the builder of cities, Government. It could be City Hall, a regional government, the state, or the feds. But it must be the public's representative, an entity charged with looking at the overall environment and its operation. As we turn our attention to government, we also turn our attention to our country's tortured and ambivalent relationship to it. Straightening out this relationship is key to building saner, more effective, and more harmonious places.

Halloween on Thirty-seventh
Avenue in Jackson Heights.
Photo by Alex Marshall.

CHAPTER 5

JACKSON

HEIGHTS

An Anachronism Finds Its Way

THE STAR RESTAURANT it was called. It sold "Chops, Steaks and Seafood." It was the kind of small Greek coffee shop that used to abound in Manhattan, but has been dwindling even there. Here, it stood out as a leftover from a bygone world.

The shop sat on Thirty-seventh Avenue, the principal shopping street of Jackson Heights. The street was a swirl of color and activity. Colombians on their way to Ecuadorean restaurants to eat yucca or ropa vieja. Koreans and other Asians came out of small stores selling herbs and spices. Indian women walked by wearing scarfs and other components of traditional dress. The street was a river of life, bustling with people and commerce.

In this flowing river, the Star restaurant sat like an island or an alley, part of this world but not of it. It somehow signaled that it was of another era, and might not be long for the present one.

The restaurant was filled, appropriately enough, with elderly Jewish women. They seemed like refugees from a storm, huddled in this sheltered place while the passions of color, language, and dress swirled and stormed outside on the street. They sat in black-vinyl booths and at square-topped tables, drinking coffee and discussing events. They eagerly surrounded me when I asked them about the neighborhood, eager to have a visitor, and a relatively young man at that. Most had lived in this neighborhood for their entire adult life, some fifty years. The stores they walked to, the candy shops, the movie theaters, the five-and-dimes, were largely gone now. They were widows, their husbands passing before them. They did not like being minorities now in ethnicity, custom, and style in a neighborhood they helped build.

"These people are so dirty, they are filthy," said a woman with big glasses who had just finished showing photos of her trip to Italy. "They throw their trash in the street. There is crime."

"They change the child's diapers in the car, and throw it out on the street, just like they do in India," said another woman.

"And let the child diddle in the curb," said still another.

"I even saw a man stand up against a wall and do it," said the first woman.

This account of the immigrants' bathroom habits seemed unfair, but probably true. Having lived in Spain for two years, I'm aware that Americans' bathroom habits are unusually fastidious compared to most. It was common in Spain for a mother to help a child urinate into the street. Men would routinely pee against a wall on a downtown street. I became accustomed to doing so myself.

One woman, less angry than the others, said she still liked it here, but that things had changed.

"There used to be so much to do here. There were the movie theaters. There was a candy store."

"There was the bingo hall down the street," said another woman.

"Even the Woolworth's is closing," said one woman. The national chain had just closed all Woolworth's in the country, but to these women it was just one more familiar friend departing.

The women's complaints were ironic, because while they noticed how much things had changed, I noticed how much things had stayed the same in Jackson Heights. Even if the color, religions, and languages of the people on the street changed, Jackson Heights was still a neighborhood that took working-class immigrants not long off the boat and lifted them into the middle class by providing them the opportunity for hard work. What makes Jackson Heights a rarity is that it is an urban neighborhood, based around the subway and elevated train line. Unlike most urban neighborhoods, Jackson Heights had not become either a slum or a giant fern bar.

WORKING IN THE CITY

As the suburbs have become ubiquitous, the urban neighborhood like Jackson Heights has become a specialized place, for the artist, the junkie, the rich, the homeless, the gay, the intellectually curious. What it isn't, generally speaking, is home to the police officer with two kids, the assistant hotel manager, the school teacher, and, of course, the factory worker. In other words, the working and middle classes. The classic working-class urban neighborhood, where a guy with a lunch pail walked to work or to a streetcar, subway, or bus, has become a rarity as the systems that produced it have become rarities.

The same goes for the classic ethnic, immigrant neighborhood. For many immigrants today, the town-house complex near the freeway ramp—in other words, the suburbs—has become the destination after getting off the boat. Only in a few cities, or parts of cities, are the walkable street, the walk-up apartment, still the first stop. The inner-city areas are either too expensive or too much of a slum.

But one urban area that is still home to the emerging middle class and the immigrant is New York City. In most cities, urban neighborhoods have become vestigial organs, either kept alive as luxury items for the well off, or abandoned to decay. In New York, urban neighborhoods still create the middle class, taking poor or less well-off people and providing them the environment by which they can make their way to a more established position economically.

One of those neighborhoods in the city is Jackson Heights in Queens. It's been a ladder for an emerging middle class for most of its existence, and it still is. Latin Americans, Koreans, and Indians have replaced or merged with Italians, Jews, Germans, and Greeks. These changes have often been wrenching sociologically. But the bottom line is that Jackson Heights is still where new immigrants come, get their first jobs, and move up.

Why does it still exist? Why has it become neither a slum nor a gentrified boutique neighborhood? What keeps its inhabitants living, with jobs, in a neighborhood where the car is still an uncommon element? In answering these questions, we see several things.

One, the uniqueness of New York City, which, after a destructive flirtation with the highway midcentury, has in the last generation become more and more dependent on mass transit. This makes it unique among America's cities. It has not been easy. It has managed to revive and enhance and build on a seventeenth-, eighteenth-, and nineteenth-century street pattern. Grids of streets where factory workers walked to jobs are now inhabited by stockbrokers or fashion executives who use limousine service. Neighborhoods like Jackson Heights still revolve around the central star of Manhattan, whose economy warms all the outer boroughs and gives life to their streets. Two, we see how transportation determines form and thus lifestyle. People live differently in Jackson Heights, and most of New York, because they get around differently. Three, we see the uniqueness of the street-based life that non-car-centered transportation produces. There is a closeness, an intimacy to life, in Jackson Heights that must at times be suffocating but which I often yearn for. We gave up something when most of our cities opted to build highways and Interstates, rather than train lines or subways.

A CHILD IS LOST AND FOUND

The "Greek" diner where the women drank coffee and chatted was actually not Greek anymore. Although the menu and the decor were both typical Greek diner, it was now run by Ecuadoreans. The women seemed quite at ease with this, despite their complaints about the habits of new immigrants. One woman paid her bill, joked with the young brown-skinned man behind the counter, and casually threw in a "mañana" as she walked outside.

A few minutes later, the woman who left with the "mañana" returned and hurried to the counter. She tugged at the sleeve of the young Hispanic man, trying to communicate, in both Spanish and English, that she wanted him to come outside. A young mother at the neighboring elementary school, P.S. 69, had lost her daughter and was in a panic. She somehow missed the child coming out of the school. But she was Hispanic and barely spoke English. The elderly Jewish woman wanted the Ecuadorean counter help to go talk to the woman.

Very quickly, the whole area around the coffee shop mobilized.

Two policemen came in and asked the diner personnel if they had seen the child. Another man did the same. On the street, people talked. Everyone seemed to know that, yes, the young mother's home had been checked, and the child was not there. Another man came in and asked to use the phone to call the mother's home. Perhaps because of its long tenure in the neighborhood, the diner seemed the place people went to ask for information, even though most did not patronize it.

The lost-child episode shows how life in Jackson Heights, because it is an urban neighborhood, still is a spectator sport. In Jackson Heights, you walk out your door, onto the street, and into the world. Only a minority step out their door and into a car, which then takes them to the world. In the suburbs, a lost child who somehow wandered from the parking-lot-enclosed schools there would create isolated moments of private panic, contained within the telephone line, the principal's office, the police station, and the family's kitchen. In Jackson Heights, it was a public affair. Have you heard? A child was lost. Where is she?

Street life is a rarity now in the United States, and particularly so for the working and middle classes. Like so many things in our swiftly changing modern world, something that was once a burden for the poor has become a luxury for the better-off.

Eventually, the child was found. It turned out that the child, not seeing her mother, walked to her aunt's home. She was fine. The entire incident was a fun one for the crowd, I sensed. It enlivened their day.

GETTING AROUND

Why was Jackson Heights still a nesting ground for upcoming immigrants working their way upward? Why were they still able to find jobs and opportunity in a traditional urban form based around the street? Why had Jackson Heights been neither abandoned nor gentrified?

The answer comes down to transportation and economics. The subway and elevated train lines give the neighborhood its urban form, and the presence of money and jobs fills the trains, homes, and businesses with people and sets the machine running.

The history of Queens is the history of cars on steel rails. No better example of how transportation creates certain types of places can be found. Because mass transportation is still the lingua franca of mobility in New York City, the urban neighborhoods created by mass transit are

Stores and shoppers carry on in the shadow of the elevated train line along Roosevelt Avenue. Photo by Alex Marshall.

still home to the bulk of the city's population, the working and middle classes. Jackson Heights sits near the axis of a network of subways, elevated train lines, and buses, including the No. 7 elevated train and the E, F, G, and R subway lines. They meet on the subway map at Roosevelt Avenue in a fat bunch of orange, purple, blue, yellow, and red cables, like electric power lines converging on a central power station.

These power cables supply all of Queens with residents and access to jobs, and give it form. Just as the freeway ramp produces a shopping mall and subdivisions, the subway stop produces urban shopping streets and apartment buildings.

At some point Robert Moses cut a freeway through Queens, almost certainly a mistake, a foreign system being laid down atop a different system. It damaged Queens but, unlike in the Bronx, did not kill it. The subway map shows the surface streets but rarely the freeways, even though their physical presence is overwhelming. They are immaterial to the system of streets and subways, and so can be ignored.

The train lines were built for the same reason new freeways are built today. As more people crammed onto Manhattan, the city and business owners looked for ways to spread people out, to have more people accessible for jobs without depending solely on foot to get them there. What they and the rest of the world came up with was the streetcar, the subway, and the elevated train line. This made it possible for more industry to come to New York and have more workers. Subway and elevated train lines started extending up the island and into Brooklyn.

In the twentieth century, they leaped across the water into Queens. The Fifty-ninth Street Queensboro Bridge was completed in 1911. Soon after came the No. 7 elevated train line. Subway lines followed. These sparked an enormous amount of development. Before the bridges and subways, Queens had been mostly farmland. A waitress at one restaurant in Jackson Heights says she still has customers who remember when Queens was mostly "farms and dirt roads."

Today, Jackson Heights is a chunk of the solid urban grid that forms most of Queens, which 2 million people call home. The neighborhood of Jackson Heights sits on the north side of Roosevelt Avenue, between Ninety-fourth Street and the Brooklyn-Queens expressway, and just south of La Guardia airport. The No. 7 elevated train line running along Roosevelt Avenue is a defining feature of the area. On its north side is Jackson Heights; on the south side, Elmhurst, another diverse, working-class area.

Because it was built between the wars, as the car was coming into use, the neighborhood is mass-transit-based urbanism transitioning to car-based suburbanism. Four-story Art Deco apartments that would be at home in Manhattan mix with one-story brick duplexes, each with its own driveway for the owners' cars.

Jackson Heights has several shopping streets, the main ones being Thirty-seventh Avenue, Eighty-second Street, and Roosevelt Avenue. Thirty-seventh Avenue is a neighborhood business street, Eighty-second Street is "downtown," and Roosevelt Avenue is a foreign place that is close but not quite of the neighborhood. All these dynamics exist within a few blocks. In suburban terminology, Thirty-seventh Avenue is the local strip mall, Eighty-second Street is the local major shopping mall, while Roosevelt Avenue might be the discount center.

The stores on Eighty-second Street, which bisects Jackson Heights, more glaringly reveal the area's mix of cultures and incomes, and the forces pushing it up and down in different ways. There is a larger corporate presence on Eighty-second, and the street feels less personal than

Thirty-seventh Avenue. I am surprised to see a Häagen-Dazs ice cream store, although it seems relatively unused. But on the corner outside the Häagen-Dazs store is a Colombian grilling intestines on an open grill. He is selling them to passersby.

On Eighty-second Street, the Hockson movie theater, a grand old palace, has been split into three screens. On two screens were showing *The Devil's Advocate* and *I Know What You Did Last Summer.* On the third screen, which was the main screen and largest, was a Spanish-language film, *Buscando La Verdad.*

It was thought that building train lines, subways, and streetcars would ease the congestion in Manhattan. It made it worse. New mass transit created new neighborhoods and new potential for economic growth. The people living there still commuted downtown, which brought more people into already congested streets and allowed developers to build tall buildings that could be easily packed with people.

The mistake in thinking that more subway lines would solve congestion in Manhattan is similar to the misguided notion of building freeways to solve traffic jams. Transportation lines cause development. The traffic congestion that accompanies our cities of beltways and shopping malls is part of their form, as much as the crowded subway car is part of Manhattan.

With the opening of Queens to development, in went the middle class. The Jews, Italians, and others that could afford to move out of the crowded tenements of the Lower East Side did so. They moved to the suburbs, to urban suburbs, which is what places like Jackson Heights were.

"There was tremendous demand to get out of Manhattan and the old- and new-law tenements," said Fred Lee, a planner in Queens. Old-law tenements were not required to sacrifice part of the property to give inner-building residents windows. New-law ones were. But in Queens, "You suddenly had windows, private bathrooms, and an elevator. That was a huge improvement."[1]

From the start, these places were generally middle class, though. The wealthy and the poor stayed in Manhattan. Jackson Heights and the rest of Queen were suburbs. At first, there were pockets of wealth, and amenities, like the golf course that used to grace the area. And some of the apartment buildings had lovely Art Deco flourishes that are today giving the area a taste of gentrification.

But the elevated train line insured that the neighborhood would never rise too far. As Lewis Mumford commented, elevated train lines are a failed transportation form. The ease in transportation and the lower cost of construction compared to subways are offset by the radiation-like effect on surrounding property. The tracks and pylons shut out the sun while spreading noise and dirt. While an elevated train line still causes growth, it inhibits growth immediately around it. As Mumford noted, it is in this dynamic exactly similar to the Interstate highway, which spurs growth but kills whatever is directly beneath or beside it.[2]

HITCH YOUR WAGON TO MANHATTAN

If the subway gives Jackson Heights its form, what gives its passengers money and jobs? How could a modern economy exist around what is considered an anachronistic urban form?

To understand why an economy still exists in Jackson Heights is to find one's eyes inevitably drawn toward the Island of Manhattan. It is the star to which the wagon of Jackson Heights and Queens is hitched. There's a lot of grousing in New York over Manhattan getting all the attention, but it is still the engine that pulls the entire city forward. Manhattan's bankers, publishers, tycoons, fashion designers, advertising executives, and playwrights, maneuvering at the summit of global capitalism, have done a pretty good job of hauling behind them the Colombian construction worker and his office-cleaning wife, and the neighborhood they live in.

"This area has always functioned as a bedroom community for the Manhattan professional business district. In the mix of professions, it is probably not that much different than in 1950 or in 1930," said Eric Kober, an economic and housing planner for New York City. "There would be more blue collar back then, but the rest would be the same."[3]

The people who live in Jackson Heights are plumbers, janitors, assistant hotel managers, and secretaries—the support crew of Manhattan. Jackson Heights is loaded with businesses, but not with industry. The butchers, grocers, dentists, lawyers, and various small businesses that line Thirty-seventh Avenue depend on the money their customers bring home from their jobs in Manhattan. Although it helps a neighborhood's health and economic base to have a healthy retail sector, it does not establish them. A city or a neighborhood cannot exist by sim-

*That's
Manhattan*

ply selling things to itself. This would be akin to a perpetual motion machine. Something must prime the pump.

I had wondered if Jackson Heights would be studded with small factories wedged into the blocks, factories that might produce paper products, boxes, tableware, or some other ordinary objects of our life. I had seen similar factories wedged into the Art Nouveau blocks of Barcelona, full-fledged industries nearly invisible from the sidewalk. But the factories were largely absent, I was sorry to say. The industry of today has moved next to a freeway off-ramp. There were some small industries in Jackson Heights—an exporter of Greek food, for example—and there were others in Queens.

*J.H. depends on
Manhattan or it's
been like.*

But if the health of Jackson Heights depends on the health of the city, that raises another question. Why does Manhattan still thrive, and with it, the city as a whole? Why isn't the entire city condemned to obsolescence? Is New York City one giant sleight of hand? How does it keep 8 million people alive using a transportation and economic system that the rest of the country has abandoned?

FOLLOW THE MONEY

The history of New York illustrates how cities exist because they employ people. To produce wealth, people generally need other people. A George Soros, who makes billions by speculating on currency, may need only a handful of people to manage his computers. But most industries even today need workers. That was much more true in the past. New York has grown to such an immense size because it has been a gigantic job creator, sucking people to it. These people in turn create more jobs. This job creation system is wrapped within a hard system of transportation and plumbing, and a soft system of governance and laws. Both incubate the creation of jobs and wealth.

"A city by definition creates jobs," said Frank Vardy, a demographer with New York City, in an obvious, but often forgotten, maxim.[4]

Cities came about because industry locates near central transportation links. Cities' raison d'être is their specialized systems of transportation that are not available everywhere—a port, a railroad, an Interstate, a canal, an airport. New York gained its preeminence not only by having a huge Atlantic port, but also by having the Erie Canal, opened in 1825, which gave shippers access to the entire Midwest by providing a direct link to the Great Lakes, "from Albany to Buffalo," as the song says.

The link between jobs and transportation explains why so many people occupied the small island of Manhattan. Industries like ship-building needed huge numbers of people. They came. This gave rise to the infamous tenements of the Lower East Side, where possibly more people per mile were crammed together than at any time in human history, before or since.

It seems almost strange now, the close link of older urban cities with heavy industry. I found myself thinking, why would you locate a big factory in the middle of a dense grid of streets, where it's hard to maneuver big pieces of equipment and other tools of industry? But of course, I had it exactly backwards. The dense grid of streets existed be-cause the factory was there. "The streets" for the factories were largely the river and rail lines, where traffic could move relatively unimpeded.

Because the waterways were the prime highways in the nineteenth century, being an island was an advantage to Manhattan because it had more main highway frontage. The city's waterfront used to be its eco-nomic engine. It was lined with docks, ironworks, shipyards, and freight yards. The United Nations site used to be the home of stockyards. The lower avenues near the East River on Manhattan's exclusive Upper East Side are still much less pricey real estate than the more inland avenues near Central Park, because the avenues near the water used to be the home of industry and worker housing. Consequently, the building stock is plainer.

Manhattan's heavy industry has gradually evaporated over this cen-tury. Once highways for cars and trucks were established, the factory moved out of town. Production lines could be placed more horizontally on big swaths of land. The waterways, whose more limited frontage had caused factories to occupy tighter plots of land, were less necessary. The waterfront, once the home to shipbuilders and ironworks, began being converted into pleasant vistas or highway routes. The dense grid of streets was left with no reason for being, unless it could reinvent itself.

An old Hagstrom subway map, dated 1936, shows well the city's changing transportation systems. The map, although for subway riders, showed as a matter of course dozens of shipping berths that then ringed the island. On the West Side of Manhattan, starting at Fifty-ninth Street and stretching down to Battery Park, were rows of shipping berths, named for their owners, the Swedish American line, Italian line, Cunard–White Star line, United States line, the Panama S.S. line, and many more. The rows of berths around the island looked like the layout of a modern airport ringed by runway gates.

The triumph of New York is that it has been able to strengthen and grow its intellectual industries to replace the muscle and brawn industries that left. Most cities have not made the leap. While "world" cities like Boston, San Francisco, and New York have thrived on globalism, cities like St. Louis, Cleveland, and Detroit have seen the bottom drop out. These cities' population loss has been exacerbated not only by the decline of industry, but by building freeways that cause new suburban centers to emerge. The political city of St. Louis, for example, has gone from 850,000 in 1950 to less than 350,000 today, while the metropolitan area of St. Louis has swelled to 2.5 million.[5]

Manhattan has thrived because it always was the center of more intellectual and creative industries, as well as heavier industry. A city can arrange itself in a number of ways as long as it promotes, or at least does not hurt, its essential economic engines. In New York, those are still banking, stock selling, composing advertising, making magazines, designing clothes, and other services that the world demands and which New York does better than anywhere else. These industries thrive in the nineteenth-century conception of a city, with its emphasis on face-to-face contact and walking proximity to many other businesses. Newer industries, like software development, can also find a home in the urban nest.

Some decisions affecting urban configuration are not optional. To thrive today, a metropolitan area needs a big airport, good Interstate linkage, good rail access, a good port, or some combination of the four. But after that, all is choice. A public choice, a political choice. You can live like Manhattanites or Portlandites, in smaller homes served by train lines, or a la Dade County, in town houses off big suburban boulevards and Interstates with round-the-clock traffic jams.

It is a mistake to see city development too linearly. That is, trains replaced carriages, and cars replaced trains, and sorry, that's just the way life goes, and attempting to keep older forms of transportation, and thus cities, is like refusing to move up to the next level of microprocessor in a computer. Following this logic, if a city refuses to "trade up" in its transportation and accompanying form, it will be left behind. But this logic is flawed because not all transportation systems are vital to a city's economy. An airport might replace a shipping berth. But if people have jobs at either, they can live in a subdivision and take the freeway, or take the subway and live in an apartment. The choice is up to them through their politicians.

THE BOAT STOPS HERE

It's twilight in Travers Park, and, against the backdrop of a blue sky turning to black, an elderly Asian woman practices Tai Chi in the unused basketball court area. She moves through the forms—repulsing the monkey, carrying the tiger to the mountain, white crane spreading its wings—expertly. She has plenty of room. The rest of the park—handball courts, chess tables, and other small areas—is full of activity but the basketball courts are unused.

This is a great commentary on Jackson Heights. In parks, basketball courts usually fill up first, particularly on a warm fall day. Basketball is the most popular street game in both white and black neighborhoods. But Latin Americans, Asians, and Russians have less interest in it. Mexicans play the game in great numbers, but there are few Mexican Americans in Jackson Heights.

Across a chain-link fence from where the woman practices Tai Chi, a group of young Latin men play an active game of handball. Some very pretty teenage girls, rail-thin in that Latin way, play on a neighboring court. The men, who are probably in their thirties, flirt with the girls casually, despite their adolescent status. In a central square in the park, a group of white-haired men play chess at a public table. Two play, and three others watch. Mothers sit on benches, children ride tricycles and swing on swings. On one corner of the basketball courts, some kids kick a soccer ball around. It's a crisp fall day, late October, and sunny, 4 P.M.

Travers Park takes up just one block in Jackson Heights, which means it's just a speck of green even on a detailed map. But it is a beehive of activity. It's a great picture of how well a small park can complement a dense urban neighborhood.

Just what role do immigrants play in Jackson Heights? It's a central question, because Queens, Brooklyn, and the Bronx, where the bulk of the city's population lives, are becoming largely cities of new immigrants. As Manhattan's star continues to shine, more immigrants come to Williamsburg in Brooklyn, Jackson Heights in Queens, and dozens of other neighborhoods in the outer boroughs and upper Manhattan.

Jackson Heights is roughly congruent with what New York City labels "Queens Community District 3." As of 1990, when the last census was taken, it had almost 130,000 people. It almost certainly has more than that now. The population has been increasing, say planners, as it did from 1980 to 1990, when the population grew by 5 percent. Queens as a whole has about 2 million people.

This gain in population is the most unmistakable sign of health. Healthy places grow, diseased ones shrink. Healthy places produce jobs. Diseased ones lose them, and people. Jackson Heights's population gain is more significant in that it comes in a city that has stayed roughly flat in population for the last two decades. For the city, though, this is a sign of relative health, because the population losses of the fifties, sixties, and seventies have stopped.

The immigrants have formed the basis of Jackson Heights's rejuvenation by coming there, working, and raising families. But this didn't happen in a vacuum. The reason Ecuadoreans, Colombians, and Koreans moved to Jackson Heights is because there were jobs in Manhattan that Jackson Heights had access to. Jobs attract immigrants, and a healthy city attracts immigration, from within and without the United States. I sense that many people don't understand this. The only reason immigrants come to New York City is because there are jobs there. Traditionally, we have associated urban places with new immigrants. They are the foundation of the classic ethnic neighborhoods like South Philly or the North End of Boston. And urban neighborhoods are ideally suited for new immigrants, because you don't need a car to live there. And immigrants seem more willing to embrace an urban lifestyle than native-born working-class Americans.

But suburban-style cities are now the big job producers, and that's where you find most new immigration now, although a huge portion still comes to New York City. In Charlotte, North Carolina, which is as suburban a landscape as you can find, your taxi driver at the airport will likely be a Nigerian who speaks English with a British accent. The Raleigh-Durham area, another vast sea of suburbia in North Carolina, has been hit by a swell of Hispanic immigrants who have come for the construction jobs. The Washington, D.C., metropolis abounds with Vietnamese immigrants who mostly live in the suburbs of northern Virginia. Los Angeles, the greatest magnet of immigrants, is almost entirely suburban in its makeup. Virginia Beach, one of the most suburban areas on the planet, has one of the largest Filipino populations in the country.

As Deyan Sudjic has noted, the presence of immigrants is the sign of a first-tier, global city. Far from signaling ill health, the converse is usually true. The confusion of immigrants with decay may be in part because they often have brown skin and so are confused with native-born blacks, Hispanics, and American Indians. These minority groups have problems revolving around generations of entrenched poverty, state-authorized oppression, and destructive cultural patterns, which make them wholly different from the immigrant fresh off the boat. Immigrants have problems, too, but they are usually more transient than those of native-born poor people of any race. Many successful African Americans, for example, are Caribbean in their heritage. Having come to this country voluntarily, they behave more like traditional immigrants in their work habits and career paths. Racism is still a problem for them, but one they can more easily overcome than the descendants of Southern slaves. To give another example, the Cuban who arrived penniless in Miami in 1961, but who had education and skills from a middle-class upbringing, is a very different person than the poor Mexican American in Texas whose ancestors might have come here in the sixteenth century.

If immigration had been more restricted, neighborhoods like Jackson Heights would be more sluggish. The jobs in Manhattan would still have drawn people to the neighborhood, but the level of population and economic activity might be lower. The population figures relating to immigration to New York are impressive. From 1990 to 1994, 563,000 documented immigrants came to the city—a number which almost exactly matched the number of residents who left the city.[6] This was 15 percent of the immigration to the country as a whole.[7] It means that New York is still a first-class destination for immigrants. Because of immigrants, the city's population grew slightly rather than declined.

The big cities that have retained an economic base in a more global economy have drawn the immigrants. "Immigrants have not only helped stabilize the population of cities such as New York and San Francisco, but have helped ameliorate population losses in cities such as Washington, Chicago and Boston," noted the report *The Newest New Yorkers*, which analyzed immigration to the city and the country.[8]

The ethnic face of Jackson Heights has turned over every generation or, sometimes, every decade. From 1980 to 1990, the number of Colombians went from nonexistent to about 12,000, or almost 10 percent of the neighborhood. The number of Dominicans went from zero to 15,000; Ecuadoreans from zero to 6,000. All told, people of Hispanic descent went from making up 32 percent of the neighborhood to 44 percent, a figure which has increased further in the seven or so years since the last census. The number of Asians almost doubled, from 6.5 percent of the neighborhood to 11.5 percent. Whites went from being the dominant minority, with 43 percent, to being just another minority, with 28 percent. Italians, Irish, and Germans, the dominant European ethnic groups, all declined by almost half. The demographics show how swiftly places change. In 1980, none of the principal population groups that now form a plurality—Colombians, Ecuadoreans, Dominicans, and mostly South American Hispanics—was here at all. Not a single unit on the census report. Whites of European ancestry were still the dominant, if shrinking, ethnic group.[9]

This rapid change causes problems. The tensions are not among immigrants of different ethnic origins—even though they come from different continents, worship different gods, eat different foods, wear different clothes, and have different color skin. Despite their differences, their priorities are similar. They need jobs, good schools, and fluency in English. Raul Bermuda, a young man who coaches soccer for his Catholic church, St. Joan of Arc, fields a multicultural team that has no problem with its members' different backgrounds. "I have eleven kids on the team and nine nationalities. Colombian, Ecuadorean, Russian, Polish, Yugoslavian, Croatian," and his voice fades out.

Rather, the tensions are between new immigrants and "old" immigrants, like the Jewish and Italian American women in the Star diner, who came here fifty years ago and now have very different needs and priorities than someone recently arrived to the country.

A woman from Spain, a Basque from the city of Vitoria, said the neighborhood is now fighting over how to use a now empty Jewish community center a few blocks away. Newer immigrants like her, with young children, want it converted into a school to relieve overcrowding. But elderly residents in apartments around the center do not because they fear noise and disruption from the children.

"They don't care about the children's education, they don't care

Public School 69 in Jackson Heights, showing the recent addition to the school. Photo by Alex Marshall.

that it's overcrowded, they only care about they might be disturbed," she said, bristling. The woman had lived here for ten years but still didn't speak English well. We spoke in Spanish, while her young daughter hugged her legs. "Can you believe it?"

CITIES NEED PEOPLE—AND CHILDREN

P.S. 69, the school from which the woman's daughter exited, is an example of New York's and Jackson Heights's rebirth. It's a milestone that they are actually building new urban schools in Jackson Heights and in other outer boroughs. The crush of new immigration by people with a lot of kids has crowded schools that formerly were dropping in enrollment. This is a challenge, but it's a sign of health. The abandoned multistory urban elementary and high schools that now dot most inner cities are a stark sign of these cities' decay.

Many cities actively discourage new residents because they say "residential growth" doesn't pay for itself, even when it occupies existing developed land or buildings. City Halls employ the twisted logic that because families have children, and children must attend schools, it's better not to have families because then you won't have to pay for their kids' education. But this logic would lead to a city devoid of people. While it's true that residences don't pay their own way, the shops, restaurants, factories, and offices that follow them do. And you can't have those without residential living quarters. A city cannot be healthy without a healthy population base. Child-filled schools are a sign of this.

In Jackson Heights, P.S. 69 was one of the neighborhood's focal points. On a weekday evening at 5 P.M., I watched as the Basque woman and about fifty other parents waited patiently for their children. Their sons and daughters were all in an after-school program where immigrant students get additional instruction in English and other subjects. This program pleased their parents very much. The parents outside were dressed in a variety of clothing styles, from Indian robes to regular Western dress. Their faces lit up as their children came out the school's grand front door and gates onto the sidewalk.

The school was renovated and added onto about five years ago. The addition is one of the best examples of respectful urban architecture I have seen. It's so seamless with the old school you don't realize at first it's an addition. But the addition, designed by Urban Associates in Manhattan, has its own style. Raised exterior medallions at the cornice lines add grace notes that weren't in the original. The parents I talk to say they are proud of the school and its reputation as a good one. The money put into the renovation a few years ago pleases them as an example of the city investing in their neighborhood, as does the after-school program.

There's a paradox here in the health of Jackson Heights and in what it represents, which is the robust health of New York City. In the age of the automobile, which has decimated so many cities, New York is arguably doing better than it has in a hundred years. With the neighborhoods of Manhattan filling up and unable to contain the continued inward flow of money and people, the middle and upper classes are spilling over to the outer boroughs. In Brooklyn, you have Park Slope, which is turning back into the upper-class neighborhood of elegant brownstones it originally was, and a dozen or so other working-class neighborhoods are returning to their roots, like Sheepshead Bay, Flatbush, and Crown Heights. In Queens, Jackson Heights, Elmhurst,

Art Deco apartments like these in Jackson Heights are attracting gentrifiers from Manhattan. Photo by Alex Marshall.

Corona, Flushing, and Astoria—all neighborhoods built around the subway or the elevated train—are on the upswing. Even the South Bronx is coming up. In both New York and other cities, you see how the growth and prosperity of a city operate like water flowing through sluice gates, spilling over from one neighborhood to the next. The Upper West Side in New York becomes too expensive, which causes people to look to Park Slope in Brooklyn. People and money spill over from one neighborhood to another, lifting first this neighborhood to a certain point, and then spilling on to the next. If this is labeled gentrification, then gentrification is a good thing. Explosive changes in a neighborhood's real-estate values, be they falling or rising, are destructive. And care and regulations can be used to protect longtime residents of an area. But rising prosperity in a neighborhood must be seen as beneficial overall, unless one allies oneself against the health of a city. Although we identify gentrifiers with appliance-carrying yuppies, the Ecuadorean immigrant in Jackson Heights is as much a gentrifier as anyone. He or she represents new blood and new wealth coming into a neighborhood and lifting it up.

Some more stereotypical gentrifiers have arrived in Jackson Heights, something I thought unimaginable at first. The neighborhood, with its polyglot of nationalities, seemed too inhospitable to the yuppie and his and her coffeehouse. But the early adopters of urban neighborhoods, gay men and women, are trickling into Jackson Heights, moving into the Art Deco apartments that are on the north side of Thirty-seventh Avenue. The apartments do not stand out as objets d'art at first glance: they are solid square brick apartments without a wealth of detailing. But on second look, they do have a cornice here, a nice entranceway there. And inside they have hardwood floors and nice trim, I was told.

THINGS CHANGE

Contemplating Jackson Heights thrills and saddens me. That the neighborhood has been able to rejuvenate itself thrills me, but the swiftness of change that makes it so exceptional, and which has swept away so much of its world, saddens me. "Ephemeral are the works of man," I seem to hear in my head.

A candy store that corrupted the palates of a generation of kids in a nameless city vanishes. As do most of the candies it served. The streetcar that once traveled by the candy store is gone. As are most of the jobs and professions its customers once had. Nothing lasts, I hear in my head. What's true culturally and commercially is true for the physical creation of places as well. Jackson Heights, with its streets and stores and homes based around subways and buses, is an anomaly. Yet, the neighborhood is not that old, built seventy-five years ago between the wars. It's bad enough for buildings to wear out in a few decades, but entire places have a life span that is often not that much longer.

I think of the subways, streetcars, and trains that for an era powered a nation, and how fleeting they were. Generations of men spent their lives inventing and perfecting these institutions, yet they occupied just a moment on the stage. Trains revolutionized cities, transformed them and overturned them, yet they began to wane in the 1920s even as they reached their zenith with the diesel engine. The age of the train lasted less than a century. I think of the streetcar, which created a whole new type of neighborhood and city structure, yet lasted only about fifty years. I think of whole systems, rising and falling and fading away. The steamship, the battleship, the ocean liner. Karl Marx and his interpreters like Marshall Berman rightly blame or credit the capitalist system for this pace of inexorable change. In the relentless search for new markets, new profits, nothing is sacred and "All that is solid melts into air."[10]

Could we ever add the car to the list of things that have melted into air? Its dominance seems complete now, but the same could once be said for the train, the ocean liner, and the streetcar. I see no easy way for its dominance to be subverted swiftly, because it rests on a network of public roads and freeways, which are not so easily abandoned. Still, if high-speed trains become widespread a new type of city would grow around them. It's one fantasy.

Then there's the New York City subway, created through so much sweat, thought, and blood. It magically still exists, is still the lifeline on which the whole city depends. Although there are still enormous opportunities for new investment, the subway is in better shape than in decades past. The graffiti is gone, and the trains are more dependable. Crowding is more a problem now than underuse. A new fare system, which allows free transfer between buses and subways, something which in most cities has been routine, has boosted both ridership and the income of the transit authority. Ridership has passed 4 million passengers daily. But the system as a whole is still a stepchild of the city and state. The politicians do not seem to understand how completely the city rests on its subway and related train lines, as well as the bus system. No better way could be found to rejuvenate New York than to relentlessly rejuvenate the subway.

But some new form of place, of city, is around the corner, even though I am not visionary enough to see it. It will be based on some new form of transportation—a high-speed train, a personal helicopter, a magical car, jet-powered tricycles—that will be adopted and will produce a new form of city structure around it. I hope it will be a denser, more communal form to balance out the fragmented physical environment built around the car. But who knows?

Government does most
everything important,
including getting us
from one side of the
water to the other.
Photo by Stefanie A.
Wittenbach.

For by art is created that great "Leviathan" called a "Common-wealth"
or "State," (in latine civitas) which is but an Artificiall Man, though of
greater stature and strength than the Naturall, for whose protection
and defence it was intended.

Thomas Hobbes (1588–1679), from *Leviathan*, published 1651

CHAPTER 6

THE MASTER

HAND

The Role of Government in Building Cities

IN 1817, THE GOVERNOR of New York convinced the state legislature to spend $7 million to finance a canal from Albany to Buffalo. Eight years later, after thousands of workers had carved a channel through rock and earth, the Erie Canal was complete. The 350-mile canal opened the entire upper Midwest to shipping, and cemented New York City's role as transportation hub for the nation, and as the country's greatest city.[1]

In 1919, the U.S. Navy, concerned that the country was losing the race in radio technology to Europe, created the Radio Corporation of America—or RCA. It was funded as a joint project between government and private business, and the Secretary of the Navy sat on its board. Later spun off as a completely private enterprise, it grew into one of the largest and most important companies in home and commercial electronics and communications.[2]

In 1995, Denver opened its enormous new international airport, its cream-colored canvas peaks glinting in the sun. It was a big risk by taxpayers. But like New York state's gamble with the Erie Canal two centuries previously, it was meant to move the Rocky Mountain metropolis into the position of a central transportation hub for the nation.

What all these actions or events have in common is government, government, government. In this chapter, I seek to make clear the role of government in creating both the architecture of place, and the related architecture of economics or wealth. In this antigovernment country, virtually founded on hostility to the enterprise, we tend to obscure government's central role in creating the places where we live, the jobs we perform, and the money we spend. Government, whether it be a republic, monarchy, theocracy, or dictatorship, is more central to our lives than many of us acknowledge or understand.

From an urban planning perspective, it's important to understand the role of government so we can more easily grasp the levers of power when we desire to make real changes.

Americans tend to think of government as something outside themselves, a kind of regulatory body that interferes with the working of both an economy and the development of places. According to this view, the shapers of cities and the creators of wealth are the individual actors: the developer, the house builder, the company owner.

But government—that is, us—almost always lays down the concrete slab that economies and places are built upon. Government not only creates the laws, and operates the courts and the police, it then lays down the roads and builds the schools. In a modern economy, it then proceeds to set up a Federal Reserve System, a Securities and Exchange Commission, the International Monetary Fund, and other more elaborate financial infrastructure.

I sense that most people do not understand this, and the reason can be laid at the feet of an insidious idea called "the free market." We tend to think that places and economies just happen, built by the invisible hand of Adam Smith if by anyone. In our mind's eye, we tend to see supermarkets and subdivisions proliferating across the countryside, driven by consumer choice and the decisions of banks to finance them. We tend not to see the government's prior decision to build an Interstate through the area that made the whole thing possible.

The intersection of place and economics is often in transportation. The decision of what transportation system to build, something almost always done by government, tends to create both an economy for an area or metropolis, and a particular physical framework organized around that infrastructure. So when Denver builds a big airport, it also creates the loose physical structure of warehouses, offices, and shopping centers that proliferates around airports. When New York City built its subway system (which was nominally private but steered and aided by government), it also created the possibility of the dense networks of skyscrapers that would follow. The Interstate Highway System created both a new economics of transportation and a new lifestyle organized around suburban living.

GOVERNMENT MAKES PLACES

The relationship of government to cities is like that of a computer's operating system to its software. Government establishes the operating system by laying out a freeway, railroad, streetcar line, a subway, or a road system. Private developers establish the software: the shopping center, the factory, or the individual business or store. But like a virus that attacks an operating system, the conduct of private enterprise now threatens to undermine the operating system of government that supports it. The system could "crash."

In analyzing the structure of cities, it is easy to put the cart before the horse and start saying things like "cars cause sprawl." Actually they don't. Roads do. And roads are a public decision, not a private one.

Eric Monkkonen, in his book *America Becomes Urban*, says we should not fall into the fallacy of thinking that the form of cities and places is an unstoppable byproduct of innovations in technology. He uses the example of Los Angeles, which people say was shaped by the automobile. This, he says, is like saying "chunks of hot metal cause death by bleeding" instead of "thousands of Americans deliberately kill one another each year."[3]

With Los Angeles, Monkkonen says, it was the "political aggression" of the city that enabled it to extend streetcar lines, build roads, and take in new territory.

> The [technological] determinists forget that political action was
> the necessary prior step for technological change. The financial

success of the Red Cars depended on a monopoly franchise and intense land speculation by the railroad owners; the acquisition of rail access to a potential port was a conscious political and economic move by the city; the conversion of dirt tracks into modern city streets came as the result of political action. Of far greater historical and contemporary importance than the shaping power of transportation technology have been the enormous political, social, and economic efforts by governments—local, state, and federal—to promote them and make them functional. In fact, very little urban history has unfolded in the purely rational way that the technological determinist model implies.[4]

The spread of the automobile, which has seemed to happen in an inevitable way, was preceded at every step by political decisions, Monkkonen says. When automobiles were first invented, they were little more than interesting toys. It was not until local and state governments committed to paving the then generally unpaved roads that the automobile was able to spread from the hobbyist to the general public. And good roads, Monkkonen reminds us, "are purely political creations."[5]

GOVERNMENT MAKES MONEY

The relationship of government to the creation of wealth is the same as its role in creating places: It tends to play a far more fundamental role than usually thought. This comes not only through the creation of a legal framework for a market, but through direct investment in innovation.

Consider the computer chip and the Internet. They are the foundation of the United States' position as leader of the global economy, and in the creation of vast sums of private wealth, from Microsoft's to America Online's.

But the history of the computer industry is completely intertwined with the U.S. military and the waging of the Cold War. Most of the major advances in semiconductors were either performed directly by government or funded by it.[6] The Internet, of course, was a defense project initially, and only later spun off by the U.S. government as a private, nonprofit commercial venture.[7] Then there is the public's role in funding the schools and universities where smart guys like Steve Jobs or Bill Gates got their education. The immense sums of private wealth present at the end of this millennium were usually built on a foundation of government capital.

Government tends to be so crucial in the economy for the same reason it does in transportation: it is the only actor with the size and scope to make foundational changes. While the Wright brothers invented the airplane, it was the U.S. government that created a passenger airline industry in the early decades of this century through research, financial support, and organizational directives.[8]

Private businesses do not invest sufficiently in research and development because they cannot capture all the additional wealth generated from it, says economic journalist Robert Kuttner in *Everything for Sale: The Virtues and Limits of Markets.*[9] In addition, few have the resources or legal power to act in sufficient scope.

If you look at every important sector of the economy over the last century—cars, computers, airplanes, and even agriculture—government has been crucial in each.

In a proper relationship, government and private enterprise exist in a mutually beneficial circle. Government supplies the foundation for the creation of wealth, private enterprise creates the wealth and passes a portion back to government, which uses it to build additional infrastructure for the creation of more wealth.

When one travels to poorer countries, it is obvious that the public sector is impoverished. In Central America and the Caribbean, I saw "towns" and even "cities" that were more conceptual than factual. They lacked almost anything public establishing them as places. They had no squares, sidewalks, or formal layout. Third World cities often lack any of the infrastructure that here is often unconsciously assumed, like a municipal water supply and a comprehensive sewer system.

It is no accident that the richest states in this country, and the richest countries in the world, all have the biggest public sectors and the highest levels of taxation. Conventional libertarian analysis is wrong. New York state and Sweden have high levels of taxation not because they can afford to, but because these high levels of taxation actually create the wealth that in turn allows for this level of taxation. The rich public sector creates the rich private sector, which in turn allows for the generation of a richer public sector.

As Peter Schrag writes in *Paradise Lost*,[10] California's wealth is underpinned by the once incredibly rich system of public secondary schools and universities. Regular folk attended these schools, and then went on to win Nobel Prizes and create computer companies. This system of wealth creation is in danger now because Proposition 13, the antitax measure which passed in 1978 by referendum, along with other antitax measures, has hamstrung government's ability to generate the social, technological, and transportational infrastructure that allows for the creation of more wealth. It was a bit chilling to read that California, one of the richest states in the union, now ranks anywhere from thirty-sixth to forty-third in the nation in per-pupil educational spending, below Georgia and on par with South Carolina.[11]

THE POLITY, THE PUBLIC, AND PLACES

We would understand government's role in both places and economies if we understood better what government is.

Government, to put it unsentimentally, is "a system of authority," from which all other forms of authority, including ownership of property, derive.[12] In a democracy, that authority derives from the consent and will of the people. Managing this authority for the highest and best use is the central task of the people.

In this country, this understanding of political community has been replaced by rigid beliefs in the free market, without an understanding that the "free" market itself only exists through its creation and maintenance by a political state. The "free market" is a political act first. Politics comes before economics. By this, I mean the economic system we live under, in both the nation and the globe, rests on a foundation of political decisions that establish said system's existence and form. Politics determines economics.

The capitalist system is a political act that creates a publicly defined set of rules enforced by the "system of authority" of government. Markets can be said to exist without governments only if we define markets as blind desire. "Free" markets exist only as created and underpinned by government. The polity creates the system of laws and courts and police that lets the "free" enterprise system operate.

The equations of economists, even at their most convoluted, seldom have a line saying something like "Right here there is a 10 percent chance that forces from a rival company will break through the factory's defenses and shoot the CEO in the head." That would be an actual free market, which we can see in operation in the drug markets nationally and globally. The illegal-drug cartels act little differently than France, England, Spain, Portugal, and the Netherlands did in the sixteenth and seventeenth centuries, as they warred to control markets, robbed each other's ships, and fought to control supply lines.

The current global economy, so often held up as an example of the benefits of the free market, was not only created by technological advances like the computer or the telephone, but from the political arrangements that allowed their introduction and peaceful operation. It was politics that allowed for the laying of a transatlantic cable, and for the creation of a system of laws and courts that governs trade. Even mailing a letter to Europe relies on a slew of postal treaties worked out in the nineteenth century.

People may forget that we had a fully functioning global economy in the sixteenth century. England no longer seizes ships from France laden with goods from India because it and most countries have a series of political agreements that allow for "free" trade. These agreements not only prohibit the use of force, but they also provide a mechanism for adjudicating disagreements and for setting standards. The peaceful creation of wealth through a market economy is always based on the establishment of a prior political system. Peaceful global trade has emerged over the last two centuries because a system of political authority has emerged that creates the structure within which a global economy has to operate.

In effect, we have a world government. We can see it in action when the World Court at The Hague in Holland orders the United States to accept tuna caught in nets that harm porpoises, even though America's own laws prohibit its sale. Sorry, says the World Court, but the system of global trade you agreed to prohibits your discriminating against other countries' products on this basis. Pull at this thread and you find a vast structure, including things like the World Bank and the World Trade

Organization (WTO), the latter supervised by the World Court, which in turn reports to the United Nations. These institutions, though, should serve the interests of their polity and not just the short-term interests of individual businesses or even countries.

The gradual ability for governments to replace the rule of force with the rule of law changed the form of cities, as well as the form of trade. Monkkonen says that the emergence of the nation-state allowed new forms of cities and towns to develop. Before the viable nation-state, only settlements that could defend themselves were possible. This took the classic form of the city-state. When "the state and the city separated," it allowed more specialized forms of cities and towns to emerge, which in turn allowed a greater percentage of the population to urbanize.[13]

The classic model of a free market, where businesses operate unhindered by government interference, is comparable to a perfect vacuum created in the laboratory. I use this analogy, though, in a way contrary to the usage of many economists. With markets, it is government that restrains the "natural" forces of power and violence from rushing in and contaminating the perfect vacuum of the free market. Another analogy is that of a soccer game. Government not only referees the game, judging when players are offside and so forth, but also creates the field, its parameters, and how you play.

Government is often thought of as a parasite on free enterprise, or at least as dependent on it. But the reverse is more true. To paraphrase architect and organizational theorist Ted Goranson, behind Adam Smith's invisible hand is an invisible arm—government.[14] Again, this should be obvious, but I suspect it isn't. The standard mental model of capitalism is that this magic system of supply and demand operates by itself, without human aid or deliberate organization of any kind. These are basic tenets of Economics 101, handed down by the priests of the system, the economics professors.

If you want to look at how markets operate without government, just look at the buying and selling of crack cocaine, or of bootleg whiskey during Prohibition in the 1920s. Without government, the act of exchanging value becomes quickly mixed with the use of force to control a market or command a sale. Indeed, since government itself is a system of authority, a system of regulated force, it can be said that in its absence, another "government" quickly emerges that establishes through force a system of rules and regulations by which trade can occur. The Mafia can be compared to a private government that is competing with the established government's authorized monopoly on the use of force and subsequent ability to establish rules and structures.

Russia and some of the newly emerging capitalist countries are having problems establishing a functioning capitalist system because they don't have *enough* government, not the converse. Capitalism only operates where there is the rule of law, including a court system to keep a record of contracts and enforce them. It operates even better if government creates a transportation system, a clean water supply, and other basic public goods. The limited liability corporation is a foundation of modern capitalism that is completely a political creation.

"All liberal rights presuppose or imply the dependency of the individual on the collectivity and on the principal instrument of the collectivity, that is, on the coercive-extractive state. This is a truism and a banality," but one that has been forgotten in the modern era, says Stephen Holmes, writing in *The American Prospect* in an article titled "What Russia Teaches Us: How Weak States Threaten Freedom."[15]

As Holmes writes, it is ironic that in this era of calls for lower taxes what Russia suffers from is the absence of sufficient taxation. Total tax revenues in Russia are at about 10 percent of the economy, which is insufficient to create a public sector to establish the rule of law and a healthy infrastructure.[16]

Part of our misconception of government is due to our emphasis on the Bill of Rights, which, as Holmes writes, is really a spelling out of a set of "negative liberties."[17] They focus on being free from government. But essential liberties also come from government's presence. What makes democracy so revolutionary is that it established the concept of being free to participate *in* government, that this system of authority, which is what government is, could be controlled by the people, the polity, the public.

The failure to recognize that a market economy is a political choice and creation first and foremost leads to a belief that an economy operates by itself. The "laws" of supply and demand magically lift all boats to their highest and best use, without the aid of human intervention, goes the standard fairy tale. Part of this confused belief system comes from economics being classified as a science, and the conviction that, because equations and numbers are used, it can be compared to physics or chemistry. But humans are different than falling apples or sodium combining with chloride. They are their own actors, and can combine and perform in a variety of ways, many of which no one can guess.

Lewis Mumford posits that with the industrial revolution, nations adopted a new religious belief in classical economics to replace the belief that an all-seeing, all-knowing father God had laid out an orderly and just path for the world.

"The most fundamental of these postulates was a notion that the utilitarians had taken over, in apparent innocence, from the theologians: the belief that a divine providence ruled over economic activity and ensured, so long as man did not presumptuously interfere, the maximum public good through the dispersed and unregulated efforts of every private, self-seeking individual. The non-theological name for this pre-ordained harmony was laissez-faire."[18]

The idea of Adam Smith's invisible hand shaping prices and production for the common good is a marvelous model that is true in some situations. The problem is, most students of economics accept it as being solid as an axe. They then proceed to pick it up and wield it indiscriminately. But the market only operates efficiently and for the benefit of everyone when the products of a market can be converted into something that can be bought and sold for money. Saving a historic building, for example, might greatly enhance the wealth and overall appeal of a town, not to mention the daily lives of its citizens. But it is very difficult to "marketize" the view of a church by charging people for the privilege of walking by it.

Not only do markets not always maximize public or individual good, they actually often degrade it through the same mechanisms meant to produce value.

There are many, many situations where people, all pursuing their maximum self-interest, make things worse for everyone, themselves included. Our treatment of the environment is the most obvious example, and the one most likely to topple the laissez-faire theology. It is simply too apparent that, left to themselves, people and companies will pollute the air, water, and land to the detriment of all without some larger system of legal control. Traffic is another. Everyone trying to get to work quickly and easily by car creates a traffic jam where no one gets to work quickly. Yet another example is the widespread distribution of guns. Individual actors, trying to maximize their personal safety, increase their physical danger, because a more dangerous world is created by the sum total of the actions of everyone arming themselves.

What's troubling is how a proper understanding of the role of government in our lives is being undermined by a steady barrage of libertarian and antigovernment rhetoric. This language obscures the real relationship people have with government. It's like criticizing the boat that keeps you afloat.

The version of the Republican Party dominant at the end of the twentieth century has been tremendously destructive in this, and should be rightly held responsible for the misconceptions many Americans hold. Republican leaders like Senator Trent Lott of Mississippi frequently wield the motto that "You know how to spend your money better than the government." According to this analysis, government is akin to a thief, robbing taxpayers of their hard-earned pay. If government should exist at all, then, goes this line of thought, it is at best a necessary evil, best kept small and minimal.

This theory obscures the fact that government creates the wealth the people hold in their hands and are now reluctant to give up. A dollar bill is signed by the Secretary of the Treasury for a reason. Money is a communication device produced by a political agreement, both literally and in a wider sense. Not only does government print the money, but it also creates the conditions under which money can be "made." It also creates the infrastructure of wealth creation, like public education and transportation systems.

America's tortured, confused relationship to government can be seen in our tortured, chaotic, and confused transportation systems. Whether it's trains, planes, or automobiles, the confusion between public and private has produced the worst of both worlds. Government puts too much money into highways and then prices the use of them too low, and so they are massively congested. Government shortchanges passenger train travel, leaving citizens with a skeletal, impoverished system. Government has ceded control of the skies to commercial airline companies, even though these for-profit companies depend on a public system of airports and air traffic controllers. This has left air passengers often running a gauntlet of high ticket prices and lousy, take-it-or-leave-it service. In general, we are a rich country with a surprisingly impoverished and incoherent transportation system.

Much of this would change if we recognized government's central role in the architecture of our lives. Once this is accepted, arguments about the size of government become less ideological ones and more practical ones. Whether government or private enterprise performs a task becomes a question of efficiency. It is often beneficial to limit the scope and role of government, but this does not change government's essential relationship to our lives.

NEW YORK CITY: WRITING THE BONES

In 1811, a state commission released its street plan for the city of New York. Meant to insure orderly growth, the commission's plan showed a system of vertical avenues and horizontal streets that stretched from the lower part of the island to 155th Street in upper Manhattan. Although a large chunk between 59th and 110th Streets would later be carved out for Central Park in the 1850s, the plan defined the shape of New York's development for the next century.

For its first two centuries, New York City's development was somewhat haphazard, as the island changed nationalities from Dutch to British to American. But as the nineteenth century began, the city and state, now part of a new country, worked to create a plan that would allow for the more orderly development of business.

The straightforward grid the commission produced, much commented on and much criticized among devotees of city design for its lack of radial and axial histrionics, determined the shape of our premier city, with its long avenues and shorter cross-streets. This action was a historic, but not a particularly unusual, one. These bureaucrats in New York were not on par with Haussmann in Paris, L'Enfant in Washington, or Cerdà i Sunyer in Barcelona. No, they were simply bureaucrats and businessmen, designing a simple plan to ensure the orderly pattern of growth for the next century.

Which it did. But it was a slow process. As late as 1900, Manhattan above Ninetieth Street was still farmland and scattered villages. When Andrew Carnegie built his mansion at Fifth Avenue and East Ninety-first Street in 1901 in the Upper East Side, "it was the good country air" that lured him to the hinterlands of Manhattan.[19] Lewis Mumford, who was born in 1895 in the West Side of Manhattan, remembered market gardens still operating in his boyhood.

This history is a particularly vivid example of government's role in the building of places. Government determines the shape and form of our cities by laying out the principal means of transportation. That's as true now as it was in 1800. But government's role in this has become more covert, and the form of our cities has suffered as a result. The history of New York illustrates how direct the role of government can be, and contrasts sharply with the typical role of government today.

In the creation of places, government is involved at both a macro and a micro level. At the macro level are things like the Interstate Highway Act or the Denver airport, and on this level, government's role is just as obvious as it was two centuries ago. Government uses its greater financial and authoritarian powers to create the central architecture of transportation. From canals to railroads to roads to airports, the basic transportation that does the heavy lifting in an economy of exporting goods and services tends to be laid out and funded by government.

But government's role on a micro level, which is the laying out of streets, is more indirect now. Gated communities have streets that are completely private, while even public streets are often laid out by a developer and then turned over to a municipality.

The history of New York's street system illustrates how the role of government has changed. Can you imagine a state or a City Hall today, anywhere in this country, doing something as far-reaching as laying out the streets a city might need a century in advance? The design of our cities is one of the few areas where government is clearly less powerful, and less intrusive, than it was a hundred years ago. Imagine sprawling suburban wastelands like Dade County, Florida, or Houston, if government had actually laid out a street pattern early on, before development occurred. These places would still be suburban, but they would be suburban more coherently. They would have perhaps had a coherent system of Interstate-style roads mixed with broader suburban boulevards, and then down to neighborhood streets, all of which connected to each other in a coherent form.

The lack of design and structure in suburban places like Houston or Virginia Beach is so subversive because it is still government that has determined their form, even if less publicly. Government builds and maintains the Interstate-style roads that created the potential for vast suburbanizing; government took the country roads and swelled them into broad boulevards; government organizes suburban infrastructure through devices like curb cuts, which determine traffic flow, property values, and use. Government maintains a coherent system of storm drainage that allows a property owner to not be underwater on the odd weekend of heavy rain and tides.

Spiro Kostof observes in his masterful book *The City Shaped* that some American cities, like Atlanta, grew up simply around the sum of decisions by independent developers, resulting in "an uncoordinated patchwork of grids."[20] But it's also true that such cities are the worst cities. Atlanta's urban history relates directly to its nature today as a fragmented, sprawling suburb that provides little sense of identity or place to its region. Cities, as Kostof hammers home, are always designed by someone, be it the private developer or Baron Haussmann. The "organic" city does not exist. The best cities in this country were always laid out with some forethought by government or someone acting in its behalf. Savannah had its Oglethorpe, Philadelphia its William Penn, Detroit its Augustus Woodward, and Washington its L'Enfant. Annapolis, Maryland, with its Beaux-Arts-style plazas and radial avenues, was laid out by Francis Nicholson.

Among the central failings of the design philosophy of New Urbanism is its insistence on putting the developer in the driver's seat in shaping places, even as the philosophy puts forth more and more talk about the public and public space. As Daniel Burnham told the city of San Francisco in 1905, "A city plan must ever deal mainly with the direction and width of its streets."[21] It shows how far we've come in the evolution, or devolution, of cities that this comment seems thoroughly foreign to the modern battles over zoning and gas-station placement. If Andres Duany or Elizabeth Plater-Zyberk want to design towns, then they should be working for the planning department of some state or county. Their often elegant streets and squares should be drawn on public documents, which should match the transportation system government is designing.

The system of zoning and land-use laws that consumes so much time and newsprint in most cities can almost be seen as an elaborate ruse to hide the real decisions being made by state departments of transportation. Frank Popper, quoted by J. Barry Cullingsworth in his book *The Political Culture of Planning*, put it rather well:

> It would help if planners grasped the real nature of the American federalist system of land use controls. It is so loose, so deliberately disjoined and open ended, that it is barely a system in the sense that European elite civil service bureaucracies understand the term. The right to make particular regulatory decisions shifts unpredictably over time from one level of government to another. No principle of administrative rationality, constitutional entitlement, economic efficiency, or even ideological predisposition truly determines the governmental locus of decisions. It is more often a matter of the inevitably uncertain catch-as-catch-can pluralism of democratic power politics.[22]

An essential challenge for building more effective cities is to get government back to the job of consciously designing them. If we look at Europe, we find government more directly and honestly controls the shape and nature of development. The countries there are still experiencing urban decay, suburban sprawl, a withering of traditional agriculture, and a fragmentation of the city form.[23] But they do a better job restraining these forces because they acknowledge that government is and should be in the driver's seat. The countries, though, vary tremendously in the mechanisms by which they control growth. Each has a separate mechanism that has grown up within its own tradition of law and property rights.[24]

The Netherlands is the country that has perhaps most precisely, and successfully, shaped growth. It accomplishes this by buying most land before it is developed. Amsterdam, when it is ready to grow, buys land and then directs development itself. The former landowner, usually a farmer, is paid the fair market value of the land plus its expected income for the next ten years.[25] So vigorously does the state control growth that land on the edge of town does not rise in price in anticipation of development. Because no growth can occur before the state wills it, the land stays at the price of other agricultural land farther out. This is not the case in Spain and Germany, where open land near a city can go for as much as forty times what land farther out costs. Nor is it the case, needless to say, in the United States.[26]

THE WRONG WAY

The wrong way to use government, or rather not to use it, can be seen in most planned communities, from the latest New Urban ones like Kentlands and Celebration, to older ones like Columbia, Maryland, and Irvine, California. In these places, private business interests have wrested the powers of government away from the public and public officials. The results are incoherent places that hide their disorder under a veneer of privatized central planning.

The impracticality of allowing a private developer to lay out a city can be seen by looking at an aerial photograph of Columbia, Maryland, the planned community outside Baltimore, with the "city" highlighted in red. Columbia was one of the biggest of the "New Towns" set up in the 1960s. The New Town theory, derived from the Garden City movement and a predecessor of New Urbanism, was to set up new cities in the countryside that would operate as perfect self-sufficient universes. Their design would marry town and country. In Europe, these new towns were set up by government. In the States, private developers, assisted by their handmaidens in governments, did the job.

Columbia was a project of James Rouse, one of the fathers of American-style urbanism and suburbanism. He made himself very rich with some of the first suburban shopping malls, then the planned community of Columbia, then festival marketplaces like Faneuil Hall in Boston and Baltimore's Inner Harbor. Rouse died in 1997, but his company, the Rouse Company, continues to this day. The company is now backing a 22,000-acre planned community in Las Vegas. Rouse is routinely cast as a savior of cities and a father figure of American urbanism. His actual track record is far more mixed. Much of what he did—his new town of Columbia and his suburban shopping malls—undermined the health of cities. His inner-city festival marketplaces were successful only in the larger cities like Boston, Baltimore, and New York. The projects usually failed in midsized cities. They were also destructive because they advanced McDonald's-like solutions to urban decay.

But his Columbia is a fascinating place to examine. In most ways, it has developed according to the plan drawn up thirty years ago, which is an incredible achievement given the vagaries of the real-estate market. The original plan called for ten separate villages with a "downtown"—an enclosed shopping mall—in the center. All of this has occurred. The tenth village is now under construction. The "city" is reaching its buildout of about 100,000 residents.

The city is utterly suburban in its style. This is ironic, because Rouse hated the suburbs. Columbia, he said, was very different from formless suburban sprawl because it was planned. It is now seen as the epitome of suburbanism, because it offers the suburban values of privacy and union with nature. When you drive through Columbia, you can almost believe you are driving through an uninhabited country. The roads wind around, trees, shrubbery, and berms on each side, concealing the houses and businesses. It can also be a difficult place to be low on gas, as even residents sometimes have difficulty finding the stations concealed with a Victorian sense of propriety.

The development has had its problems in recent years. Crime and decay have come to some villages. The village centers—small strip shopping centers—have struggled financially. In part, this is because they are threatened by new big box stores out on the main highway, ironically built by the Rouse Company itself. But to a large degree, Columbia works as advertised. It's fascinating to compare with other New Urban creations, for Columbia actually does a better job of being a relatively self-contained city for its residents, even though they do not live behind the fig leaf of Georgetown-style row houses.

But back to that aerial photograph. What you see is that Columbia, the master-planned community where everything is planned, down to the height of the shrubbery and the color of the house paint, lacks any coherent form. When James Rouse went out and surreptitiously bought up 14,000 acres in between Washington and Baltimore, he was limited by whether private landowners would sell to him. Many did not. So Columbia's ten villages are spread out over a patchwork quilt of territory. Large chunks of land that are physically in the middle of Columbia are not part of the city at all and, in fact, are governed under a different set of laws because they were not part of the New Town zoning passed by Howard County.

If a city was to be built in between Washington and Baltimore, a government should have done it. It could have laid out a street system with a clear design that did not have to avoid the noncooperative property owner. This did not even have to happen through eminent domain or vast expenditures of the public treasury. Howard County or the state could have laid out a street system on paper that simply dictated that, when development occurred, it should happen in this fashion.

Regardless of the merits of New Urbanism and the older New Town theories, their essential problem was and is attempting to have private developers do what should only be done by government. Private developers do not have the political authority to effectively shape places, because they cannot, yet, condemn land. Speaking on a broader level, they also, unlike government, cannot be content with generating "positive externalities," but must try to capture their created wealth through profits. Which doesn't work very well.

The dishonesty of Columbia is that you find government structures, financing, and institutions lurking behind the facade of privatism.

Who created Columbia? The standard answer is Rouse, who gathered the millions in capital through Connecticut Life Insurance and his own deep pockets. He bought the land and assembled the city's team of designers. But another answer, just as real, is the government of Howard County, which, in 1965, passed a package called New Town zoning that created the underlying system of laws that governs the use of the land. The county passed over nominal control of the land to a private company, only stating that the development follow a model and loose plan submitted by Rouse. This act was dishonest because, although a private company was running Columbia, it was the public entity of Howard County that was legally responsible for its fate.

Who created Columbia? An even more fundamental answer is the state and federal transportation departments. They built I-95, which courses between Baltimore and Washington. Columbia lies just a mile or so off it, and depends on it for its existence. Columbia, still a bedroom community economically, is possible only because the Interstate allows its residents and business owners to quickly reach the centers of Baltimore and Washington. New forms of transportation create new forms of cities. The postwar Interstate, which was a new form of transportation, created Columbia. The Interstate, of course, was laid out and paid for by the federal and state governments. Columbia is an example of private enterprise living off the "positive externalities" created by government. Compare Columbia to the nearby "New Town" of Reston, which lies in Virginia, also near I-95. Robert Simon, Reston's founder, lost control of his creation because he did not ensure that his community had a freeway exit ramp nearby before beginning his project.

Just as the physical structure of Columbia masks its dependence on government, so does its internal organization. Columbia is "governed"—a misnomer here—through a system of covenants and restrictions that rest in the property deeds. These create the intricate set of regulations governing life there. It is these, for example, that prohibit a householder from painting his or her wall pink, or placing a birdbath in the front yard, or putting up anything other than the prescribed type of basketball goal. These instruments also create the homeowners association, which enforces their rules, giving it the legal power to do so above and beyond what a conventional government can do.

WHO PAYS THE BILLS?

In discussing how cities are created, no concept is more confusing and destructive than that of "subsidies." So thoroughly has the notion of the free market invaded our conception of life that we apply it to places where it doesn't belong. It comes up most often in discussions of railroads or mass transit, with their detractors stating that they should not be built or maintained because they will need to be, or are, "subsidized."

In reality, government subsidizes all the basic infrastructure of a city, be it the suburban or urban model. No one asks whether a sidewalk, which is a mode of transportation as much as a subway, is paying its way. Nor does anyone ask for toll gates on every city street to stop their subsidization. It is a rare highway that has a toll. In general, roads are built from revenue from the gas tax, which is not the same as a user fee, and through general tax revenues of cities and states. Then there's the cost of paying for police and ambulance service. Maintenance means everything from fixing potholes to plowing the snow off. Roads do not pay for themselves, nor should they. The direct cost of roads is tremendous, even without getting into what economists call negative externalities like pollution and traffic deaths.

A better way to think about things is that highways, train lines, sidewalks, and bike paths are a service, or an investment, around which the rest of society and an economy constructs itself. They resemble that other basic of a healthy community which we massively subsidize: education. Government plays a key role in transportation because it is the only entity capable of building a transportation "system." As one transportation engineer remarked to me, "Transportation is a system. You can't have a little bit of transportation." One cannot have a half-mile of a bus route, and then a half-mile of rail, and then a half-mile of Interstate. Transportation is not the accumulation of individual decisions in a marketplace.

Trains and subways and buses are easy targets for budget cutters because their funding mechanisms and internal dynamics appear to offer the opportunity for an in/out, cost-benefit analysis. A train line takes in so much through the fare box. Does that match or exceed the operating cost plus a share of the capital cost?

No similar questions are asked of highways and cars because their funding is so diverse and fragmented, much like the cities they create. Figuring out how much highways or cars cost would mean calculating the cost of building the highways, the cost of maintaining them, the cost of supplying the police to patrol them, just for a start. Then we move into "negative externalities," like pollution from tailpipe emissions and the cost of disposing of rusted metal and dirty oil. This calculation is difficult because a lot of different sectors pay the car's way. A state government might pay to build a city road, but a city government might pay to maintain it out of its general fund, and then to police it. But the cost of police will come out of the police department budget, not public works. In addition, unlike a lightly used train line, a lightly used highway is not seen as something to be shut down because it doesn't pay its own way.

The Surface Transportation Policy Project, a transportation re-form group in Washington, estimated that federal, state, and local governments spent $70 billion on building and maintaining roads in 1989. Of that, only 40 percent came from gas taxes or user fees like tolls. The rest of the money came from sales and property taxes and other forms of direct taxation. The authors of the Project's study broke expenditures down as $33 billion on road construction, $20 billion on maintenance, $6.4 billion on police and safety services, $5.4 billion on administration, and $6.3 billion on interest and debt retirement.[27]

Highway lovers compare a gas tax to a user fee. But the gas tax is not a user fee because it is neither voluntary nor related to a specific road or destination. The Interstate near my home gets money from the gas tax I pay whether I use the road or not. One cannot choose to pay it or not pay it depending on where one goes. This is very different from boarding a bus or subway, where one calculates whether the $1.50 fare is worth it to get the ten blocks or ten miles one is traveling.

It is almost impossible to make any transportation system "pay for itself." The owner has to set the rents so high that usage inevitably declines, establishing a vicious circle of higher prices and fewer customers. In the summer of 1997, the government of Mexico took control of more than a thousand miles of highways that private companies had built at a cost of $7.7 billion.[28] The government assumed the debt. The private companies could not meet their expenses. People will not use highways when they have to pay the full cost. The same rule holds for mass transit. Which is why both are public, not private, goods, and should be.

There is a strong argument that people shouldn't have to pay anything to ride a subway or a trolley as a direct fare. After all, you are not charged every time you swing out onto a highway. Your taxes pay to build and maintain roads. In the same way, taxes are used to build and maintain subway lines. People know instinctively that it doesn't make sense to charge admission to every street and highway. In the same way, it doesn't make sense to charge to use buses or subways. As economists say, the optimal efficiency of a public facility is usually not delivered if a fee is charged, because it reduces the numbers of users. Probably some fare should be set to discourage frivolous use of a public asset, but it should not be much.

THE DARK SIDE OF GOVERNMENT

My preaching about the centrality of government in our lives does not blind me to its inefficiencies or its capacity for harm in the urban arena. I am thinking principally of the horrors of urban renewal and the devastation wrought by freeways carved through the middle of neighborhoods. I need only to say the words "Robert Moses" (name of the longtime New York park commissioner) to conjure up the terror of a heavy state hand.[29] But this underlines the fact that governments are the essential builders of cities and places. The question is whether their role should be covert, or more open and direct.

Cities seem to work best when government sets the form of places, but does not try to fill that form. Like dictating that a poem be a sonnet but not actually writing it. Government determines form by laying out streets and other means of transportation, be it superhighways or rail lines. Once that is done, it can dictate the height and massing of buildings, setback requirements, and other such rules. In suburbia, this would include things like curb cuts and parking requirements. After that, however, government could let go and let private developers fill in the spaces.

I favor eliminating design review boards and other aesthetic arbiters. These boards tend to be composed of nit-picking control freaks who get their kicks by nibbling to death everyone from the guy putting on an addition to his house, to the office developer trying to use a different-color brick. Such boards homogenize cities and render them bland. They usually have no say over or conception of the larger questions that actually determine the shape of our cities. Better that government dictate the form through setback rules, height limits, and other regulations, but then let the developer determine the style and exact shape.

I am not arguing so much for greater state power as recognition of the power it already has. The rights of individuals should be respected, although there should be greater recognition of where these "rights" come from. Often, when a government takes away property value it is only taking something that it gave in the first place through building a road or extending some other type of infrastructure.

It's interesting to ask whether some method of growth control could be found that is uniquely American; something that harnesses the individual appetite, rather than using centralized planning. Could the equivalent of a voucher system be found for city design? Something that, through rules, would direct growth in ways that make sense? I have difficulty imagining such a system. Still, it is an idea.

Contemplating the relationship between private and public, I am struck by the dance of power, the continual changes of partners and who has the lead. Whether it be the construction of cities, or the production of films, for example, the path of power is not predictable or logical. Who could have predicted, for example, that a park commissioner like Robert Moses would manage to swing the entire region of New York around him, transforming its built environment. Who could have predicted that in Hollywood for a time, Michael Ovitz would make the humble agent—not the producer, not the director, not the actor— the person who decided what movies would be made and by and with whom. In the computer world, it was never imagined that the lowly operating system would be more important than the box within which it was housed. It's who can manage to be the axis around which the world turns.

A Portland light-rail car at rush hour. Notice the low numbers of African Americans. Photo by Alex Marshall.

CHAPTER 7

PORTLAND

AND OREGON

Taming the Forces That Create

the Modern Metropolitan Area

STARTING IN GRADE SCHOOL nowadays, kids have drilled into their heads that nature is a system, an ecosystem, where pushing on one end pushes out on another. The toxins that get dumped in the stream affect the bay downstream. Too many deer mean they will eat too many of the plants that hold the topsoil together. Air pollution can kill the plants that feed the deer. The marshes strain the pollution from the water that drains from the fields. And so on.

A similar propaganda campaign should be begun on behalf of cities. Its message that they, too, are ecosystems. The true city today is the metropolitan area. And like the ecosystem in nature, it has only a limited supply of inputs and outputs, and manipulating one manipulates the others. Its inputs are jobs and people. Its outputs are houses, shopping, and places. These resources are finite and can only be "spent" once. A metropolitan area has a limited market for housing, which is generated by its economic development. If the capital resulting from development is spent in the suburbs, it's not available for the inner city.

A metropolitan area has a limited capital for shopping, which is again generated by its supply of jobs and dollars. If spent in the suburbs, it is less available for the inner city.

The metropolis of Portland, and the state of Oregon with it, are two places, among very few, where people have started to grapple with the actual forces that create the places where they live. They are starting to understand this ecosystem, make choices, and live with the results.

They have done this by recognizing the big three: government, transportation, and economics. Through their state and local governments, they began twenty-five years ago expressly deciding where growth occurs. Also through government, they began more consciously laying out transportation systems in line with where and how people would live. Finally, they have recognized that economic development means more new residents, and they have tried to decide consciously where to put them.

The policies are conceptually simple. A growth boundary to push growth inward. Stop building freeways (and even tear some down), and spend money on mass transit. The results? Portland is arguably the only midsized city in the country that still has major department stores and dozens of healthy streets downtown. It does not depend on a few force-fed city projects to "create" a downtown. The countryside is a concise pattern of towns and country because of the growth control laws. Thanks to the changing pattern of development and the investment in mass transit, you can live in Portland without a car, or with only one car, as a household, instead of two. This again is unheard of in a midsized city.

The city and state aren't perfect. But it's not about perfection. It's about making choices, and living with the consequences. That's called civic maturity. What we are starting to see in Portland is a city that recognizes you can have easy suburban growth with big homes on large lots, or a coherent city with a vital mass transit system, but not both. What we see is a region grappling honestly with the choices that actually face a metropolitan area today.

THREE FACES OF PORTLAND

Here's a glimpse of three people who are living differently because of the choices Portland and Oregon have made in the last generation.

Elizabeth is a middle-aged woman sitting in a plastic seat in a crowded light rail car at rush hour, heading home from her downtown job. Surrounded by standing commuters, she looks down at her book until I start talking to her.

Light rail, she said, has changed her life. When she first started using it regularly, she says, "I hated it." But she had no choice, she said. Parking was simply too expensive.

"I didn't want to ride it at all," she said. "I didn't like being so close to other people. I wasn't used to that. But now I really like it. One interesting thing is that it's turned me into a reader. I didn't used to read at all, but now I read about twenty books a month. I've become so accustomed to using the MAX [the acronym for the light rail system here], that now I forget I have a car. My boss recently asked me to bring something downtown, and I told him I couldn't, forgetting that I had a car. I've become a total MAX person."

Because Portland and Oregon have invested in trains instead of freeways, because they have a growth boundary, this woman reads more books. As anyone who has used mass transit regularly knows, the time spent on a bus or subway or trolley does open up a window of opportunity to use your time differently.

Because of Portland and Oregon's policies, this woman also has a different conception of people. She now is comfortable being in groups of people she doesn't know. As we talk, the train is standing room only. Around her are workmen, kids, women in elegant dresses, and children with schoolbooks. But she is at ease.

Here are two more people.

Sally is a teenager who works at a fruit stand in Beaverton, on the edge of the Portland metropolitan area. The fruit stand carries thirty or forty different varieties of Northwest apples. They sit in bins that surround the small stand. The apples have weird shapes and names like Priscilla Orange Beauty.

Sally is nineteen and aggressively normal. She likes clothes and shopping. Her eyes glaze over when I ask her about light rail lines and growth boundaries. She appears to be a representative sample of a standard American teenager. But she goes downtown four or five times a week, she says, even though she lives on the fringes of the metro area. She drives, and pays the hefty parking fees. It's the only place to go if you want to really shop and watch the people, she says.

In nineteen out of twenty other cities, a young woman like this—

probably unsophisticated, not an artist or an intellectual—wouldn't go near downtown. She would occupy her days at the nearby mall. Downtown, and the sense of connection with some older city, would be a distant, fading concept. Because she goes downtown she is likely to have a more sophisticated view of the world than if she had just gone to the local mall.

Michael Easley is a rancher I encountered eating in the food court of the Clackamas Town Center Mall, another suburban area on the other side of the city from Beaverton. Easley is different from most ranchers in several obvious respects. He takes a bus downtown regularly. He takes a bus when he goes to the airport. He likes having mass transit, he says.

But what makes Easley worth singling out is that Easley is a cattle farmer, with land on the edge of the growth boundary, and he's working for the boundary to be held. He and his father like raising cattle, he says, and they like the protection the growth boundary gives from building interests. In another city, Easley would be campaigning for a rezoning so he could sell his land out. But in Oregon, so entrenched has become the direction of growth and development that a rancher feels comfortable working to continue his livelihood, rather than to keep his options open to change it.

"No, I don't want to sell," he said when I asked him about this. "That kind of defeats the purpose, doesn't it. . . . I like it, the urban growth boundary. [In this country in general,] we're ripping up a lot more farmland that could be used to produce food."

I could keep going. I could also find people who have lost out because of Portland's direction. Someone who might have liked to build a house in the countryside, but couldn't. The point is that people are living differently in Portland because of the policies they have chosen. Actual shaping of cities requires making choices. More of this, less of that. Some people lose, some people win.

THE CENTER HOLDS: PEOPLE ARE THE PROOF

We can get a sense of Portland's uniqueness by looking at its population figures. Virtually alone among center cities of all sizes, it has managed to slightly increase its population over the last two decades, avoiding the moderate to massive population losses that have afflicted other cities.

In 1980, Portland had 368,000 people, virtually identical to its population in 1950, and a slight decline from its population in 1970. By 1997, it topped a half million people at 508,000.[1] This is part of a metropolitan area of 1.5 million. Most of this population increase was due to annexation, but about a fifth of it was not. The city has managed to grow despite a decrease in the size of families and despite economic downturns in the 1980s.[2]

It's no coincidence that the population increase began after the introduction of the growth boundary in the late 1970s and the start of more investment in mass transit. It's also no coincidence that this is when the downtown and older center-city neighborhoods began their rapid rise in health and vitality.

New York City's population hit its peak in 1950, and was lucky to stabilize not too far below that today, at 7.4 million. Like Portland, New York has grown since 1980, although it is still below its 1950 size of 7.9 million. This compares with cities like St. Louis, with a population of 856,000 in 1950 and 368,000 in 1994.[3] Virtually every established city has lost substantial population in the last half-century, if you rule out population increases that include expanding the political boundaries. Portland's almost singular trajectory can be seen by comparing it to Norfolk. In 1970, these two port cities were close in size, with Norfolk having a population of 308,000 and Portland 380,000. By 1998, Norfolk had dropped to 230,000, while Portland had swelled to more than 508,000. After subtracting for annexation, Portland had still managed to grow by more than 20,000 people. Meanwhile, the overall metropolitan areas of both cities remained about the same size over this time period, with each growing to about 1.5 million. But in the Portland region, some of the population growth had gone to the inner city.

CIRCLES WITHIN CIRCLES:
UNDERSTANDING THE METROPOLITAN AREA

The Portland metropolitan area, and, like it, most metropolitan areas around the country, can be understood best as a series of circles, each affecting the performance and dynamic of the whole. Understanding how these circles interact helps us understand how the metropolitan area functions.

At the center of the bull's-eye is Portland's downtown, an extraordinarily vital urban grid of about 150 square blocks. Low-rise nineteenth-century buildings on short blocks compose the city's character. It's a downtown finely marbled with everything from small nondescript stores to big department stores. It is the only midsized city in the country where the downtown still functions in this way, as the center of the metropolitan area in retail, business, politics, and culture.

The second ring of the circles is the older neighborhoods and urban districts that surround downtown. They are urban in that they have grid streets, and their own shopping streets rather than strip shopping centers or malls. While many metropolitan areas have maybe one or at most two funky urban neighborhoods, Portland has at least a half dozen, with more emerging all the time. There are Northwest Twenty-third Avenue, Hawthorne, Pearl, Belmont, Northeast Alberta Street, and the emerging Martin Luther King Boulevard district.

The third ring is the outer suburbs of Happy Valley, Beaverton, Gresham, Hillsboro, and others. These are the suburbs with the typical pattern of highways, malls, office parks, and the like. But they are held in check by the UGB, the urban growth boundary that surrounds the entire metro area. It limits their outward growth, forcing them to turn inward and pushing them to work with Portland.

The fourth ring is the area outside the first three circles: the countryside of fields, forests, and small towns that surrounds the metropolitan area. Although outside the first three circles and the metropolitan area, it is as much a part of their dynamic as downtown.

Each of these circles within circles reveals something about the nature of Portland and why it works, and how the contemporary metropolis functions. The true city today is the metropolitan area, and that is the level where effective city design must start. Actually, as we shall see, effective city design must start outside the metropolitan area. We'll look at each of these circles, and how it operates and interacts with the others.

THE FOURTH CIRCLE: FIELDS AND FORESTS AS PART OF THE CITY

Let's take a drive out of Portland, past the suburbs and the highways and the new homes, out past the growth boundary. You'll find your journey a pleasant one. You'll drive over rolling hills of farms and forests, until

A vineyard as seen through the windows of a tasting room of a small winery outside Portland. Viticulture has flourished in the protected farmland the Oregon growth controls have created. Photo by Alex Marshall.

you come to small towns, sitting compactly in the countryside. These small towns, like Yamhill, Dundee, or Forest Grove, will be surrounded by new development that hugs the existing town. You will not be greeted by the usual display of scattered subdivisions, Pizza Huts, and strip centers that now rings most smaller towns in the country. Because of this, the downtowns of these smaller towns are more viable and alive than most.

This landscape is as much a part of Portland, and its success, as its bustling downtown. Because these small towns are limited in their outward growth, there is no way they can pluck the growth off the metro Portland area, by standing just outside of it and feeding off of it, like parasites. A newcomer to Portland cannot buy a house outside a small town in a new development within easy driving distance of Portland, a development that would doubtless be followed by other developments until a sea of sprawl was built up.

This landscape shows that growth can no longer be controlled by a city itself, or even a metropolitan area. It must be done by an entity larger than the city or metro area itself, likely the state. A metropolitan area cannot effectively limit its own growth, because there is no way to get outside of itself. It's a Zen thing. A tongue cannot taste itself; a metro area cannot limit itself. Wherever it draws a growth boundary, a developer can always go just on the other side and build houses that siphon off the growth pressure. Only a state can limit this kind of parasitic development.

Legally, it makes growth control both more difficult and more simple. If effective growth control must usually come from a state level, then activists have the sometimes more difficult, but conceptually easier, task of persuading the state to manage growth. It's ironic that states have generally shown little interest in urban management. It's ironic because legally, states have the rights and powers to do so, if they choose. Legally, towns and cities are creatures of our states. They have their existence only by authority of the state constitution, which usually grants the legislators the right to pass charters which delegate some of the powers of the state to a municipality. Theoretically, the state could revoke these charters and control the actions of cities directly, from school boards to cops.

In Europe, the more controlled nature of growth is due in part to the more clearly subordinate status of cities. Their growth is controlled and ordered by a larger entity, usually the nation-state itself. It seems odd that the states in the United States do not exercise powers that are available to them.

It's important to realize that the forces that shaped Portland and Oregon were both progressive and reactionary in nature. That is, policy makers did not set out to create great urban places, although some were interested in that. They set out to stop certain things. Mostly, they set out to stop the hills, farms, and forests they love from being turned into shopping malls and freeways.

That, to me, is the ultimate irony of Portland and Oregon. We urbanists from all over the country turn to the area to see how we, too, can fashion great urban places. But those places are largely an afterthought, almost an unintended byproduct. The leaders and people of Oregon set out to protect the streams, rivers, farms, and mountains that they loved.

"They [growth boundaries] were means to an end," said Ethan Seltzer, director of the Institute of Portland Metropolitan Studies at Portland State University, who often explains the area to visiting journalists. "The point was to call an end to farmland development. The kind of press we're getting is mostly about what we're doing, not why. The why is the incredible landscape of the Willamette Valley.

"This is not a city that stands back and looks at its skyline and says, 'What a great city!' It's a city that stands back and says, 'Look at those mountains!'"[4]

As Seltzer and others explained to me, it was a coalition of farmers and tree huggers that got the state growth control laws passed and have kept them in place. Governor Tom McCall, the progressive Republican governor who led the fight for the statewide planning law in the early 1970s, was a nature lover first and a city lover a distant second. The group that has been so influential, 1,000 Friends of Oregon, is bound together by its members' deep love of nature. The Friends have become true lovers of urbanism as they have seen how that is a means to their end. They have come to love urbanism, I believe, but it was a discovery, not a goal.

Robert Caldwell, editor of the editorial page for the Portland *Oregonian* and a native, talks of often seeing "a cowboy" or a blue-collar worker stooping to pick up a piece of litter, or sharply telling someone else to do the same.

To me, this trait is cheering, but it is also saddening, for it suggests Americans are unlikely to unite around an urban vision. Cities are still too misunderstood, still too prone to inspire suspicion, for people to unite around a goal of streetcars, walking streets, and the diverse milieu of urbanism. They may like it once they get there, and even come to love it, but it is unlikely to be a strong enough goal to inspire the necessary work.

It also suggests that place, in the urbanistic sense, cannot be built from scratch, but only preserved, enhanced, or rebuilt. A Greenwich Village or an East Side or even a midtown can evolve, change, building on its essential form of streets and buildings. A Portland can come back, resprouting and reinvigorating its old homes, and building new ones again. But I'm not sure such a place can be built again. Cities may be a dead art form, or a limited one. It may be possible, but I've never seen it. I haven't seen any collection of streets and buildings built after World War II that has a coherent sense of place.

CARPE DIEM

Other places have nature lovers, too. Why were Portland and Oregon able to weld them into an effective political force?

Shakespeare's Brutus said that "there is a tide in the affairs of men which, taken at the flood, leads on to fortune." While it didn't work with Brutus (he killed himself after losing the battle of Philippi, where he had wrongly persuaded Cassius to march their troops with his eloquent phrase), it did with Portland and its master, the state of Oregon. In 1973 the state passed a landmark statewide growth control law, called Senate Bill 100, that mandated that cities and localities draw precise growth boundaries, submit them for state approval, and stick to them. This was the slippery slope, the camel's nose under the tent, the path not taken by the rest of the country, which made all the difference, that led to a cascading series of laws and events that made the state and city the wonderful places they are today.

Senate Bill 100 led to an elected Metro government for Portland, which now decides land use on a regional level. Senate Bill 100 made it possible for the city to build a light rail line and improve bus service, because it could be confident that the density would be there or emerge to support these facilities. Senate Bill 100 held the center together and allowed it to regrow. From this legislation, all riches, or possibilities, flowed.

There has been a lot of criticism of growth boundaries, particularly by some New Urbanists, and particularly by Miami architect Andres Duany, the most prominent New Urbanist. This criticism shows how many New Urbanists are primarily suburbanists, not urbanists. What interests them is not revitalizing the center city, but building cute new subdivisions on the edge of town. Growth boundaries limit these because they limit the supply of open land. Growth boundaries push responsibility for growth away from developers, be they New Urbanist or conventional, and back to where it should be, with city and regional planning departments.

Duany has been speaking out steadily against growth boundaries. In the Winter/Spring 1997 issue of *Harvard Design Magazine*, Duany says, "There has never been a growth boundary that has held, not even Portland's. And the reason for this is simple: such boundaries are arbitrary. . . . It is not organic."[5]

Actually, Portland's growth boundary has held remarkably well. In fact, builders complain that the boundary has achieved such permanence politically that moving it at all, much less getting rid of it, is close to impossible. The region has been debating whether to move it for an increase of 3,500 acres, an increase of less than 1 percent. As for "organic," this begs the question whether anything in city design is organic. As Spiro Kostof said in *The City Shaped,* organic is a slippery word that is often better left out of discussions of city design. Growth boundaries are like cups holding water; they work to the extent that they are solid and nonporous. Portland's growth boundary works, compared to many others that haven't, because it has been solid, and has genuinely pushed development inward. That Duany should lead a campaign against the most effective tool for urbanism in the last half-century is telling.

Oregon was able to embark on its different approach to city-building in part because it is small, and relatively homogeneous both ethnically and politically. The overheated horses of California's economy would be difficult for any driver to rein in, not to mention the unwieldy wagon load of ethnic groups and immigrants, legal and otherwise, who live there. Oregon is more manageable.

Costa Rica is the only stable democracy in Central America, with a larger, more prosperous middle class, because it had the blessing of not being blessed with large quantities of gold or other forms of natural wealth. Thus unblessed, it escaped the attention of the Spanish, the Americans, the French, and other marauding colonizers who turned its neighbors into plantations with semifeudal regimes, leading, in turn, to the problem-ridden countries of today. Costa Rica, which was ignored by that day's global powers, had a chance to work out its own problems and destiny.

Oregon might be said to be similarly blessed. It lacked Seattle's aerospace industries or California's dynamic combination of defense, banking, computer, and other industries that led to explosive growth there. Not poor, but not rich either, Oregon could go about its business in the early 1970s relatively unnoticed by the marauding band of developers and pirates then carving up its neighbors. Oregon had its timber industry, some ports, and some fishing, but was a relatively quiet place. In fact, until recently, it was a difficult place to make a living for a newcomer.

This relative isolation allowed the state and the city to begin their journey away from the rest of the country in the early 1970s, when events and luck conspired to give the state and city the critical mass to do things differently. The three factors were: One, the culture of the times. The 1960s had just ended, the environmental movement was just flowering, and things were still in flux, making big changes possible. Two, the maverick culture of the state, which allowed for new things to happen. Three, the leadership of courageous individuals who dared to do things differently and were supported.

This was about the same time that the state had passed a handful of progressive laws. Between 1969 and 1971, Oregon passed laws to provide public access to the beach, to issue bonds for pollution abatement, to ban billboards, to build bike paths, and to mandate returnable bottles. The Land Conservation and Development Act of 1973 (also known as "Senate Bill 100") was part of a wave of public-interest laws passed at the time.

At the helm of the state was Governor Tom McCall, part of a now-extinct tribe called progressive Republicans. It was the same tribe that would produce Oregon Senators Mark Hatfield and Bob Packwood. Theirs was the type of go-your-own-way attitude that produced Sen. Wayne Morse, one of only two senators in 1964 to vote against the Gulf of Tonkin resolution. At the helm of Portland in the early 1970s was a progressive Democrat named Neil Goldschmidt, who would go on to become governor. Supporting these men was State Senator Hector Macpherson—a Republican and farmer who was the principal author and legislative herder of Senate Bill 100, which required statewide planning, and out of which came the Land Conservation and Development Commission, which governs growth on a statewide basis.

What McCall did was push through Senate Bill 100, which required localities to establish growth plans and have them approved by this commission. And they had to be drawn with the priority of preserving "farms and forests." From this initiative would eventually emerge Portland's growth boundaries. What Goldschmidt did was stop one freeway, tear down a wide arterial boulevard, and establish a more urban vision of a finely grained downtown and city. This contrasted with the superblock, freeway, parking garage, and bulldozer strategy of his predecessor.

Although Portland is a city lover's dream now, the sad state of the city twenty-five years ago can be seen by the remarks of then–*New York*

Times architectural critic Ada Louise Huxtable. She visited the city in 1970 and described it as a place of "towers, bunkers and bomb sites." As Randy Gragg, architectural writer for the Portland *Oregonian*, noted, "In a little over a decade [Portland] came to be rewoven around Waterfront Park, Pioneer Courthouse Square, the transit mall, a collection of historic districts and arguably the best retail district of any city its size."[6] An elderly man told me that the revitalization of downtown seemed miraculous when seen after a twenty-year absence. "We left downtown in 1971, and it was pretty dingy, full of Triple-X bookstores and saloons. We came back in 1990 and couldn't believe it. It was a place transformed."

The journey away from bunkers, bomb sites, and Triple-X bookstores began with a vision of something different, and proceeded with the tools of growth boundaries, metro governments, light rail lines, and fine-tuned regulation of development.

RACE: WHY THE CENTER HOLDS

In turning away from the expanding suburbs, Portland turned back toward the center. And at the center it found . . . a whole lot of white people. The center city indicates the cohesiveness of the whole, and Portland and Oregon were more able to embrace each other, to have a center, because they're a less diverse society than the rest of the country.

Of course, Oregon at first seems very diverse. It's got left-of-center to right-of-center, earring-wearing grungeites to dress-shirt-wearing Bible thumpers, urban-loving to cattle-farming . . . white people. Oh sure, it's got a few Asians, a few Hispanics, a few Native Americans, and even a few African Americans. But what it doesn't have is a large entrenched underclass of Others. In the South and Northeast, this is poor blacks, the descendants of three hundred years of slavery. In the Southwest, this is low-income Mexican Americans, the descendants of those who stole the country from the Indians before we stole it from Mexico.

The presence of an "Other," whatever its color, serves as a reverse magnet, propelling the middle classes of all colors out of the center, toward the enclaves of suburbia. It is sobering to think that most cities with relatively prosperous downtowns are in regions that lack the burden of a racially defined underclass. The Northwest as a whole has more cohesive center cities because of this.

Race is not the only reason for the suburbs. In fact, it isn't even a principal factor. The car and the highway are. And as I've said before, homogeneous countries in Europe are struggling with suburban sprawl as well. But race is a force multiplier, spinning the centrifuge at a faster rate and making it more difficult for the center to hold.

I rode the light rail lines and buses while I was in Portland. I saw cars crowded with all types of people, leaning to the working class but also with wealthy or better-off folks in nice suits and dresses. Public transportation builds social cohesiveness. On the light rail line at rush hour, I'd see a construction worker in soiled clothes, kids holding knapsacks of books, a chic woman in jeans, gold jewelry, and a tweed jacket, and a whole lot of other folks. But then I counted the black people. Usually one or two would be the most I would come up with. For most white people, including me, I'm sorry to say, being part of the whole is easier when it's not mostly black or brown, particularly poor black and brown.

It's easy to be tolerant and progressive where there aren't that many poor racial minorities to be tolerant of. According to the 1990 census, the Portland metro area was 91 percent white and less than 3 percent black. The state as a whole had a nearly identical composition. The implications of this go beyond just the racial polarization that still exists in our society, and into all the other factors that the presence of a low-income, minority population implies. Portland has a low violent crime rate in part because of this.[7] It also has better schools, more equitable funding across school districts, and a higher percentage of its children in the public schools. Portland has never had the entrenched slums of Northeastern cities.

Portland and Oregon's less racially diverse population is not the only factor in their success; neighboring Washington has a similar population, but has not gotten its act together as well as Oregon. But even in Washington, I suspect the more homogeneous population is a reason the center city is more alive there than most other places.

So where does that leave us? Perhaps in a more hopeful place than one might think. Although race and racism are still big factors, the country is changing for the better on this. White and black people are getting more used to being around each other. A larger black middle and upper class has started to change the image in many whites' minds of black as synonymous with poor. Interracial dating is becoming so common now that it is hardly even worthy of comment anymore. Although race has been a big factor in the past, it may be less so in the future. Even in the entrenched neighborhoods of the Northeast and South, people may be more willing to support a light rail line or improved bus service, even if it means mingling more with different ethnic groups. The more homogeneous populations of the Northwest have made their task easier, but the rest of the country can still catch up.

THE THIRD CIRCLE: A QUESTION OF QUANTITY

Portland has the usual carpet of subdivisions, malls, and office parks bordering fat suburban boulevards with multiple left-turn lanes. And despite some attempts at innovation, they generally look no different, nor function differently, than suburbs anywhere else.

There's no reason they should. Places are created by transportation systems, and here, the highway still reigns supreme, so the places resemble those anywhere else in the country. An active bus service makes a difference, but not enough to make the changes visible to the naked eye. The light rail lines, both under construction and proposed, will make a difference, but they are not completed yet.

What the Portland suburbs show us is that achieving urbanism today is not so much about refashioning the suburbs, which is the New Urban vision, but limiting their quantity. Urbanism is a result of putting people and their activities under pressure. That pressure can only be achieved if government restricts or does not facilitate the outward expansion of the suburbs.

Because of the growth boundary and a lack of new highways on the periphery, development opportunities are limited. Metro planning officials tell me that large corporate developers have steered clear of Portland, because there is no area where they can buy five thousand or even five hundred acres at once and build large mega-subdivisions. They have left the terrain to the local developers, who are forced to buy forty acres here, ten acres there, and build more compactly. Because of this, in Portland, the odd spaces of open land that usually lie between suburban developments are being filled in. Most suburban cities that are considered "fully developed" have literally thousands of acres of undeveloped land that are simply left over, like pieces of cake left on a plate after a greedy but indiscriminate eater.

Jacking up the pressure necessary to create urbanism must be done

Subdivisions and shopping centers crowd in on farmland on the outskirts of Portland near the growth boundary. Photo by Alex Marshall.

in the suburbs because that is where the growth occurs first. In Beaverton and Hillsboro, you have Intel, Nike, and a dozen other high-tech and high-profit companies. It's a landscape of fresh office buildings popping out of dirty fields, of bulldozers on the horizon, and still-vacant or farmed fields mixing with wide highways and freeway off-ramps. But the regional policies of limiting outward development have forced these cities to have more of a relationship with the center city. The policies build on an underlying economic relationship that is already there, but usually ignored by governments.

Unlike in my own city of Norfolk, the suburban cities have not become prosperous suburbs trying to avoid responsibility for a struggling inner city. Instead, the inner city has a complementary relationship with the suburbs. High-tech companies go to the 'burbs, where, despite the growth controls, there is still open land for development. But because the relationship to the inner city is closer, these new workers will travel downtown and to other urban districts regularly. They might even live there. As Portland prospers, the example of a compact metro area with a prosperous and appealing downtown and neighborhoods, and the countryside close by, draws more companies and more residents. The trick is to keep building the circle at the right pace. There are other benefits to companies as well. A better mass transit system means lower-income workers can get to their jobs more easily.

Nowhere is this different relationship between city and suburb illustrated better than in the light rail line cutting its way through virgin land in Beaverton and Hillsboro. Portland is doing something unprecedented here, extending tracks into virgin or semivirgin land. It's much as New York extended the subway and elevated train lines into Queens and Brooklyn in the early part of this century. The stations around the Westside Line have land already zoned for offices and homes that should fit in with the higher density and walking environment a rail line can serve.

Portland has a chance to produce something unique in the century, a new urban neighborhood or area. With transit as its base, the major station stops in Beaverton and Hillsboro could produce an urban city as naturally as the ones that produced Queens or the East Side of New York.

In Portland, we'll see. The places produced at the Sunset Transit Center, Beaverton Central, and Orenco, to name a few of the new stops, will be new places, not copies of Beaux-Arts cities or streetcar suburbs. They will be hybrids, mixing in parking garages for commuters with street-oriented businesses and apartments. I'm not sure it will work, or what the final flavor of these developments will be. Will you be able to stroll down a street and walk into a store? Will there be a sense of place, even if it's a new kind of place? I hope it is a new kind of place. It would be great to prove that urbanity is not a lost art.

The contemporary places I have seen built in the latter half of the twentieth century around transit in Europe, like the Part-Dieu shopping center in Lyon, or La Défense in Paris, or the "Lyngby Storcenter" outside Copenhagen, inevitably feel like Tyson's Corner with a train line attached. They function differently, in terms of how people get there, their density, their effect on the environment, but they don't *feel* that different. There is a unidimensionality about the places, the sight lines of the planner's drawing board still visible in the buildings and streets. It's hard to imagine these European places growing and evolving into comfortable urban places. But I hope I'm wrong. I'm sure whatever new city that does emerge around the Portland rail lines will be a new form, perhaps recognizably urban, but still new, shaped by the contemporary demands of space and time, and the balancing act with the automobile. History does not repeat itself.

PORTLAND: ANOTHER BOULDER, COLORADO?

A generation ago, Boulder, Colorado, instituted some of the first growth controls in the country. They sharply limited the quantity of development within the city. The result has been a pristine city, and an increasingly elitist one. With nowhere to live within Boulder, the fast-food managers and store clerks live in distant suburbs and drive in.

Portland has a chance to be a different model. Through its growth controls, it is becoming an urban city again. But to keep this process going, it must continue to accept more people within its borders.

The biggest question facing Portland in the next decade is where it will put the 500,000 people and 250,000 new homes estimated to be coming there by 2017. Most of these people will go to the 'burbs, although, because of the growth controls, some 50,000 new homes are aimed at the existing city. Under the 2040 plan approved by the Metro government, most of these new residents will go within the existing growth boundaries.[8]

The danger is that the citizens of Portland, Beaverton, Sherwood, and other political districts will *say* they will accept the additional housing, but resist the case-by-case rezonings to accomplish it, and so end up not accepting the additional residents. If this happens, the Portland metro area risks becoming a larger version of Boulder, where an upscale elite live within its boundaries and the working class and poor go somewhere else.

Because of Oregon's growth control, it's not clear where the poor or working class would go. But some shift in population would occur. Perhaps, as housing prices went up, economic development would stop and so would growth.

Douglas McClain, planning director of Clackamas County, said most of the growth battles in the last two decades have been fought outside the growth boundaries, not within them. The debates were over whether to let a farmer split off a lot for a son-in-law, whether to let a rich advertising executive build a country farmhouse, even though he and his family didn't farm themselves. (For under Oregon law—another incredible feature of the state—one must get a certain amount of one's income from rural land to build a home there, even if other zoning requirements are met.)

For the most part, the antidevelopment forces won. But restricting a few home builders in the countryside is a lot easier, probably, than demanding that existing residents accept more neighbors in their neighborhoods.

Density is a dirty word, and already signs have sprouted in neighborhoods seeking to stop the placing of apartments or town houses that Metro and various councils have decided the neighborhoods can handle. Jon Chandler, an often-quoted leader of the home builders association, said that local governments are "lying through their teeth" when they say they will accept thousands of new residents within existing boundaries. They don't want to accept the political heat for moving the growth boundary; but they also don't want the heat for more people. Unfortunately, you have to choose one or the other.

"Sixty to 70 percent of the people don't want to move the UGB and 60 to 70 percent don't want higher density," said Chandler.

If Portland refuses higher density and refuses moving the growth boundary, it risks becoming a larger version of Boulder—a rich, unreal place where a schoolteacher is forced to live thirty miles away in another county because it's the only place that she can afford a home. If Portlanders, however, accept more people, they have the chance of living in one helluva good city. Increased population will help mass transit work. It will help neighborhood business districts and downtown. It will further push the center of gravity away from the suburban malls and subdivisions, and toward the center city areas and the train stops.

Speaking of housing prices, there has been a lot of talk that Portland's high home prices, in the upper reaches of home prices nationwide, are caused by its urban growth boundary. I originally thought this true myself. If you restrict the supply of something, in this case land, it seemed logical that its price would go up, and therefore so would the prices of homes.

But, after observing Portland, I've changed my mind. Housing prices, I suspect, are determined more by demand than supply. In the 1990s, the Portland metropolitan area was producing more units of new housing annually than at any time in its history. And still the prices went up. Which is simply because the market could bear it. High-tech jobs were flooding into Portland and wages were going up, which drove up housing prices.

Reducing the supply of land probably did not reduce the production of housing. The housing market and industry are flexible. Because of the shortage of large tracts of land, developers instead built on the many smaller parcels of open land within the growth boundary they otherwise would have ignored. There are still thousands of acres of such land within the growth boundary. They also redeveloped areas within the existing city.

If you compare Portland's rate of housing price increases to that of other fast-growing areas, you'll find that it is no higher than in Phoenix or Las Vegas, two fast-growing areas which are laissez-faire, let-'er-rip types of cities that would consider a growth boundary a Communist plot.

What does increase housing prices, and this accounts for Phoenix and Las Vegas, is economic development and big increases in wealth. That's why home prices are shooting up in Phoenix, Las Vegas, and the Silicon Valley despite the absence of growth boundaries in any of those places.

MAKING THE POLITICAL REFLECT THE ACTUAL CONTEMPORARY CITY

Look in the blue pages of the Portland metropolitan phone book and you'll see a clear view of what makes Oregon work and what makes it different.

First you'll see the local governments, all thirty-one of them, listed in equitable alphabetical order, ranging from the town of Tigard to Portland itself. Then you have the counties, Multnomah, Clackamas, and Washington. Then—and this is a big one—you come to the regional government, simply titled "Metro." After that, you get state, then federal.

How orderly, and proper. In every other phone book in the country, you skip from town and city directly to the state. No regional government.

This regional government is an incredible achievement. It is the only elected regional government in the United States, but being first is no achievement if what is achieved is not worthwhile. What makes it noteworthy is that Portlanders have attempted to recognize the city for what it is: a sprawling megalopolis, spilling over hill and vale, and encompassing dozens of once separate towns. Because of this act of cognition, they have reaped rewards. Because they have allowed themselves to see the world they inhabit, they have reaped control over it. A fair exchange.

People don't like to admit that their world has grown more complex. They don't like to admit that their "city" is an entire metropolitan area, sometimes a hundred miles across. They don't think about it much, and when they do, it threatens them. They hug their old conceptions of a city. There are practical reasons, in the short term, for this.

To the people in the suburbs, admitting they are part of one city would usually mean taking responsibility for the center city and its problems. It would mean recognizing that their own lives are dependent on the center city, and merely one-half of a coin. This is obviously true in a city like Norfolk that still possesses more jobs, about 250,000, than it does people, about 230,000. But it's also true in more depressed areas, like Detroit. Not only do the center cities still have some economic engines, but their inhabitants work out in the suburbs, or their suburbs' inhabitants work in the center. It is one city.

In Portland, the Metro government was a gradual evolution from a typical bureaucratic metropolitan planning organization. Has Metro been responsible for Portland's success? In part. Metro does everything important. It draws and manages the urban growth boundary. It, through the transit authority, runs and designs the light rail line and the bus system. It does not, technically speaking, manage downtown Portland, but what it does is what Portland depends on.

What local-area governments have done is turned over to Metro, in large parts, the pleasures and pains of land use—deciding what goes where.

It was so startlingly otherworldly to see the representatives that make up Metro sitting in a meeting trading population like cards—"I'll take 25,000, if you agree to keep the forests over there." They were divvying up the expected population growth in the next few decades. It was bizarre on two levels. The first was the implicit assumption that growth could be directed, or accepted or rejected, and was not something that just happens. The second was the implicit assumption that growth happens on a regional level, and so can be shaped on a regional level.

Several things threaten Metro government.

Much or most of the population is ignorant of why Portland works better than most other cities, although many are aware that it does. It's a fine line here, because taken as a whole, the masses have a more en-lightened conception of how a city works. But many people don't know about the regional Metro government, and are only vaguely aware of the growth boundary.

"I love downtown," said one woman at the Clackamas Town Center Mall in the southeastern suburbs of Portland. She sat at a table in the food court, surrounded by shopping bags. "I love the diversity of the Hawthorne area. I love the Saturday Market. . . . [But] I don't know what the Urban Growth Boundary is. I don't know what Metro is."

Many people were like that. They appreciated the effects of things like urban growth boundaries, even if they didn't know what they were or how they operated. Still, it was a scary and unsettling observation.

Aside from ignorance and apathy, there are the more focused forces of conservative right-wingers who have taken aim at the land-planning and governmental tools as examples of—take your pick—activist government, too much government, or antibusiness regulations. Of course, Portland's planning policies are none of these. They are no more activist than building freeways for more malls and subdivisions; they are just activist in a different way. Building a train line promotes different businesses and homes than a freeway. Nevertheless, the newly elected Republican majority in the Oregon state legislature in the mid-1990s took aim at getting rid of the statewide system of growth control but found a mass of public opposition prevented them.

A more specific threat has come from a committed referendumer and sometime candidate for governor, Bill Sizemore, who has taken aim at Portland's system of regional government as an unnecessary layer of government. He has at various times sponsored a statewide ballot measure that would repeal the state authorization for Metro governments. It would be an ironic thing if it passed. An antigovernment guy would be using a higher layer of government, the state, to take away a system of local government that people support.

THE SECOND CIRCLE: NEW BLOOD TO OLD NEIGHBORHOODS

Many cities, even if their downtowns are a mess, have at least one funky older urban neighborhood. Because these neighborhoods are smaller in scale than a downtown, and often originally suburbs themselves and crafted closer to the time of the automobile, they more often are easier

A Jaguar cruises by some old apartments in the Hawthorne neighborhood. In another city, these apartments might be crumbled and decayed. Photo by Alex Marshall.

to adapt to the automobile. A single shopping street of storefronts, with a neighborhood around it, is easier to make work than a downtown of denser buildings filled with stores on the bottom and offices above. Because of this, many metropolitan areas whose downtowns are a mess of dysfunctionalities, like Charlotte, Columbus, or Norfolk, to name three, still have at least one lively urban neighborhood where the gays, the artists, the lawyers, the journalists, and other urbanites can make a place for themselves.

Portland is unique, though, in having at least a half dozen such neighborhoods, with more emerging. They reveal how urban growth works. They reveal the process behind gentrification and why it is mostly a good thing.

In the Portland area, the first secondary urban area to emerge was Northwest Twenty-third Street, about a mile west from downtown. It has the typical story for such neighborhoods. It was a charming, but seedy, area in the early 1970s. Its Victorian homes and apartments were filled with a mixture of the aging, the funky, and the lowlifes. As it took off with the wave of gentrification that went around the country in the 1970s, it gradually became a more prosperous neighborhood of gays, yuppies, and singles, while holding on still to some longtime residents.

Now, with Portland itself being the object of so much growth, Twenty-third Street has become so overheated that it resembles a shopping mall, with Pottery Barns and the like, and wall-to-wall traffic on the weekends.

As Twenty-third Street overheated, its growth spilled off into other urban neighborhoods, which function like pressure-release valves. There is Hawthorne, a long street on the other side of the river which is funky in the way perhaps Twenty-third Street used to be. It has used-book stores, New Age stores, and restaurants, and people with ropelike hair standing on the corners. A few blocks over is Belmont, a less intense street that still has its own dynamic. Then there is the Pearl district, which is an area of old warehouses that are being converted to apartments and galleries, and which has new town houses being built into it as well.

"There isn't a section of the city that isn't improving," said Gordon Oliver, a transportation reporter for the Portland *Oregonian*. Even neighborhoods considered semislums have new people moving in and old residents fixing up their homes. Property values are rising in virtually all center-city neighborhoods, not just in the suburbs or an isolated upscale center-city neighborhood.

Why is this so? Because these neighborhoods are the beneficiaries of the growth pressure that is usually limited to just the outer neighborhoods. Having a growth boundary means that development is pushed inward, prompting developers, real-estate agents, and residents to look at neighborhoods they might otherwise avoid. Building a light rail line that works with a much larger bus service means that these neighborhoods get the natural growth pressure that comes from transportation systems. In an *Oregonian* story in August of 1997, staff writer R. Gregory Nokes revealed that nearly three in every ten new homes are being built on redeveloped land. This is an incredible statistic. As Nokes put it:

"It's like finding land the region didn't know it had, in areas already served by roads, waters and sewers, police and firefighters, and schools, which eases the potential development costs to taxpayers and ratepayers. About 37 percent of new jobs are in redeveloped businesses."[9]

This overall process of new growth in the inner-city neighborhoods can be labeled gentrification. Whatever its name, rising prosperity in older neighborhoods is only a bad thing if it occurs so explosively that older or poorer people are forced out unwillingly. To declare all such new growth bad is to say that older neighborhoods should be condemned to decay or be isolated from all change. Much of the usual rhetoric on gentrification, for example, ignores that poor homeowners often benefit from rising property values.

"You have low-income homeowners who for the first time have equity in their homes," said Seltzer of Portland State University. "And people say that's not good, that only suburban homeowners should have that."[10]

THE FIRST CIRCLE: THE CENTER IS THE MESSAGE

We arrive finally at downtown. It's a wonderful place, but only because its success is built on the structure of the last three areas we looked at: countryside, suburbs, and inner city. A downtown can no more succeed by itself than a capstone can hold itself up without the tower beneath it.

Downtown is the bellwether of a city. With a glance at it you can tell how much of an identity a place has, how much of a center, both in a symbolic and cultural way. Downtowns don't lie. No matter how much money a city or region has spent on a downtown, it takes only a quick glance to see through the city-subsidized performing arts center, the new museum or aquarium, to see how much life it really has. With a glance at a downtown, you can tell how effectively a city has handled its region, and how much a region has handled its general common problems. For a downtown is still the center, the only center, of a region. And by looking at its health, you can see how well a region has handled things that its parts face together, whether that is recognized or not. Things like growth control, and transportation policies, poverty, and business development.

For a city of Portland's size, its downtown is phenomenal. Most often, alive downtowns are those of big cities like New York, Boston, or San Francisco. Small to midsized cities generally have decaying or artificially preserved downtowns. To get an idea of what I mean, think about virtually any other midsized metropolitan area of around one to two million souls—my own city of Norfolk, or Indianapolis or St. Louis. These places do not have downtowns that still serve as retail centers of their areas. Indianapolis, Norfolk, and Columbus have huge, city-subsidized enclosed shopping malls. But, partly successful though they are, these are alien, car-centered environments imported into the hostile, foot-walking land of a nineteenth-century downtown and kept alive by means of artificial respiration.

Even the downtown of neighboring Seattle is, by comparison, a struggling, uneven place. Downtown is active, but there is also a patchy quality about it. The big department stores are all gathered around a big city plaza and convention center. There is Pike Place Market, touristy but still a real produce, fish, and meat market. But there is a lack of the broad number of midlevel stores, things like a cutlery shop, that are not aimed at tourists or bohemians or the convention market. It's easy to see why this is so. There's the huge freeway, built in anticipation of the World's Fair in the early 1960s, that carves the city in half. There is the strangulation of freeways around the waterfront. Most importantly, there's an absence of a growth boundary, which dissipates the region's energy and makes the Seattle region a fairly hellish place to drive through and, I suspect, to live in.

For me, walking Portland's streets is a bittersweet exercise. Portland was founded in 1843, and hit its stride in the last half of the nineteenth century. It's older than neighboring Seattle and it shows. The buildings are mostly late-nineteenth-century brick and stone structures, with elaborate cornices, lintels, and moldings, and often only five or ten stories in height. The city was built with short, two-hundred-foot blocks, which give buildings more street frontage and make it even more of a pleasure to stroll around. The number of viable healthy blocks downtown is very high, especially when compared to other midsized cities. While other cities struggle to have even one successful shopping street, Portland has roughly a ten-by-fifteen-block area that is thriving, which means roughly 150 square blocks in all, crammed with stores, restaurants, businesses, and cultural facilities.

I say bittersweet because Portland's downtown reminded me, quite surprisingly, of my own city of Norfolk. Although it was founded in 1680, Norfolk had a growth spurt about when Portland did, in the late nineteenth century. Thus, much of Norfolk's downtown has, or had, the feel of Portland, with the ornate, low-rise, and human-scale buildings of the times. But in Norfolk, urban renewal cleared away most of the city in the 1950s (including most of the pre–Civil War architecture and streets). Granby Street, the original main street, remains but is lined with empty department stores and boarded-up theaters. It is a downtown of parking lots, with here and there poking up a city-funded project, or buildings from some of the few remaining old streets.

In Portland, I see a picture of what might have been, had my own city and region pursued a different path. Indeed, Norfolk and Portland's downtowns sounded nearly identical in the early 1970s. Both were described as landscapes of vacant lots, boarded-up buildings, and parking garages. But starting then, Portland built itself inward, filling in its gaps. Meanwhile, Norfolk tore itself apart even further.

So why else is Portland's downtown vital? It comes down to the car, or the lack of it. Speaking frankly, a viable, old-fashioned downtown in not possible where the car is the principal means of transportation. The classic downtown that we all have in our minds, where people stroll the streets past shop windows, was created before cars. It is, in its fullest flowering, a product of the streetcar, the subway, and the elevator, which allowed late-nineteenth-century cities to reach densities not possible a generation earlier. In its pattern of walkable streets, though, it continued patterns that had served several millennia. The car broke this thousands-of-years-old pattern apart, shattering the city. Having a real downtown, and, I would posit, having a sense of place at all, are not possible where the car reigns supreme. Highways and cars do not produce places—that is, places with streets, and buildings that enclose a street, that prepare one for walking. Cars produce parking lots and driveways. It is thus and ever will be.

To have a cohesive downtown, or really even older neighborhoods, a city has to have a cohesive system of mass transit, and it has to make it dominant, or at least close to dominant. Urbanism is a result of pressure. It's about putting people, activities, and movement in a confined space. Only mass transit has the ability to raise the pressure to enough people per square inch; cars release pressure as surely as puncturing a hole in a tire.

This maxim is simple, but most city fathers don't get it. A downtown is produced from the bottom up, not the top down. No big city-funded convention center or aquarium will change that. They may bring people into town, but they will have to be housed in parking boxes, which will actually corrupt rather than enhance the ground-level concept of a downtown.

Portland increased its urban pressure by prohibiting, in the mid-1970s, the construction of more parking spaces. This was a master stroke, a strategy opposite that of most other places. Other cities perversely *required* the construction of parking spaces. If you built an office building, you were required to build an even larger parking box beside it to house the cars. (Usually, the space required to house all the workers' cars is larger than the space needed for their bodies.) And even without laws, office builders would usually construct parking so their customers or workers would have an easy way of getting to and from their offices or stores.

By prohibiting the construction of parking, Portland managed to reverse this dynamic. It was a pressure builder. Any new businesses or stores or homes would have to make do with the parking that was there. This pushed people onto the buses and eventually onto the light rail line. Of course, without a growth boundary businesses and stores might have just left downtown altogether. But with the growth boundary, it was not as easy to move outward, even though a significant chunk of open land remained within it. The boundary kept the pattern of development still relatively constrained.

A side note on the parking cap, as it is called. The Environmental Protection Agency may be the real father of the law. The EPA required the city to find some way of dealing with its status as a poor-air-quality city, and of limiting automobile emissions. The city fathers came up with the parking cap. So the EPA is one of the fathers of Portland's success. In recent years, the Portland City Council has begun relaxing its parking cap—a mistake, I believe.

THE DESIGNER'S HAND

Portland has succeeded in proving that the city is still the largest art form in which we work, and still a very viable one, in which the painters— working mostly for the government—still have a variety of colors and brushes at their disposal.

But a city is, finally, an economic unit. On that, its existence depends. Go look at a ghost town in Wyoming to see what happens when a city's economic base dries up, or at Flint, Michigan. And it appears that a successful city, given this definition of success, can be built in either the Portland model or the more typical suburban-sprawl model that can be seen in the Raleigh-Durham area in North Carolina. I mention Raleigh-Durham because, like Portland, it supports a thriving high-tech center and, also like Portland, is one of the fastest-growing regions of the country. Go to one area and you get suburbs spilling into farmland and dead center cities. Go to the other and you get thriving downtowns and older neighborhoods, and neat, compact towns in the countryside, as well as the possibility of traveling somewhere without four tires under you. I prefer the latter, but either one appears to work in the economic sense.

It's taken me awhile to work out what a city is. Cities are primarily about creating wealth, whether it be computer chips, software, new ideas, or new cars. A university town's "product" is educated kids and new thought. New York's is advertising, finance, and media; Portland's is a mixture of computer chips and older industries relating to shipbuilding and repair. Cities, to quote Jane Jacobs, are export producers. Without industries that continually export something, a city doesn't exist. Without money coming in from outside, a city has no way to pay for newspapers, groceries, dentists, and all the other sundries, including things like houses, schools, and performing arts centers. It's often mentioned that residential real estate is a big industry in a town, but it always depends on something else for its existence.

Stopping a subdivision no more stops growth than putting your hands under a waterfall stops the water. Growth, seen another way, is less something to be stopped or started than a tool with which to craft the form of a city or a region. Computer chips or software, it seems, can be manufactured whether their makers arrive by light rail line or on a highway, and the chips can be exported by either truck or rail.

It is the big decisions that determine a region's economic viability—does it have Interstate access; does it have a big airport; does it have a port? These decisions are all public ones, and they are the most important. But once these decisions are made, the specific contours of the city can be shaped a number of ways, with either short or long hemlines, wide or thin lapels. And the final product can be what I would judge as beautiful and harmonious, on both a social and aesthetic level, or hideous and discordant, and still be viable.

I am sorry to jump on the "I love Portland" bandwagon. The deification of Portland can be compared to the deification of many of the land patterns of many Western European countries. The point is not that Europe or Portland has completely avoided the challenges of sprawl and decay; neither has. The point is that both have more honestly grappled with them.

This center city market is an example of community, commerce, and government together in an indivisible bundle. Photo by Teresa W. Wingfield.

Another question: what is a community at the end of the 20th century? A focus group, a concentration camp, a chat room on the Internet, an address book, a dance club, all those afflicted with a particular incurable disease, a gender, an age bracket, a waiting room, owners of silver BMW's, organized crime, everyone who swears by a particular brand of painkiller and a two-block stretch of Manhattan on any weekday at lunch hour.

Herbert Muschamp, from "The Miracle in Bilbao," *New York Times Magazine,* September 7, 1997.

CHAPTER 8

NO PLACE

CALLED

HOME

Community at the Millennium

COMING HOME

It's a Saturday night and my house is filling with people. Some carry musical instruments. Some have sheets of poetry or fiction by their sides. Some carry nothing, but are prepared to stand up before a crowd of people and dance, perform theater, or tell a story.

We call it the Coffeehouse. We've been doing it now for seven years. The first Saturday of every month, friends and friends of friends come to our house to entertain and be entertained. Usually about fifty people show up. It's a great time.

This coffeehouse is the highlight of the month, both for me and many of the people who attend. It's not just the music, poetry, and other acts that bring people back, although these are good. It's the chance to meet, connect, and talk with other people during the breaks. Through it, my wife and I have met many of our now good friends, and other people have made similar friendships and bonds. In a city where people come and go, it provides us a mechanism to make new friends as older ones leave town.

Why do I mention it? Because our coffeehouse is a replacement for what does not exist in the outer world. And the fact that it does not exist says a lot about our society at this stage in its history. I would prefer that a corner tavern or bar be down the street, where I could magically meet my friends and make new ones. I would prefer to be held up in a naturally emerging web of friends and family, growing out of the physical place where I live and the work that goes on there.

Our situation is ironic, because if anyone should have community "naturally," it's my wife and I. We live in Norfolk, Virginia, a port city on the Elizabeth River, the Chesapeake Bay, and the Atlantic Ocean. Huge carriers make their home here, as do huge cargo ships that freight millions of tons of coal all over the world.

It's been the home of my family on my father's side for five generations. My great-grandfather came here before the Civil War. He was the first publisher of the newspaper where I started my career in journalism, *The Virginian-Pilot*. My father grew up one block from where I write this. My wife is a native of the area as well. My newest niece lives down the street.

Looking at my background, one might think that I live a life rich in contacts with the past and the world that molded me, a place where an intricate and perhaps suffocating web of family and friends who have centuries of combined experience support, argue with, and love each other. Which is not the case. I have no close friends from my childhood or high school years that still live in this town, or even the state. Most of my siblings have scattered themselves around the country, as is the wont of professional people these days. Various relatives—second cousins once removed and so forth—do live near me. I know none of them well. As one commentator remarked about Europeans in contrast to Americans, "They still have cousins." Americans do not.

Various forces operating in the country and world today have pulled apart my "natural" community and scattered it to the winds. My own more cosmopolitan bent figures into this. I lived in Europe for a few years, attended college and graduate school in Pittsburgh and New York City. I am not able, nor do I desire, to sink back into the old-boy culture that does still exist here to a degree. I have a community around me, but it is one that I created or sought out, more than one I was born into. My community is in my coffeehouse, in the arts organizations I belong to, and in the civic work I do.

Community—the network of formal and informal relationships that binds people together—is a thin, tepid brew in this country. It has declined to the point where improving it, saving it, nurturing it have become slogans of a variety of movements in different, seemingly unrelated fields. In urban planning, New Urbanism promises to revive community through building subdivisions more cohesively. In political theory, Amiti Etzioni hopes to reduce crime and improve social health through his philosophy of Communitarianism. In journalism, the philosophy of Public Journalism, sometimes labeled Community Journalism, promises to rebuild community and a newspaper's circulation base by having the press foster public dialogue and political participation. Our politics, our places, our press—all of these things run across power lines that jolt us with the message that something is missing in too many of our lives, some sense of cohesion and togetherness.

This desire many people have for richer, more connected lives is a valid one. I believe that a society grows out of its social, religious, and political compacts, on which ultimately even market relationships depend. But like the construction of coherent physical places, the construction of coherent communities is not something to be attempted directly. Rather, one has to understand what produces both places and communities, and what weakens them, and address those forces.

Most of what we call community in the past has been produced as a byproduct of other things: making a living, shopping for food, keeping ourselves and our families well, protecting them and our society from physical harm, educating them. We shopped for groceries, served in the military, and went to a doctor and along the way got to know the butcher, the fellow soldier, and the local doctor. All of these actions have become less communal, and so our society has become less community-minded. We buy our food at the warehouse-style supermarket, do not serve in the military unless we volunteer, and go to the impersonal HMO to get our cholesterol checked. If we want to revive community, then we should look at the trade-offs involved in making some of our decisions more communal again.

Place has something to do with all this as well. Walking to a neighborhood cafe for breakfast is a more communal thing than using the drive-through at a McDonald's for an Egg McMuffin, although relationships can occur at either place. Driving on the freeway is less likely to generate relationships than riding a streetcar. Living in an older neighborhood fashioned around the foot is more communal than living in a contemporary one fashioned around the car. But the physical makeup of our places is just one factor in this trend.

John Perry Barlow, computer sage and former Grateful Dead lyricist, commented once that community is largely generated by shared adversity. This gets at the notion, true I believe, that our social ties, while beneficial, are not necessarily produced by situations we would choose. Although many of us miss community, we don't miss poverty, disease, and war, things that produce community with some regularity. The problem for contemporary Americans is that enhancing social cohesion may mean giving up some things we really like, like personal mobility, low taxes, and a footloose economic structure. We have not figured out yet that creating wealth is not the same as creating community.

I speak without any sentimentality or nostalgia for the past. I believe, however, that the generally fragmented lives so many of us lead break up marriages, disturb childhoods, isolate people when they most need help, and make life not as much fun. We live, to speak frankly, in one of the loneliest societies on earth. If we are to change that, then we should look more closely at the various relationships in our society—political, social, economic, and others—and attempt to construct them in more communal ways. Deciding how to structure these relationships comes back to what I increasingly believe is our most fundamental relationship—politics.

COMMUNITY AND THE MARKETPLACE

The act of buying and selling has always been wrapped up with building and maintaining community. Exchanging things of value in the spirit of peace and mutual support, rather than one of armed fear, is an example of civilization and the triumph of community, or politics, over fear, violence, and aggression.

What's happened over the last two centuries is that buying and selling has become less and less concentrated in a physical place. The near divorce of commerce from a physical community is one of the causes and effects of the fragmentation of our community.

The general trend has been bigger wholesalers and retailers gobbling up or displacing smaller ones, until we arrive at our present era of OfficeMaxes, CompUSA's, and Home Depots. The history of retail is one of prices getting lower in exchange for fewer and fewer steps between producer and consumer. The end result of this may be all of us going to one huge store located in some midpoint of the country, say Kansas City.

In the late nineteenth century, the newly emerged department store gobbled up customers from the old-fashioned general store and specialty stores of the time. Like all new forms of both commercial and residential activity, the department store was created by changes in transportation and communication. In this case, it was the new national railroad system and a national telegraph system. The railroad allowed goods to be shipped, and telegraph and other changes made it possible to order stock or keep in touch with the home office.[1]

The chain store made its appearance at about the same time because it could, in effect, turn a wholesale point into a retail point. One of the first chains was the Great Atlantic and Pacific Tea Company (A&P). There were ninety-five A&P stores in 1880.[2] These bigger, but more impersonal, stores gave people more goods for less money. They were also all decried by smaller, more established merchants. And all changed the social fabric.

Before World War II, the country made some effort to stop discount and chain stores and to protect smaller merchants. The fair-trade laws of the 1920s allowed manufacturers to set minimum prices for goods, thereby prohibiting deep discounts by stores in attempts to gain customers.

The Wal-Mart, Target, Super K-Mart, and other big box stores are the current stage of this evolutionary process toward fewer and bigger. Wal-Mart has come to symbolize the destruction of traditional downtowns and community. From its start thirty-five years ago, Wal-Mart now has stores in all fifty states (with the larger ones being over 200,000 square feet). In 1997, it had a U.S. workforce of more than 700,000 people and $118 billion in sales. The landing of these big boxes has become a symbol and sometimes an example of big, car-centered retail sucking the life out of Main Street businesses.

There's some truth in this, but this storyline ignores the last century of retailing. It's as if we went from the general store to Wal-Marts with nothing in between. Before Wal-Mart, there was the shopping mall, the strip center, and the fast-food restaurant on the out-parcel, all designed around the car.

Keith Moore, Director of Community Affairs for Wal-Mart, said in an interview that "When we go into towns where there is opposition, it's almost like they long for the way it was thirty or forty years ago. They stand up at public meetings and say they used to walk to Joe's corner store, why can't it be like that now. It's like the automobile was just invented. In a lot of communities, people would say, 'Why aren't there stores we can walk to? When I was growing up, we used to know people by name, and be able to walk places.' Well, sorry, cars were invented, highways were built, and you can shop at a range of places, from power centers to shopping malls. I don't know all the reasons that happened, but it did. The arguments people give don't really make a lot of sense."[3]

He's basically correct, although that doesn't invalidate people's feelings. People have a right to long for stores they can walk to. But I don't think they realize that creating them would mean giving up some of their cars, paying more for gasoline, tearing down highways, living in smaller homes, and paying more for their food, televisions, and clothing. The simplest means toward this end would be to put a $2 to $3 tax on a gallon of gasoline. This would push people out of their cars and densify communities, as well as more equitably pay for the true cost of driving. I support such a tax. But I don't hear most people clamoring for a $3 tax on a gallon of gas.

The link between value, price, and access, and community and connectedness, is there. One cannot have twenty-four-hour-a-day access to everything—and a more stable society bound together by common rhythms of life and work. Kenneth E. Stone, a professor of economics who has studied Wal-Marts, advised merchants who compete with Wal-Marts to give up such "outdated customs as closing on Sundays, 5 P.M. on weekdays, and Wednesday afternoons, 'primarily so everybody can go fishing.'"[4] Stone was not saying this ironically. He was realistically giving advice on how to be more competitive. But he apparently did not see that it might be nice to go fishing every once in a while, as well as enjoy a Sunday dinner with one's family. And that in the long run society might be more stable and prosperous because of it.

How much are you willing to pay? There is ample evidence that warehouse-style supermarkets and stores deliver goods at lower prices.

They also do so more impersonally, and with perhaps greater environmental and social collateral damage. One of the often-unasked questions at the heart of the debate over urbanism is how much Americans are willing to see prices rise on homes and the basic goods they buy in order to have a saner, more livable lifestyle.

COMMUNITY—WHATEVER IT IS, WE WANT IT

What is community anyway? Here's my definition. It's a network of relationships among individuals, families, and groups that binds them in a mutually supportive and dependent construct. Like family, it can be both a joy and a burden.

As individuals, we value privacy, wealth, mobility, and choices, all of which conflict at times with community. But as a society, and as individuals, we depend on community. Some form of it, whether it's constructed around a city block or the Internet, is necessary for life to go on. It is not possible to organize society purely around market relationships. The important work in society—raising children, instilling in them values and a moral code, educating them—is all done outside the market, and through something that is in some ways a community. In fact, the market itself arises through shared social arrangements, which are one aspect of community.

Here's the kicker. As a society, we enter into these relations through politics. Community is a political choice, as is so much of life. As I have said elsewhere, many of the other relationships of our lives—like the physical form of our places, the architecture of our commerce—are really political choices as well.

As a society, we are so poor in community because we have been so uncommunal in our political choices. Whether it's health care or transportation, we choose the individual avenue over the collective. We reject universal health care. We reject mass transit. We reject family leave policies and equitable school funding across a state. And then we lament that we have high crime rates, high rates of juvenile delinquency, high rates of alcoholism, and that we don't know our neighbors. The absence of community and the malady of political neglect are related.

Community comes from making shared decisions through the political infrastructure that underpins our lives. We can build stronger community and communities in this country, but it does not involve pushing houses closer to the street, constructing front porches, or redesigning subdivisions, at least not initially. It means investing more in the political choices that combine our collective interests. It might mean building mass transit lines that carry people together at the expense of more freeways that depend on individual car drivers. It might mean establishing growth boundaries at the expense of not letting individuals build isolated houses in the country. It might mean establishing universal health coverage at the expense of the salaries of individual doctors and the tax rates of individual citizens. It might mean better family leave policies at the expense of less flexibility and more expense for employers. It might mean equalizing school funding across districts of unequal wealth, at the expense of the tax rates in richer areas.

Really choosing community means giving things up. They might include, just for starters, low taxes, physical mobility, cheap prices, cheap housing, and lack of collective responsibility. In return, we get neighbors and friends and a healthier society. Our problems and our scarcities stem from scarcities of collective wealth, not individual wealth. I am free to buy a house in the country, but not to ride a bike there unhindered by traffic; or to get easily out of my city to the country on a weekend; or ride useful public transit when unable to drive. I may be able to get medical care for myself but not for the classmate my son attends school with.

One day my wife and I bicycled in the countryside an hour outside Norfolk. We could not find a road uncluttered by traffic, even when we selected the tiniest, most obscure country roads. Random suburban housing was popping up on all of them, thanks to Virginia's lax growth policies. Traffic was literally everywhere. We compared this to France, from which we had just returned after a cycling trip in the Loire Valley. There, in a country that has a much higher gross density, you could cycle for hours on peaceful country roads and barely see a car. There's no way I could buy that experience in the United States. That's something I would have to "buy" through political work engaged in with others of like mind.

A key point is that individual prosperity is not synonymous with collective health. In the past half-century, our per capita wealth has risen immensely in all sectors, even allowing for a flattening of incomes in the lower half of society in the last twenty-five years. But along with income has risen the per capita crime rate, including murder and rape, the divorce rate, the illegitimacy rate, and virtually every other indicator of social disease. Although the crime rate has fallen over the past few years, it is still many times higher than in the 1940s and previous decades. New York City in the 1940s had about fifty murders a year, less than a tenth of the murders today even under the city's newly lowered crime rate, and even though the city's population today is nearly identical in size to what it was in the 1940s. The two states with the highest crime rates in the nation are, perhaps surprisingly, Florida and Arizona.[5] Is it a coincidence that these two states also have transient, suburban populations who live in communities that are fragmented physically? These two states also have a similar hostility to government.

There are some "goods," to use econo-speak again, that cannot be bought through the marketplace. They can only be bought with social cooperation, through government, or something that takes its place. I cannot buy a healthy, friendly, and harmonious community for my child to grow up in, where people from many walks of life mingle, even if I have the wealth of Bill Gates. I cannot buy a reduction in infant mortality, or a decrease in the crime rate. I cannot buy a trip downtown on a commuter train. I can buy a television, but not better TV shows on that television.

A point of this book, perhaps its main point, is that we can choose to change this, but that it involves real decisions with real consequences and real trade-offs. To foster community, our society needs to become more conservative, in the sense of conserving more of the past, and be less open to change. Both our places and our society need to be "stickier," less flexible, less elastic. Being more conservative as a society has drawbacks, but the one plus is giving people more time to form relationships. The patterns of living are less easily swept away, and persist longer, which means friendship and family relationships have more time to flourish. The drawbacks are more on the individual side. Individual initiative would be squelched some; proceeding with the brilliant new idea would be slower.

Bill Powell, in an article in *Newsweek*, said that Germans and Japanese have a different conception of what an economy is for than Americans. Germans and Japanese (and I suspect many Europeans) believe an economy, or economic growth, is for fostering social stability. This attitude comes from countries that have seen foreign troops sweep over their lands, their cities bombed, and their own populations swept up in virulent ideologies of hate and war. They know what happens when society loses its moorings.[6]

We in the United States see an economy's purpose as providing wealth for individuals. This comes from a land that has not been invaded by foreign aggressors for 150 years, that has had fewer pestilences and dislocations of its social fabric, and in addition, is not a "nation" in the literal meaning of a group of people of common ethnic, religious, and genetic background. Instead, we are united by ideas and goals, most of which relate back to the possibilities of individual success and mobility. We have been relatively unimpeded in this journey.

True, there was the Great Depression. And for black Americans, history has been a series of chains to be thrown off, from slavery to Jim Crow laws. But, with perhaps the exception of the experience of African Americans, our society's struggles don't compare to Verdun or the Holocaust. Having less concern with social stability, we see an economy's purpose as providing personal wealth.

Neil Postman writes of the social and political biases of technology.[7] Television pacifies and desocializes man. Cars atomize and splinter humanity; streetcars pull people to a point. Architects love to wax about how a room can stimulate sociability with a window placed just so: so also can a streetcar pull people together and a car pull them apart. Of course, it's difficult to predict how a technology will change us. Computers pull us apart and pull us together. But in what ways? They build new communities while fragmenting old ones.

Still, as Postman says, we have been a profoundly unconservative society in our willingness not only to unleash, but also to actively promote and subsidize, new forms of technology that will inevitably rip apart our communities and put them back together in new shapes. I believe that is why we are a violent society prone to disease and dysfunction, while at the same time a creative, fermenting place as well.

The problem with community, and with place, and with our cities, is not one of scarcity. It is the problem of setting limits, of making choices. Our problems with our cities and places and communities are the same as our problems with our diet: too much quantity, not enough quality. We have too much land, too much cheap gas, too many highways. We have too many chickens costing a nickel or so apiece, and too little flavor in each of their hormone- and antibiotic-stuffed bodies. In a similar way, we have Wal-Marts and Homearamas delivering dish sets and 2,500-square-foot houses for a quarter, but with little value, longevity, or character in either. To live a more full life, a more sane and balanced life, we need less of everything. It is a tough message to a society built on doing your own thing, and lighting out for the territory.

Prosperity is not synonymous with health. Postman writes that between 1950 and 1985, serious crime by fifteen-year-olds increased by 11,000 percent.[8] Postman blames television. This may or may not be true, but what the statistic and others like it suggest is that there is not a clear one-to-one correspondence between health and wealth.

THE CITY MARKET

The near disappearance of the central city market conveys well the fragmentation of our communities and the less visible role of government in creating commerce and community. I speak of the cavernous central markets, usually housed in a building built and owned by the city, that served as a home for vendors of fruit, meat, fish, vegetables, and other wares. These were the central marketplaces of a town, where the producers came with their goods and transferred them, perhaps through a middleman, to the consumer. The vehicle for this transference was a publicly built structure. Such a structure was as much a part of the infrastructure of commerce as a highway is today.

To create a place for the most basic human transaction, buying and selling food, city governments all over the country created public buildings in the center of town for this to take place. They didn't wait for a private developer to build one and then lease out space. For various reasons, it was more efficient and beneficial to everyone to have government do it. The old city markets show a time when the architecture of commerce was more directly tied to the architecture of the city and government. The city "created" the opportunity for commerce, directly, through building and designing a home for it in the center of town.

Public spending still creates the architecture of commerce, but the chain is less visible. When the state highway department builds a freeway interchange, this is creating the possibility for a shopping center, even though it is not, as is the case with the old city markets, actually building the shopping "center" itself.

Like the classic urban city, the old city markets that survive have become specialized places, re-creations of themselves, servicing a smaller, more elite population that can afford their wares and has a taste for them. In this country, they exist in specialized places that see their value: a college town like Missoula, Montana, or a New England town of rich retirees. Like the vine-ripened tomato or the chicken that eats its corn off the dirt rather than from a trough in a thousand-hen shed, the central market has become something only the rich and the cultured enjoy.

Norfolk's old City Market was at its center for three hundred years. About every fifty to seventy-five years, the city would build a new one, which would open with great fanfare. The last two were memorable. In the 1880s, an elaborate brick building with turrets was constructed. In the 1930s, an Art Deco structure was opened. It had the heads of lambs, cows, and other animals adorning the cornice line, symbolizing the food sold within. The city fathers, who built it with public money, announced that it was the premier city market on the East Coast, in much the same way that an aquarium, sports stadium, or museum is heralded today. The new market sat beside the "old" city market of the 1880s, which was used for other civic activities.

The city tore both old and new City Markets down in the 1950s, despite a referendum campaign to save at least the "new" market. It was part of the misguided urban renewal strategy that ripped out one of the greatest collections of pre–Civil War housing in the nation. It's a tragedy these buildings no longer exist, and an example of the lack of vision by city leaders. But, if they had survived, they would probably be reconstructed imitations of themselves, no longer the central place of commerce, but stylized imitations of such places.

The real thing does survive in some cities. In Barcelona vendors sell blood sausage, Manchego cheese, fish, and produce under a huge roof right off Las Ramblas, the grand promenade through the heart of the city. In Seattle, Pike Place still survives, and not just as a tourist trap. Through hard work, and careful controls, the city has maintained it as a place where you can still buy the best meat and fish, as well as a T-shirt or a cappuccino. But both Seattle and Barcelona manipulate the markets to counter wider societal and economic trends.

Daniel Kemmis, mayor of Missoula, begins his book, *The Good City and the Good Life*, with a description of the central vegetable and produce market in the center of his city.[9] It's a glowing, romantic account. Kemmis tells of buying his morning sweet roll, of the battle between newer, more industrious immigrant vegetable sellers and older native farmers, and of his conception that the market itself embodies the idea of the good city, the good place, the good community.

The market in Missoula that Kemmis lionizes is, as he states clearly, a recent invention, a mere twenty years old. It thrives now as a flowering of a combination of trends, the resurgence of organic farms, which are not yet industrialized, along with the more selective tastes in a college town. I applaud the market's existence, even while recognizing that its existence is a thing different than it once was. Like an actor as he grows older, we must now do consciously what once was intuitive.

As Kemmis says, the market and community are inexorably linked. The decline of the central marketplace is both a cause and a symptom of the fragmentation of community. But I wonder whether Kemmis does not realize, or just chooses not to say, how deep the structural changes are that have ended city markets in most places. Reversing such structural changes involves everything from ending the tyranny of the free market over our farm policies to building more mass transit.

Kemmis's praise for things like Baltimore's Inner Harbor area, a Rouse festival marketplace project, bothers me. Kemmis must see how shallow and insubstantial such a place is. There is very little public about it, nor does it provide much in the way of essential buying and selling. It is, instead, an urbanistic sleight of hand, a meringuelike confection of color and taste that, if swept away, would leave no real loss other than the renewed question of what to do with the space. Outside of major cities like Baltimore, New York, and Boston, such festival marketplaces have usually failed. And in Baltimore, the Inner Harbor has done nothing to stop the steady drain of the city's population, year after year. For this to be addressed, Baltimore would probably have to merge politically with surrounding counties, and institute growth controls in the suburbs.

A more finely grained pattern of buying and selling ties us more closely to a community and creates community. But I wonder if people realize just how far we have come from the corner grocery store. In Norfolk, a city councilman, Herbert Collins, runs a one-room grocery store called Long's Market. Its principal customer base is the housing project across the street. The cans of peas and loaves of Wonder Bread he sells he actually buys at various supermarkets nearby. He does this because the distribution system that once supported such stores, trucks that threaded their way among small city streets, no longer exists.

It's telling that the networks of small grocery stores and businesses that do still exist are in cities like Manhattan. New York, the symbol of gigantism and impersonality to many, is the last haven to the small business.

ZONING DOESN'T MATTER

The growing centralization of our retail has followed the changes in our transportation system that have made such centralization possible. The infrastructure of our marketplace is bound to the architecture of our cities.

The increase in Wal-Marts, power centers, and other warehouse-style stores is due to the increase in the cables of freeways and interchanges that encircle most metropolitan areas now. These systems of freeways, although terribly destructive in many ways, do provide many residents a means to get across much of a metropolitan area in less than thirty minutes. Consequently, major retail points have grown up around freeway interchanges, particularly those that connect several different freeway lines. Find a Super K-Mart or a Home Depot and you'll usually find a freeway interchange nearby. Moving away from freeways and toward smaller roads and more mass transit will produce smaller stores— and higher prices.

It's important to understand that the suburban pattern of separating uses—a subdivision here, a Wal-Mart there, a megaschool here—is the product of a transportation system that encourages such separation, not from zoning codes that require it. Government regulation follows markets; it rarely dictates them. If you abolished all zoning codes tomorrow, it would change the pattern of land use very little. Houston proves this. It has no zoning code, but its physical landscape is, if anything, even more sprawling than other American cities. Mixed use is a product of pre-automobile transportation systems. Cars and arterial-style highways separate uses.

The dilemma of modern retailing is that progress in retailing means serving greater and greater numbers of people, in order that prices can be lower and lower. The newest Wal-Mart Supercenter stores require a customer base of 500,000 households within a twenty-minute drive.[10] This is a long way from the neighborhood store. In addition, the drive to bigger and bigger stores is accompanied by lower and lower profit margins. A small neighborhood store might have profit margins of 50 percent, Wal-Marts 20 percent, Supercenters 13 percent.

I believe we must choose between more for less, and a fuller, more connected community. It's getting so that stationery, tools, breakfast cereal, computers, stereos, and more are bought at huge warehouse stores, with rock-bottom prices, that sit near a freeway interchange. But the clerk at the Circuit City who sells you a washing machine, not surprisingly, will not know your name. It is a trade-off. For the most efficient distribution systems in the modern world, for the elimination of all middlemen, we get a life devoid of intimate contact between the home and the market.

COMMUNITY AS COMMODITY

Rather than address the substantive changes that might enhance community, by which I mean everything from national health care to mass transit, people are trying to buy community or create it in patchwork ways. New Urbanism is an example of this. Although its theorists talk about things like more mass transit, most New Urbanism results in isolated subdivisions, appearing to be nineteenth-century towns, that people can buy in one easy package.

This philosophy of community as commodity is seen in a book titled *A Good Place to Live: America's Last Migration*, by Terry Pindell.[11] In it, Pindell describes his own transition from an active, involved community member, a city councilman in fact, to someone restlessly searching for "a good place to live."

"I quickly discovered that I was participating in a widespread contemporary phenomenon. . . . I met people searching for a good place to live everywhere I went—on trains and planes and buses, in bars and roadside diners, in real estate offices and at chamber of commerce desks, and on street corners of communities large and small across the country."[12]

Pindell's book is about his visit to a dozen or so of the hippest places in the country, from Santa Fe to Minneapolis. It's sickening somehow. Here's his list: Santa Fe; San Luis Obispo in California; Napa,

California; the Willamette Valley in Oregon; Puget Sound in Washington; Southern British Columbia; Missoula, Montana; Ithaca, New York; Burlington, Vermont; Portsmouth, New Hampshire; Ashville, North Carolina; Wilmington, North Carolina; Minneapolis; and Charlottesville, Virginia. In all of them you can find high-priced Italian restaurants, natural foods stores, and earnest young couples with the right number of bumper stickers on their cars. It's also telling, and irritating, how Pindell calls Seattle "Puget Sound" and Portland "Willamette Valley." Even in his terminology, he is rejecting the idea of a city, a center, and some responsibility to it.

Pindell is not unsubtle in his observations. At one point he says: "We on this continent have never resolved the problem of place, partly because we have seldom stayed in our places long enough to get them right and rarely comprehended the connection between place and human community."[13]

Which doesn't quite square with his own continuation of that pattern. But I have no answer to my criticism. I have thought many times of leaving my own, quite unhip town, and perhaps I will someday. Perhaps it is like most things, a question of balance. If we want community, we need to be a little more committed to the places where we are, and not so eager to move on.

Our consumer culture and economy have given us the biggest houses, cheapest televisions, and most plentiful supermarkets in the world. Unfortunately, they have also given us the highest crime rates, the highest levels of fractured families, and endemic loneliness. These are two sides of the same coin. In return for a dynamic and flexible economy, we have a rootless culture and society. The European Union may face similar trends. Making one economy out of Western Europe means making labor migration easier and, thus, fracturing local communities.

The powerful isolation of American life is a fact. Ray Oldenburg's book *The Great Good Place* is a romanticized view of the gathering spots he calls "Third Places." Like Pindell and others, he glowingly describes European life without mentioning that the cafes, bier gartens, and pubs he admires have been declining in number and usage for decades, caught in a crossfire of the car and television just like here. But it is also true that they exist in greater number than any similar institution here. European society still has big differences with American society,

even if they are more a question of degree than of kind. Oldenburg
quotes a transplanted European who had lived all over the world, and
her remarks ring true.

> After four years here, I still feel more of a foreigner than in any
> other place in the world I have been. People here are proud to
> live in a "good" area, but to us these so-called desirable areas
> are like prisons. There is no contact between the various house-
> holds, we rarely see the neighbors and certainly do not know
> any of them. In Luxemburg, however, we would frequently
> stroll down to one of the local cafes in the evening, and there
> pass a very congenial few hours in the company of the local fire-
> man, dentist, bank employee or whoever happened to be there
> at the time. There is no pleasure to be had in driving to a sleazy,
> dark bar where one keeps strictly to one's self and becomes fear-
> ful if approached by some drunk.[14]

A powerful statement. But diminishing the isolation of American
life is less about building Third Places than about constructing the conditions that produce Third Places. Which might have as much to do
with national health care, family leave policies, or equalizing school
funding, as it does with trying to build walkable streets with cafes on the
corner.

WHY WE PUT UP WITH EACH OTHER

In praising a common, more group-centered society, I recognize that
we have progressed in ways that often have reduced "community." The
stronger, more stable communities we had in the past were built in part
because of the presence of hunger, disease, poverty, and a more limited
horizon of human potential.

We still struggle with violence, education, societal disrepair, and
slums, but our poor are not facing polio, diphtheria, rickets, and starvation. In a best-seller like *Angela's Ashes*, by Frank McCourt, we see how
the family faced starvation, disease, and death at every turn, both here
and in Ireland, during the 1930s. In *Down and Out in Paris and London*,
George Orwell's account of living for a time among the bottom rungs
of both societies, Orwell and his compatriots faced starvation in Paris

when they failed to secure employment at the hotel washing dishes, not just eviction or a lowered lifestyle.

I paradoxically learned about how our society had changed by reading Neil Sheehan's extraordinary book about Vietnam, *A Bright Shining Lie*. It tells the history of the war through one man, John Paul Vann, whose own career stretched from the war's beginning to nearly its end. But Vann, as it happens, was from Norfolk and grew up a few blocks from my house. A good part of the book is dedicated to showing Vann's childhood in Norfolk.

Vann grew up mostly in a neighborhood called Atlantic City, a working-class neighborhood dating back to the early nineteenth century. Sitting on the Elizabeth River, it was made of solid homes that today would be considered charming. The neighborhood no longer remains, not even in name. The Norfolk Redevelopment and Housing Authority tore it down in the late 1950s during the urban renewal era. In its place rest now a tangle of highways, some vacant lots, and a huge medical complex.

I had always been bitter about this clearance. In the city's actions, I saw a typical disregard for the worth and rights of a working-class people. The neighborhood's destruction, like most of Norfolk's urban renewal, also worsened the city's long-term health by reducing its supply of historic urban housing. There are also hints of more nefarious reasons for the neighborhood's destruction. Forrest R. White, in a book about the battle to desegregate the schools in Norfolk called *Pride and Prejudice: School Desegregation and Urban Renewal in Norfolk, 1950–1959*, argued that the city tore down Atlantic City as a way to avoid integrating the schools.[15] The neighborhood was largely white. But in the 1950s, a few black families had moved into Atlantic City, breaking the color line. Under the interpretation of the Supreme Court ruling then in effect, only schools that had black families living near them had to be integrated. This was before busing had been introduced. So one way to avoid school integration was simply to tear down any neighborhood that had any degree of residential integration.

Because I had often thought about the neighborhood's fate, I was excited to learn that a group of former Atlantic City residents still held an annual reunion, almost forty years after the neighborhood's destruction. It seemed proof that something vital, something different, had really existed there. Still, as I prepared to attend the reunion, held at a Norfolk park far from the old neighborhood site, I expected at most to see a handful of graying heads. Instead, I found a good crowd, some fifty people, graying to be sure, but all enthusiastic to see their old friends and talk about old times. Attending were Frank and Dot Vann, brother and sister of John Paul Vann.

"It was the greatest place I ever lived," Frank Vann said. "Everyone lived right together. But you got closer to people that way."

It was clear as they and others talked about the neighborhood, and their lives there, that it had been something special. They talked of walking down the street in the evening and hearing the cascading chorus of hellos from front porches. They talked of hanging out in the stores on the small shopping street at neighborhood's edge, of fidgeting together inside churches and schools that were torn down by the city. It was tempting to dismiss these memories as yellowed photographs of the past, edited to improve what must have been a pretty average place. But their very presence in the park seemed to deny that their memories had been just sentimentality or rose-colored hindsight. I believed them.

Theirs and other stories confirm that the city destroyed a community when it ripped out the streets and houses of Atlantic City. But this community would almost certainly have vanished regardless of the city's actions. It would have vanished more gently, more humanely, and perhaps been replaced by other communities, perhaps yuppies like myself, but vanished it would have. For one thing, practically all the people attending now lived in the suburbs and probably would have moved there regardless of what the city did. Moving to the suburbs was and still is what you do in the working class when you have moved up.

Marshall Berman writes of this paradox in his masterful work, *All That Is Solid Melts into Air: The Experience of Modernity*. He writes of watching from an overpass with rage and horror as Robert Moses destroyed his own childhood neighborhood with the Cross-Bronx Expressway. But with thought, he realized his anger at Moses could not be pure, because Berman also realized he and others would have left the Bronx regardless of Moses's actions.

What if, like [Jane] Jacobs' lower Manhattan neighbors a few years later, we had managed to keep the dread road from being built? How many of us would still be in the Bronx today, caring for it and fighting for it as our own? Some of us, no doubt, but I suspect not so many, and in any case—it hurts to say it—not me. For the Bronx of my youth was possessed, inspired, by the great modern dream of mobility. To live well meant to move up socially, and this in turn meant to move out physically; to live one's life close to home was not to be alive at all. Our parents, who had moved up and out from the Lower East Side, believed this just as devoutly as we did—even though their hearts might break when we went. . . . But when you see life this way, no neighborhood or environment can be anything more than a stage along life's way, a launching pad for higher flights and wider orbits than your own.[16]

Of course, it does not have to be either/or. Creating more community simply means slowing our mobility as a society, not ending it.

Reading the description of a family's life in Atlantic City in the 1920s and '30s in A *Bright Shining Lie*, I realize how much smaller the horizons of life were back then. The legs of Vann's brother Gene were bowed horribly because he got rickets from the family's vitamin-deficient diet of fried potatoes and biscuits. Although Vann's family was worse off than most, it was not an unusual set of circumstances. And of course, Vann and Atlantic City were white. Blacks lived within an even narrower set of circumstances, a good rung below working-class whites.

Community was something we once enjoyed but did not choose. And when we escaped various limitations, we escaped community as well. But our liberation has produced a brutal situation: we no longer know our neighbors. I have found this to be true almost everywhere in the country. At some point, starting about a decade or two ago, the traditional Welcome Wagon and custom of greeting the new neighbors with a pie ended. My own hunch is that many factors, particularly less organized religion, added up to bring us to what statisticians call "the tipping point." It suddenly is just not worth the trouble to bake that pie to bring to the new neighbors across the street. Why bother? They will probably attend a different church or no church at all, watch different TV shows, listen to different music, vote for different politicians if they vote at all, and they will move on in a few years anyway.

COMMUNITY: A MYTH OR REALITY?

In *The 100 Mile City*, Deyan Sudjic dismisses the desire for community as something akin to indigestion; a phantom, transitory ill not suffered by those with heartier physiques and souls.

"The most cherished of contemporary myths is the recurring dream of community. . . . it's a fantasy that celebrates the corner shop, borrowing a cup of sugar from the neighbors, and all those other unimpeachable suburban virtues that range from motherhood to apple pie."[17]

Sudjic paints community as a retreat into tribalism and a wish to stop the city from being the dynamic, changing place it is. Sudjic is sharp. But to argue, as Sudjic does, that community is an illusion is to support a form of nihilism. The core of our lives and places is built on public institutions that need to be maintained by someone. It starts with schools, for one, and moves on to City Hall itself. To argue, as Sudjic does, that we are merely a shifting, nomadic people, moving onward forever and ever, is to not recognize that the places and societies we move to were created by someone. Social and community ties, as well as stability, are a necessity for the establishment of human settlement, without which civilization collapses. Balance is a word that has escaped Sudjic's vocabulary. There is a point between being either restless nomads or stick-in-the-mud, xenophobic stay-at-homes.

Like the creation of places, the creation of community can happen, but it requires making choices that give us less of some things and more of others. Community is my coffeehouse. It is a mass transit system. It is a family leave policy. It is both an opportunity and a responsibility.

Is there a way out of the "dead end" of sprawl to coherent, pleasing places and cities? There's "hope." Photo by Teresa W. Wingfield.

GETTING

THERE

Building Healthy Cities

OUR FRUSTRATION with the sprawling conglomeration of subdivisions, shopping centers, and loosely placed buildings that composes our contemporary cities seems to arise every few years with fresh vigor. It's as if every decade or so we turn around and go, "You know, this really is horrible, we have to do something."

So it's somewhat startling to realize that this horror, this determination to do things differently, has been at full throttle for at least a half-century. In the 1950s, when most of what is now decried was not even built, Lewis Mumford and others condemned the soulless, plastic suburbs that were beginning to multiply across the country.

To be sure, some perspective is necessary. Life is a balance of tensions. People have always wanted more of this and less of that. In the past, however, crowding, or too little space, was the principal complaint. Since about 1950, we have been dealing with the flip side of that, too much space, and too little place.

As we as a society choose among various goods and lesser evils, are there any rules of thumb I can list that would better put us in the driver's seat in shaping our places? What I desire is not so much the triumph of a particular city planning philosophy, but for the public and leaders to more consciously make their choices, with a better understanding of the pluses and minuses of each. In doing this, we can recognize as misconceptions some of the ideas we have about how cities and places work. We can understand better the ingredients that go into place-making—business, transportation, and government—and how they interact.

So here briefly are some of Marshall's rules of thumb for shaping places.

ONE

Change the idea that development emerges primarily from the decisions of the individual property owner. It does not. Creating places is almost wholly a product of public, political, and taxpayer-financed decisions. This is fine, and I know of no other way to structure it. Our habit, though, of conceptually putting the individual or corporate actor in the driver's seat, and thinking of the emergence of a place or city as the sum total of that actor's decisions, causes us to pursue development in a back-handed, peeking-between-our-fingers, one-eye-closed manner. We, the public, structure development with our decisions on how to lay out the infrastructure of our places, starting with the lowliest backcountry road, the biggest freeway, the nicest airport, or the fastest train line.

The individual property owner can do nothing without the assistance of the state, unless we are speaking of a Ted Kaczynski–like existence in the middle of the woods. Every other decision to develop property, from a farm to an office building, involves hooking up to the infrastructure of the state. The simple house must be accessible by a public road. It usually requires public drinking water and waste disposal. Then there are flood control systems and a dozen other systems. Then there is the public software that a property owner buys into. Education for one's children. A court system to adjudicate disputes. Access to whatever city or county services are available.

Property owners should be treated fairly. In fact, they should be treated more fairly and equitably than they are today. Today's system of zoning and land use rewards mostly the developer able to muscle his or her way through the mass of bureaucratic and political thickets surrounding it. Establishing clear and simple rules for when and where development should occur would be better. But where development goes is essentially a public decision, not a private one. Once this is established, then we can start to understand my second rule of thumb, the relationship of transportation to place development.

TWO

Of all the public decisions that go into place-making, the most important is what type of transportation systems to use. They will determine the character of the city and much of its economy. Do we pave roads or lay down tracks? Do we fund buses or subsidize cars? Do we lay down bike paths or more highway lanes? Do we build airports or high-speed train lines?

What is transportation for? That's the essential question Lewis Mumford asked forty years ago.

In the first place, it's for building the economy of a city. A city's external links to the outside world, its freeways, train lines, airports, ports, and others, will determine the potential of its industry and people. The big links a city has to the outside world determine its economic potential, something most people do not grasp. Thus, people should think hard about, and usually be ready to fund, the new airport, the new train lines, the new port, and even the new Interstate if it actually travels somewhere new, though this is not likely these days.

As these external links are established, attention can be paid to the internal transportation network. We should recognize that the internal transportation serves a different purpose than the external transportation systems of a city. The layout of a region's internal transportation will determine how people get to work, how they shop, how they recreate, how they live. The standard choice today of lacing a metropolitan area with big freeways for purely internal travel means we will have a sprawling, formless environment. Simply getting rid of the freeways—forget mass transit—would establish a more neighborhood-centered economy and dynamic. But we don't have to forget mass transit. Laying

out train lines, streetcar tracks, bus lanes, bike paths, and sidewalks—
and forgoing freeways and big roads—will mean a more place-oriented
form of living. Both the drawbacks and the benefits of such a style dwell
in its more communal, group-oriented form of living. You will have the
option of not using a car. But to get this option, you have to accept that
using a car will be more difficult.

Transportation is not the only public decision. Policies on growth
and development can help implement a transportation policy. Such policies are far less important than usually thought, however. The major
transportation systems dictate the pattern and style of developments. Once
those are established, ways will be found over and around zoning and
land-use laws to build the type of development that fits with a big highway or train line.

But zoning and other land-use laws can be used to facilitate or
support the type of development that goes along with a particular style of
transportation. The best way to do this would be to move away from
zoning and go back to actually designing cities. Governments would
actually lay out street systems on paper, and then private or public developers could build them as needed. This would give a coherent structure
to a metropolitan area. It would also mean better coordinating the relationship among states, metropolitan areas, and smaller localities.

Growth control laws and boundaries are a wonderful tool for shaping development. Conceptually they are great because they help the
public and the planners focus on where they want growth to occur. But
growth boundaries are misleading because they give rise to the percep-
tion that without them, houses and shopping centers would magically
pop up like mushrooms after a good rain. They would not. In reality,
development only occurs after the public has made a decision about
where to lay out roads, train lines, sewers, and other public infrastructure. Growth boundaries are as much about inhibiting public development as private. They are lines that tell government, beyond this point,
go no farther with your services. A better way to think about growth boundaries is that they are lines that demarcate to what point the public is
going to extend its blessings, both in the form of transportation and in
things like educating children, police services, and libraries.

But growth boundaries are not possible usually without addressing the tangled political structures of our cities. Which leads us to our third rule of thumb.

THREE

A city's political structure should match its economic structure. Cities are vast organisms today, with money, people, jobs, and products coming in one end, and cars, buildings, streets, waste, and commerce coming out the other. And our true cities today are our metropolitan areas, our Citistates, to use the term coined by writers Neal Peirce and Curtis Johnson, because that is the level at which most of these systems function. Ultimately, our political structure determines our physical and economic structure. It's governments that lay out Interstate highways and train lines, hard roads and streets, bike paths and sidewalks. But our governmental structures are a mishmash of overlying and crisscrossing authorities. The most effective—which isn't the same as admirable or well-designed—action is usually taken by state transportation departments, which have the authority to act on the level of metropolitan areas, the level at which effective city design usually starts.

Metropolitan areas usually gather together anywhere from a dozen to a hundred municipalities. These separate localities usually resist any effort to form a more regional government. Their citizens should consider that they do themselves a disservice by resisting forming a government that can act on a metropolitan level. The smaller governments can still remain to act on concerns that are more local, and there should be a balance of power between local and regional. But all the stuff that makes up a city—transportation, commerce, and the environment, to name a few—operates at the level of the metropolis or region. In fact, the only level at which cities today are not regional is usually political.

To handle this, I believe states must take a more direct role in the politics of the entities that are legally their responsibility and creation, local governments. An effective state policy would be to pull and push municipalities, with both carrot and stick, toward more regional governments. Ultimately, states have the right to declare regional governments by fiat, and should perhaps consider doing so. Effective urban design and controls increasingly must begin at a level of authority beyond that of the metropolis itself, because the shape of the metropolis is affected by so many forces outside its borders. Portland, perhaps the only city in the country to effectively shape itself, is able to do so because the state both gives the Portland metropolis the power to act as a single entity, and controls those forces outside of Portland's borders with the state's requirement that all growth occur inside designated growth boundaries.

WHAT'S LEFT? Given these rules of thumb I have laid out, we can imagine returning to the magic of designing great cities. People design cities, whether it be a state commissioner laying out Fifth Avenue in New York City in 1810, or a state transportation engineer laying out a new beltway around Raleigh, North Carolina, in the year 2000. Cities can be designed well or badly, just like buildings. But we will at least have more of a chance of good design when we understand that is what we are doing. If we want to return to great place-making, we can make government officials great artists again. Central Park, New York City as a whole, Washington, D.C., and Savannah were all created by the public sector. But great place-making requires some entity acting on the level of the entire metropolis. It requires consciously designing cities, rather than having it done unconsciously, usually by state transportation departments.

We design our places through the actions of that marvelous instrument of the founding fathers, representative democracy. When I started this book, I asked, where do places and cities come from? They come from us. We make them. Let's do so consciously, effectively, and beautifully.

ACKNOWLEDGMENTS

THIS BOOK BEGAN as a criticism of the design philosophy New Urbanism. It is ending as an attempt to locate and describe the actual forces that create our cities and places where we live.

In this journey, many people helped me sort out what I was writing about and why. I thank them all. The final product, of course, is solely my own responsibility.

I thank first my editor Randy Swearer, who first came to me in December 1996 asking if I had a book inside me. Throughout the following years, he has been a great midwife in the difficult birth process of a first book, even while he himself moved from being a professor of design at the University of Texas in Austin to being the dean of the Parsons School of Design in New York.

I thank the following people, who either reviewed the manuscript or helped in some way: the librarians at the Chapin Planning Library in Chapel Hill, who let me open a window in the summer to escape from the frigid air-conditioning; Professor Robert Fishman, who lent his ear during moments of crisis; Shep Siegel, who in one intense conversation in Montana helped get the book back on track; Hugo Lindgren, now at *The New York Times*, who steered me toward Jackson Heights as an interesting urban neighborhood to examine; Philip Smith, who in Portland poured me great wine and showed me the city through the eyes of a native; Randy Gragg, the architecture critic for the Portland *Oregonian*; David Fenza, who kept telling me "it was time" for me to write a book; Jack Junkins, who passed me nifty building info; David Levy, who reviewed the manuscript and is Norfolk's best bulldog for good design; my brother John "Paco" Marshall, who read the manuscript and badgered me to come up with solutions; Ted and Susan Goranson, who each contributed greatly to the book's evolution; Joy Hakim, who has always been a stern writing mentor; Jan Eliassen, who helps me play outside the box; Patrick Masterson, who has helped me in innumerable ways; Tony Wharton and Patrick Lackey, who showed me buildings and streets in a new light; Dennis Hartig, the *Virginian-Pilot* editor who first recognized my talent in writing about cities and encouraged me to develop it; the Vaalers and Caldwells for their friendship during this book's germination; J. D. Crutchfield, who knows so much; Kevin Doyle, who as a great friend steered me toward original thinkers like William Irwin Thompson; Neal Peirce and Curtis Johnson, who have been great mentors to me; Greg Avila, Norfolk's literary dean, who asked me so many tough questions; and Richard Bulis, the sage of Reno, who helps me keep my eyesight clear and my feet on the ground. And finally, I thank all my friends and family and readers in and around Norfolk, who have always been so supportive.

I thank most of all my wife, Andrea, who helped me in countless ways, put up with my research trips, edited some first drafts, and moderated the curve of my mood swings about the project with her steady love and support.

ALEX MARSHALL

Loeb Fellow, 1999–2000
Harvard University, Cambridge

NOTES

INTRODUCTION

1. H. W. Burton, *The History of Norfolk, Va.* (Norfolk: *Norfolk Virginian*, 1877).

CHAPTER ONE

1. Kissimmee City Manager Mark Durbin, telephone interview with author, March 20, 1998.

2. Notes from lecture by David Pace, head of residential development for Disney Imagineering, at conference of the American Institute of Architects at Celebration, February 1998.

3. Sandra Vance and Roy Scott, *Wal-Mart: A History of Sam Walton's Retail Phenomenon* (New York: Twayne Publishers, 1994).

4. Lewis Mumford, "The Marseilles 'Folly,'" in *The Highway and the City* (New York: Harcourt, Brace & World, 1963), pp. 53–66.

5. Data taken from *Celebration Chronicle*, a Disney publication, vol. 3, no. 2,

6. Steven Levy, *Insanely Great: The Life and Times of Macintosh, the Computer That Changed Everything* (New York: Penguin Books, 1994).

7. David Pace lecture, February 1998.

8. Professor Andrew Ross, a New York University scholar who is living in Celebration so as to observe it, confirmed my own reporting on this issue in an interview March 22, 1998.

9. Evan McKenzie, *Privatopia: Homeowners Associations and the Rise of Residential Private Government* (New Haven, Conn.: Yale University Press, 1994), p. 11.

10. Ibid. This number represents an extrapolation of figures McKenzie gives. In 1992, there were an estimated 150,000 homeowners associations, while in the year 2000 there were expected to be 225,000.

11. McKenzie, *Privatopia*.

12. Ibid., p. 21.

13. Ibid., p. 16.

14. Michael Pollan, "Town Building Is No Mickey-Mouse Operation," *New York Times Magazine*, December 14, 1997, p. 56.

15. Russ Rymer, *Harper's Magazine*, October 1996.

16. Harry Northrop, interview with author, March 22, 1998. Harry is the husband of Angie Lee Northrop, who owns the mansion at 420 Sumner Street in Kissimmee. He told me the history of the house and the family there. His wife's parents built the house, and Angie Northrop was raised there.

17. Jerry Williams, a Kissimmee city assessor, interview with author, October 7, 1997, in Williams's office in Kissimmee.

18. Data from author interview with Brent Herrington, Celebration Community Manager, April 27, 1998.

19. David Pace lecture, February 1998.

20. Alex Marshall, "Suburb in Disguise," *Metropolis Magazine*, July/August 1996, p. 70.

21. Herrington interview, April 27, 1998.

22. Despite his apparent upbeat mood, Dickson would eventually abandon Celebration and return to North Carolina. This was reported in Andrew Ross, *Celebration Chronicles* (New York: Ballantine Books, 1999), p. 74.

23. Herrington interview, April 27, 1998.

24. Robert Fishman, "The Mumford-Jacobs Debate," *Planning History Studies*, vol. 10, no. 1–2. (This is a fascinating paper on the great war between Lewis Mumford and Jane Jacobs, and the roots of it.)

25. Peter Calthorpe, *The Next American Metropolis: Ecology, Community and the American Dream* (New York: Princeton Architectural Press, 1993).

26. Rob Steutiville, telephone interview with author, August 1, 1997. The December 1997 issue of *New Urban News*, a publication Steutiville edits, listed 141 projects in twenty-nine states, up from 119 projects in twenty-seven states a year earlier. Steutiville estimated that the large majority of these were new developments, as opposed to infill.

CHAPTER TWO

1. James Howard Kunstler, *The Geography of Nowhere* (New York: Simon & Schuster, 1993), p. 10.
2. Kenneth Jackson, *Crabgrass Frontier* (New York: Oxford University Press, 1987).
3. Robert Fishman, "Megalopolis Unbound," *Wilson Quarterly*, Winter 1990, pp. 25–45.
4. Stuart Leavenworth, "Atlanta Offers Glimpse of Triangle to Come," *News and Observer*, July 23, 1997.
5. Victor Gruen, *Centers for the Urban Environment* (New York: Van Nostrand Reinhold Company, 1973), p. 86.
6. Delbert A. Taebel and James V. Cornehls, *The Political Economy of Urban Transportation* (Port Washington, N.Y.: National University Publications, 1977), p. 16.
7. Jane Jacobs, *Cities and the Wealth of Nations* (New York: Random House, 1984).
8. Jim Wahlbrink, "The Lure of Jobs," *Raleigh News and Observer*, July 27, 1997.
9. Mark Kingwell, "Fast Forward: Our High Speed Chase to Nowhere," *Harper's*, May 1998, p. 38.
10. Donald J. Bowersox, Pat J. Calabro, and George D. Wagenheim, *Introduction to Transportation* (New York: Macmillan Publishing Co., 1981), p. 33.
11. Lewis Mumford, *The City in History* (New York: Harcourt, Brace & World, 1961), p. 451.
12. Ibid.
13. Morton and Lucia White, *The Intellectual versus the City: From Thomas Jefferson to Frank Lloyd Wright* (Cambridge, Mass.: Harvard University Press; Joint Center for Urban Studies, 1962), p. 59.
14. Ibid., p. 19.
15. Forrest R. White, *Pride and Prejudice: School Desegregation and Urban Renewal in Norfolk, 1950–1959* (Westport, Conn.: Praeger Publishers, 1992), p. 20.
16. Thomas Parramore, with Peter C. Stewart and Tommy L. Bogger, *Norfolk, the First Four Centuries* (Charlottesville: University Press of Virginia, 1994), p. 366.
17. Ibid., p. 368.
18. Harvey M. Choldin, *Cities and Suburbs: An Introduction to Urban Sociology* (New York: McGraw-Hill, 1985), p. 125.
19. Ibid.
20. Ibid.
21. Elizabeth Hawes, *New York, New York: How the Apartment House Transformed the Life of the City* (New York: Henry Holt, 1993), p. 44.
22. Lewis Mumford, "The Highway and the City," in *The Highway and the City* (New York: Harcourt, Brace & World, 1963), pp. 235–236.

23. Ibid., p. 237.

24. Ibid., p. 236.

25. Tom Downs, quote from column by syndicated columnist Neal Peirce, December 7, 1997, published by Washington Post Writers Group.

26. Based on interviews done in Tours, France, in September 1996.

27. Deyan Sudjic, *The 100 Mile City* (New York: Harcourt Brace & Co., 1992), p. 64.

28. Naomi Wolf, "Return of the Village People," *George Magazine*, November 1997.

29. Michael Tolkin, *New Yorker*, February 23, 1998.

CHAPTER THREE

1. Deborah Olson, *Life Is a Bowl of Olson's Cherries*, no publishing date. This is a recipe book that Olson puts out where she also tells the history of the Valley. Having studied in France as a chef, Olson includes recipes like lamb with cherry and vanilla, which, I can personally attest, is excellent.

2. Taken from National Public Radio, *All Things Considered*, July 7, 1997, one of a four-part series by Ray Suarez.

3. Peter Hall, *Cities in Civilization* (New York: Pantheon Books, 1998). Hall has a chapter on the development of the Silicon Valley, pp. 423–455.

4. Company report for 1997. Taken from Web site for Intel, http://www.intel.com.

5. Eric H. Monkkonen, *America Becomes Urban: The Development of U.S. Cities and Towns, 1780–1980* (Berkeley and Los Angeles: University of California Press, 1988).

6. Po Bronson, "Silicon Valley," *Wired*, January 1998.

CHAPTER FOUR

1. William Irwin Thompson, *Coming into Being: Artifacts and Texts in the Evolution of Consciousness* (New York: St. Martin's Press, 1996), p. 8.

2. Richard Hell, *Go Now* (New York: Simon & Schuster, 1996), p. 149.

3. Alex Marshall, "Eurosprawl," *Metropolis Magazine*, January 1995, pp. 62–65, 77, 79, 81, 106.

4. Ibid.

5. Deyan Sudjic, *The 100 Mile City* (New York: Harcourt Brace & Co., 1992).

6. Ibid., p. 187.

7. Morton and Lucia White, *The Intellectual versus the City: From Thomas Jefferson to Frank Lloyd Wright* (Cambridge, Mass.: Joint Center for Urban Studies, 1962), p. 14.

8. Ibid., p. 227.

9. Harvey M. Choldin, *Cities and Suburbs: An Introduction to Urban Sociology* (New York: McGraw-Hill, 1985), pp. 46–48.

10. Ibid.

11. White and White, *The Intellectual versus the City*, p. 193, quoting Frank Lloyd Wright from *The Living City*.

12. Frank Lloyd Wright, *The Disappearing City* (New York: William Farquhar Payson, 1932), p. 21.

13. Wright, *The Disappearing City*, p. 61.

14. Lewis Mumford, *The Culture of Cities* (New York: Harcourt, Brace & World, 1938), p. 267.

15. Ibid., p. 261, Illustration 19: "Metropolitan Routine."

16. Ibid., p. 269.

17. Ibid., p. 273.

18. John Keats, *The Crack in the Picture Window* (Boston: Houghton Mifflin, 1957), p. 1.

19. James Howard Kunstler, *The Geography of Nowhere* (New York: Simon & Schuster, 1993), p. 10.

20. Robert Fishman, *Bourgeois Utopias—The Rise and Fall of Suburbia* (New York: Basic Books, 1987), p. ix.

21. Ibid., p. x.

22. Lewis Mumford, *The City in History* (New York: Harcourt, Brace & World, 1961), p. 477.

23. Lewis Mumford, "The Wilderness of Suburbia," taken from an online article by James Surowiecki published April 2, 1997, by "Atlantic Unbound: The Atlantic Monthly Magazine Online."

24. Anthony Downs, *New Visions for Metropolitan America* (Washington, D.C.: Brookings Institution, and Cambridge, Mass.: Lincoln Institute of Land Policy, 1994), p. 209.

25. Herbert Gans, "The Suburban Community and Its Way of Life," in *People and Plans, Essays on Urban Problems and Solutions* (New York: Basic Books, 1968).

26. Ibid., p. 138.

27. Ibid., p. 206.

28. Fishman, *Bourgeois Utopias*, p. 16.

29. Mumford, *The City in History*, pp. 486, 491.

30. Lewis Mumford, "The Highway and the City," originally published in *Architectural Record* in April 1958, pp. 179–186, later in *The Highway and the City* (New York: Harcourt, Brace & World, 1963).

31. James Rouse, "Master Builder with a New Concept," *Business Week*, August 20, 1966, p. 106.

32. Fishman, *Bourgeois Utopias*, p. ix.

CHAPTER FIVE

1. Telephone interview with Fred Lee, October 1997.

2. Lewis Mumford, "The Highway and the City," *Architectural Record*, April 1958, pp. 179–186, taken from a book of collected essays of the same name (New York: Harcourt, Brace & World, 1963), p. 240.

3. Telephone interview with Eric Kober, October 1997.

4. Telephone interview with Frank Vardy, October 1997.

5. John W. Wright, ed., *The New York Times Almanac*, 1998 edition (New York: Penguin Reference Books, 1997).

6. *The Newest New Yorkers, 1990–1994*, (New York: New York City Department of Planning, 1997).

7. Ibid.

8. Ibid.

9. "Selected Social Characteristics–Queens Community District 3," Summary of Tape Files 3 and 4 (New York: New York City Planning Department), p. 328; "Population Characteristics—Queens Community District 3" (New York: New York City Planning Department), p. 228.

10. Marshall Berman, *All That Is Solid Melts into Air: The Experience of Modernity* (New York: Penguin Books, 1982, 1988).

CHAPTER SIX

1. Carol Sheriff, *The Artificial River: The Erie Canal and the Paradox of Progress, 1817–1862* (New York: Hill & Wang, 1996).

2. Robert Kuttner, *Everything for Sale: The Virtues and Limits of Markets* (New York: Alfred A. Knopf, 1997), p. 214.

3. Eric H. Monkkonen, *America Becomes Urban: The Development of U.S. Cities and Towns, 1780–1980* (Berkeley and Los Angeles: University of California Press, 1988), p. 285.

4. Ibid., p. 167.

5. Ibid.

6. Peter Hall, *Cities in Civilization* (New York: Pantheon Books, 1998), pp. 423–454.

7. Ibid., p. 945.

8. Kuttner, *Everything for Sale*, p. 213.

9. Kuttner, *Everything for Sale*.

10. Peter Schrag, *Paradise Lost: California's Experience, America's Future* (New York: New Press, 1998).

11. "How the States Rank in Public Education, 1995–1996," in John W. Wright, ed., *The New York Times Almanac*, 1998 edition (New York: Penguin Reference Books, 1997), p. 371; John Cassidy, "The Comeback," *New Yorker*, February 23, 1998, pp. 122–127.

12. Charles E. Lindblom, *Politics and Markets: The World's Political-Economic Systems* (New York: Basic Books, 1977), p. 8.

13. Monkkonen, *America Becomes Urban*, p. 34.

14. Theodore Goranson, conversation with author, Eastern Shore, Virginia, September 1997.

15. Stephen Holmes, "What Russia Teaches Us: How Weak States Threaten Freedom," *American Prospect*, July–August 1997, p. 35.

16. Ibid.

17. Ibid.

18. Lewis Mumford, *The City in History*, pp. 452–454.

19. Elizabeth Hawes, *New York, New York: How the Apartment House Transformed the Life of the City* (New York: Henry Holt, 1993), p. 151.

20. Spiro Kostof, *The City Shaped* (London: Thames and Hudson Ltd., 1991), p. 138.

21. John W. Reps, *The Making of Urban America: A History of City Planning in the United States* (Princeton, N.J.: Princeton University Press, 1965), p. 517.

22. Frank Popper, quoted in J. Barry Cullingsworth, *The Political Culture of Planning—American Land Use Planning in Comparative Perspective* (New York: Routledge, 1993).

23. Alex Marshall, "Eurosprawl," *Metropolis Magazine*, January 1995. In this article I describe the suburbanization of much of Europe and the related phenomenon of urban decay. Each is more widespread than most American observers believe.

24. Nicholas N. Patricios, *The International Handbook on Land Use Planning* (Westport, Conn.: Greenwood Press, 1986).

25. Hiam Darin-Drabbkin, *Land Policy and Urban Growth* (Oxford, England: Pergamon Press, 1977), p. 347.

26. Ibid.

27. Daniel Carlson, with Lisa Wormser and Cy Ulberg, *At Road's End: Transportation and Land Use Choices for Communities*, (Washington, D.C.: Island Press, 1995).

28. "Failed Private Roads Get Bailout," *Raleigh News and Observer*, August 27, 1997.

29. Moses's own autobiography provides fascinating reading on the heavy-handed state (Robert Moses, *Working for the People* [New York: Harper & Brothers, 1956]). It is interesting how the Cold War so colors his thoughts. He says, in arguing for better public administration, that the Communists have an edge because they don't have to compete with private enterprise. He says Communists hire the best, even though they may be "liquidated" later after the job is finished. He says that:

> We should not let our abhorrence of Communism blind us to the fact that we are in competition with an aggressive, ruthless government that is exerting every effort to train scientists and technicians to carry out their objectives. The Soviet regime does not have to compete with private interests to man its government.

Moses is defending his own fascism by referring to another, more authoritarian state.

CHAPTER SEVEN

1. Metro government, planning department, provided 1997 figures.

2. Author interview with Barry Edmonston, director of Population Research Center, Portland State University, November 3, 1999.

3. John W. Wright, ed., *The New York Times Almanac*, 1998 edition (New York: Penguin Reference Books, 1997), p. 236.

4. Ethan Seltzer, telephone interview with author, Portland, September 1997.

5. Roundtable discussion with multiple participants, including Andres Duany, *Harvard Design Magazine*, Winter/Spring 1997, pp. 46–49.

6. Ada Louise Huxtable, quote taken from copy of speech by Randy Gragg in Portland, Oregon, in 1997. Copy of speech given to author by Gragg.

7. Crime statistics, Wright, *The New York Times Almanac*, 1998 edition, p. 318.

8. *Metro 2040 Framework Update*, Fall 1996/Winter 1997, (Portland: Portland Metro Government, 1997).

9. R. Gregory Nokes, "City Recycles More Land for Housing," Portland *Oregonian*, August 4, 1997.

10. Seltzer, telephone interview.

CHAPTER EIGHT

1. Sandra Vance and Roy Scott, *Wal-Mart: A History of Sam Walton's Retail Phenomenon* (New York: Twayne Publishers, 1994).

2. Ibid.

3. Telephone interview with Keith Moore, July 1997.

4. Vance and Scott, *Wal-Mart*.

5. John W. Wright, ed., *The New York Times Almanac*, 1998 edition (New York: Penguin Reference Books, 1997), p. 317.

6. Bill Powell, "Keep Your Profits," *Newsweek*, November 6, 1995, p. 98.

7. Neil Postman, *Conscientious Objections* (New York: Borzoi Books, 1988), p. 106.

8. Ibid.

9. Daniel Kemmis, *The Good City and the Good Life* (Boston and New York: Houghton Mifflin, 1995), pp. 1–27.

10. Vance and Scott, *Wal-Mart*.

11. Terry Pindell, *A Good Place to Live: America's Last Migration* (New York: Henry Holt and Company, 1995).

12. Ibid., p. xiii.

13. Ibid.

14. Ray Oldenburg, *The Great Good Place* (New York: Paragon House, 1989), p. 45.

15. Forrest R. White, *Pride and Prejudice: School Desegregation and Urban Renewal in Norfolk, 1950–1959* (Westport, Conn.: Praeger Publishers, 1992).

16. Marshall Berman, *All That Is Solid Melts into Air: The Experience of Modernity* (New York: Penguin Books, 1982, 1988), p. 326.

17. Deyan Sudjic, *The 100 Mile City* (New York: Harcourt Brace & Co., 1992), p. 279.

SELECTED

REFERENCES

Abbott, Carl. *The New Urban America: Growth and Politics in the Sunbelt Cities*. Chapel Hill: University of North Carolina Press, 1981.

Alexander, Christopher, Sara Ishikawa, and Murray Silverstein, with Max Jacobson, Ingrid Fiksdahl-King, and Shlomo Angel. *A Pattern Language*. New York: Oxford University Press, 1977.

Allen, Mike. "Virginia Wants Safety Fears Laid to Rest; Guards, Cameras Planned for Stops on Interstates." *Washington Post*, May 12, 1997.

Barna, Joel Warren. *The See-Through Years: Creation and Destruction in Texas Architecture and Real Estate, 1981–1991*. Houston: Rice University Press, 1992.

Barnett, Jonathan. *The Fractured Metropolis*. New York: IconEditions, HarperCollins, 1995.

Berman, Marshall. *All That Is Solid Melts into Air: The Experience of Modernity*. New York: Penguin Books, 1982, 1988.

Bowersox, Donald J., Pat J. Calabro, and George D. Wagenheim. *Introduction to Transportation*. New York: Macmillan Publishing Co., 1981.

Brand, Stewart. *How Buildings Learn*. New York: Viking, 1994.

Braunfels, Wolfgang. *Urban Design in Western Europe.* Chicago: University of Chicago Press, 1988.

Bronson, Po. "Silicon Valley." *Wired,* January 1998. Available online at http://www.wired.com.

Burton, H. W. *The History of Norfolk, Va.* Norfolk: *Norfolk Virginian,* 1877.

Calthorpe, Peter. *The Next American Metropolis: Ecology, Community and the American Dream.* New York: Princeton Architectural Press, 1993.

Campbell, Robert. "Celebrating Community." *Boston Globe,* February 2, 1997.

Carlson, Daniel, with Lisa Wormser and Cy Ulberg. *At Road's End: Transportation and Land Use Choices for Communities.* Surface Transportation Policy Project. Covelo, Calif.: Island Press, 1995.

Cassidy, John. "The Comeback." *New Yorker,* February 23, 1998, pp. 122–127.

Chevalier, Louis. *The Assassination of Paris.* Chicago: University of Chicago Press, 1994.

Choldin, Harvey M. *Cities and Suburbs: An Introduction to Urban Sociology.* New York: McGraw-Hill, 1985.

Cullingsworth, J. Barry. *The Political Culture of Planning: American Land Use Planning in Comparative Perspective.* New York: Routledge, 1993.

Darin-Drabbkin, Hiam. *Land Policy and Urban Growth.* Oxford, England: Pergamon Press, 1977.

Downs, Anthony. *New Visions for Metropolitan America.* Washington, D.C.: Brookings Institution, and Cambridge, Mass.: Lincoln Institute of Land Policy, 1994.

Duany, Andres, and Elizabeth Plater-Zyberk. *Towns and Town Making Principles.* Edited by Alex Krieger with William Lennertz. Essays by Alex Krieger. Cambridge, Mass.: Harvard Graduate School of Design; Rizzoli International Publications, 1991.

Fishman, Robert. *Bourgeois Utopias--The Rise and Fall of Suburbia.* New York: Basic Books, 1987.

———. "Megalopolis Unbound." *Wilson Quarterly,* Winter 1990, pp. 25–45.

———. "The Mumford-Jacobs Debate." *Planning History Studies,* vol. 10, no. 1–2.

———. *Urban Utopias in the Twentieth Century: Ebenezer Howard, Frank Lloyd Wright, Le Corbusier.* Cambridge, Mass.: MIT Press, 1982.

Frieden, Bernard J., and Lynne B. Sagalyn. *Downtown, Inc.: How America Rebuilds Cities.* Cambridge, Mass.: MIT Press, 1989.

Gallagher, Winifred. *The Power of Place: How Our Surroundings Shape Our Thoughts, Emotions, and Actions.* New York: HarperCollins, 1993.

Gans, Herbert. "The Suburban Community and Its Way of Life." In *People and Plans, Essays on Urban Problems and Solutions.* New York: Basic Books, 1968.

Garreau, Joel. *Edge City.* New York: Doubleday, 1991.

————. *The Nine Nations of North America.* New York: Avon Books, 1981.

Gratz, Roberta Brandes. *The Living City.* New York: Simon & Schuster, 1989.

Gruen, Victor. *Centers for the Urban Environment.* New York: Van Nostrand Reinhold Company, 1973.

Hall, Peter. *Cities in Civilization.* New York: Pantheon Books, 1998.

————. *Cities of Tomorrow.* Oxford, England: Blackwell Publishers, 1988.

Hawes, Elizabeth. *New York, New York: How the Apartment House Transformed the Life of the City.* New York: Henry Holt, 1993.

Hell, Richard. *Go Now.* New York: Simon & Schuster, 1996.

Hiss, Tony. *The Experience of Place.* New York: Random House, 1990.

Holmes, Stephen. "What Russia Teaches Us: How Weak States Threaten Freedom." *American Prospect,* July–August 1997, pp. 30–40.

Hughes, Robert. *Barcelona.* New York: Alfred A. Knopf, 1992.

Hylton, Thomas. *Save Our Lands, Save Our Towns.* Harrisburg, Pa.: RB Books, Seitz & Seitz Inc., 1995.

Jackson, Kenneth. *Crabgrass Frontier: The Suburbanization of the United States.* New York: Oxford University Press, 1987.

Jacobs, Jane. *Cities and the Wealth of Nations.* New York: Random House, 1984.

————. *The Death and Life of Great American Cities.* New York: Vintage Books, 1961.

James, Henry. *New York Revisited.* New York: Franklin Square Press, 1994.

Karatani, Kojin. *Architecture as Metaphor: Language, Number, Money.* Cambridge, Mass.: MIT Press, 1995.

Katz, Peter. *The New Urbanism: Toward an Architecture of Community.* New York: McGraw-Hill, 1994.

Kay, Jane Holtz. *Asphalt Nation.* New York: Crown Publishers, 1997.

Keats, John. *The Crack in the Picture Window.* Boston: Houghton Mifflin, 1957.

Kelbaugh, Douglas. *Common Place: Toward Neighborhood and Regional Design.* Seattle and London: University of Washington Press, 1997.

Kemmis, Daniel. *The Good City and the Good Life.* Boston and New York: Houghton Mifflin, 1995.

Kingwell, Mark. "Fast Forward: Our High Speed Chase to Nowhere." *Harper's,* May 1998.

Kostof, Spiro. *The City Assembled: The Elements of Urban Form through History.* Boston: Bulfinch Press; Little, Brown and Company, 1992.

————. *The City Shaped: Urban Patterns and Meanings through History.* Boston: Bulfinch Press; Little, Brown and Company, 1991.

Kunstler, James Howard. *The Geography of Nowhere.* New York: Simon & Schuster, 1993.

————. *Home from Nowhere.* New York: Simon & Schuster, 1996.

Kuttner, Robert. *Everything for Sale: The Virtues and Limits of Markets.* New York: Alfred A. Knopf, 1997.

Langdon, Philip. *A Better Place to Live: Reshaping the American Suburb.* Amherst: University of Massachusetts Press, 1994.

Leavenworth, Stuart. "Atlanta Offers Glimpse of Triangle to Come." *News and Observer* (Raleigh, N.C.), July 23, 1997.

Levy, Steven. *Insanely Great: The Life and Times of Macintosh, the Computer That Changed Everything.* New York: Penguin Books, 1994.

Lindblom, Charles E. *Politics and Markets: The World's Political-Economic Systems.* New York: Basic Books, 1977.

McCourt, Frank. *Angela's Ashes.* New York: Simon & Schuster, 1997.

McKenzie, Evan. *Privatopia: Homeowners Associations and the Rise of Residential Private Government.* New Haven, Conn.: Yale University Press, 1994.

Marshall, Alex. "Eurosprawl." *Metropolis Magazine,* January 1995, pp. 62–65, 77, 79, 81, 106.

———. "Putting Some 'City' Back in the Suburbs. Sounds Interesting— Too Bad It Doesn't Work." *Washington Post,* Outlook Section, September 1, 1996.

———. "Suburb in Disguise." *Metropolis Magazine,* July/August 1996, pp. 70–71, 100–103.

Monkkonen, Eric H. *America Becomes Urban: The Development of U.S. Cities and Towns, 1780–1980.* Berkeley and Los Angeles: University of California Press, 1988.

Morrish, William R., and Catherine Brown. *Planning to Stay.* Minneapolis: Milkweed Editions, 1994.

Moses, Robert. *Working for the People.* New York: Harper & Brothers, 1956.

Mumford, Lewis. *The City in History.* New York: Harcourt, Brace & World, 1961.

———. *The Culture of Cities.* New York: Harcourt, Brace & World, 1938.

———. *The Highway and the City* (collected essays). New York: Harcourt, Brace & World, 1963.

Muschamp, Herbert. "The Miracle in Bilbao." *New York Times Magazine,* September 7, 1997.

Nasaw, David. *Going Out: The Rise and Fall of Public Amusements.* New York: Basic Books, 1993.

New York City Department of Planning. *The Newest New Yorkers, 1990–1994.* New York, 1997.

Nokes, R. Gregory. "City Recycles More Land for Housing." Portland *Oregonian,* August 4, 1997.

Oldenburg, Ray. *The Great Good Place.* New York: Paragon House, 1989.

Olsen, Donald J. *The City as a Work of Art.* New Haven, Conn.: Yale University Press, 1986.

Olson, Deborah. *Life Is a Bowl of Olson's Cherries.* Self-published, n.d.

Parramore, Thomas, with Peter C. Stewart and Tommy L. Bogger. *Norfolk, the First Four Centuries.* Charlottesville: University Press of Virginia, 1994.

Patricios, Nicholas N. *The International Handbook on Land Use Planning.* Westport, Conn.: Greenwood Press, 1986.

Peirce, Neal. "Regional Strategists and CDCs: Time to Start Working Together." Washington Post Writers Group (taken from online version
distributed by columnist), July 20, 1997.

———, Curtis W. Johnson, and John Stuart Hall. *Citistates: How Urban
America Can Prosper in a Competitive World.* Washington, D.C.:
Seven Locks Press, 1993.

Pindell, Terry. *A Good Place to Live: America's Last Migration.* New York:
Henry Holt and Company, 1995.

Postman, Neil. *Conscientious Objections.* New York: Borzoi Books, 1988.

Reps, John W. *The Making of Urban America: A History of City Planning
in the United States.* Princeton, N.J.: Princeton University Press,
1965.

Rusk, David. *Cities without Suburbs.* Washington, D.C.: Woodrow
Wilson Center Press, 1993.

Rybczyk, Mark Louis. *San Antonio Uncovered.* Plano, Tex.: Wordware
Publishing, 1992.

Schrag, Peter. *Paradise Lost.* New York: New Press, 1998.

Sennett, Richard. *Flesh and Stone: The Body of the City in Western Civilization.* New York: W. W. Norton, 1994.

Shaffer, Carolyn, and Kristin Anundsen. *Creating Community Anywhere.*
New York: Jeremy P. Tarcher/Perigee Books, 1993.

Sheehan, Neil. *A Bright Shining Lie: John Paul Vann and America in
Vietnam.* New York: Random House, 1988.

Sheriff, Carol. *The Artificial River: The Erie Canal and the Paradox of
Progress, 1817–1862.* New York: Hill & Wang, 1996.

Sucher, David. *City Comforts: How to Build an Urban Village.* Seattle:
City Comforts Press, 1995.

Sudjic, Deyan. *The 100 Mile City.* New York: Harcourt Brace & Company, 1992.

Taebel, Delbert A., and James V. Cornehls. *The Political Economy of Urban Transportation.* Port Washington, N.Y.: National University
Publications, 1977.

Thompson, William Irwin. *Coming into Being: Artifacts and Texts in the
Evolution of Consciousness.* New York: St. Martin's Press, 1996.

Tucker, George. "Documents Reveal Norfolk's Founding May Be Two
Years off the Mark." *Virginian-Pilot,* December 15, 1997.

U.S. Congress, Office of Technology Assessment. *The Technological
Reshaping of Metropolitan America.* OTA-ETI-643. Washington,
D.C.: U.S. Government Printing Office, 1995.

Vance, Sandra, and Roy Scott. *Wal-Mart: A History of Sam Walton's
Retail Phenomenon.* New York: Twayne Publishers, 1994.

Vergara, Camilo José. *The New American Ghetto.* New Brunswick, N.J.:
Rutgers University Press, 1995.

Warner, Sam B. *The Urban Wilderness: A History of the American City.*
New York: Harper & Row, 1972.

Weber, Max. *The City.* New York: Free Press, 1958.

White, Forrest R. *Pride and Prejudice: School Desegregation and Urban Renewal in Norfolk, 1950–1959.* Westport, Conn.: Praeger Publishers, 1992.

White, Morton and Lucia. *The Intellectual versus the City: From Thomas Jefferson to Frank Lloyd Wright.* Cambridge, Mass.: Joint Center for Urban Studies, 1962.

Whyte, William H. *City: Rediscovering the Center.* New York: Doubleday, 1988.

Wolf, Naomi. "Return of the Village People." *George Magazine,* November 1997, p. 74.

Wright, John W., ed. *The New York Times Almanac,* 1998 edition. New York: Penguin Reference Books, 1997.

INDEX